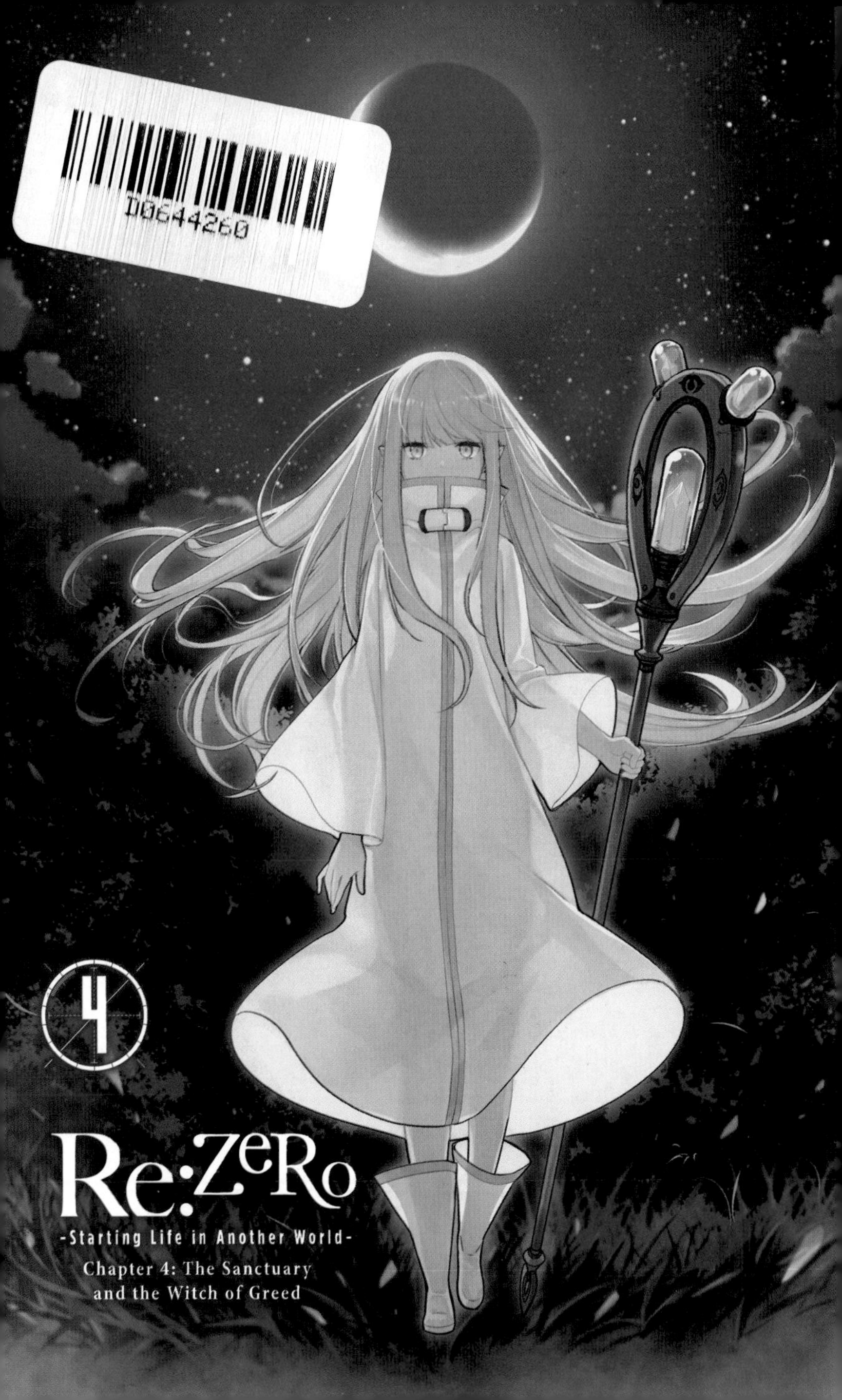
4
Re:ZeRo
-Starting Life in Another World-
Chapter 4: The Sanctuary
and the Witch of Greed

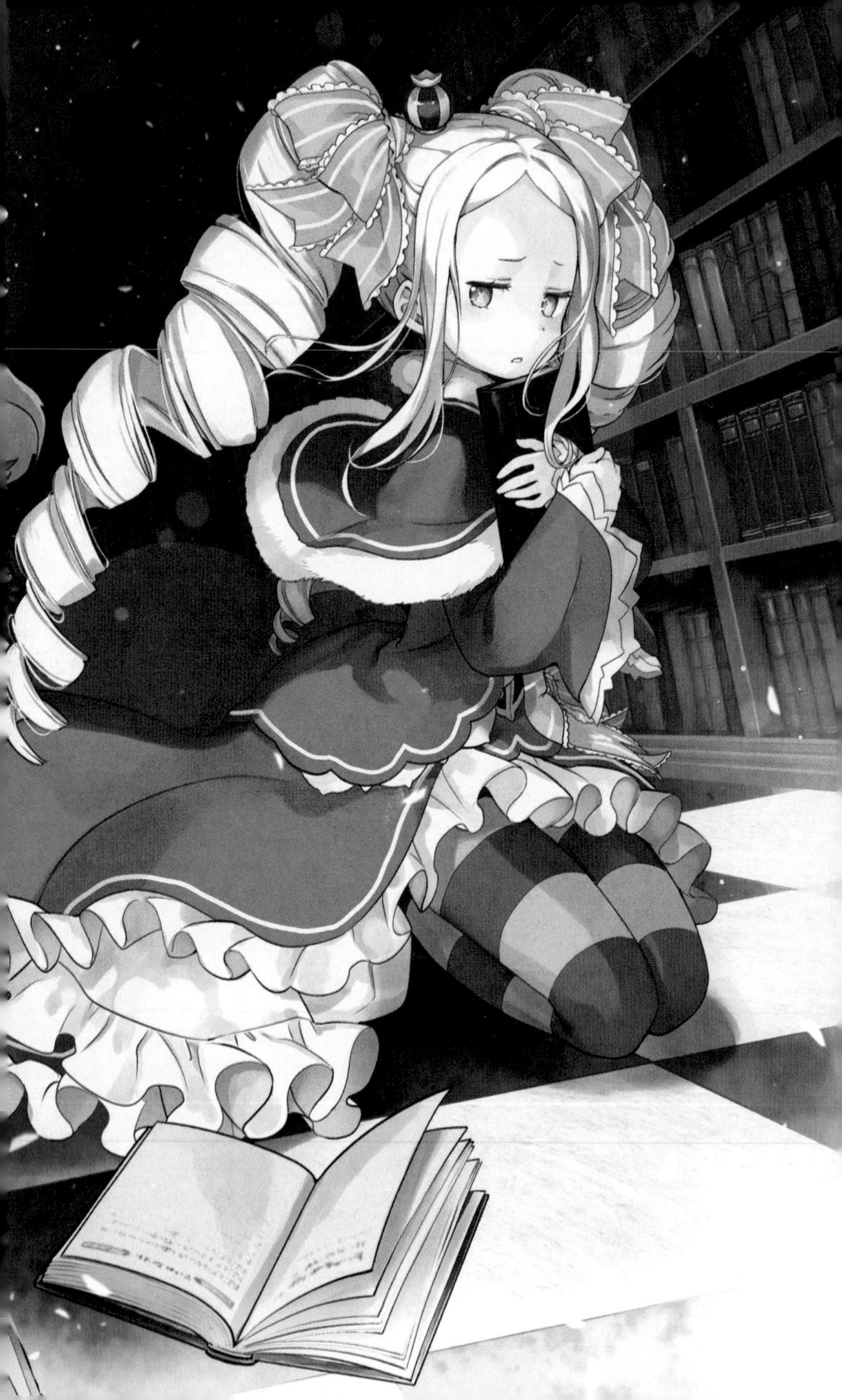

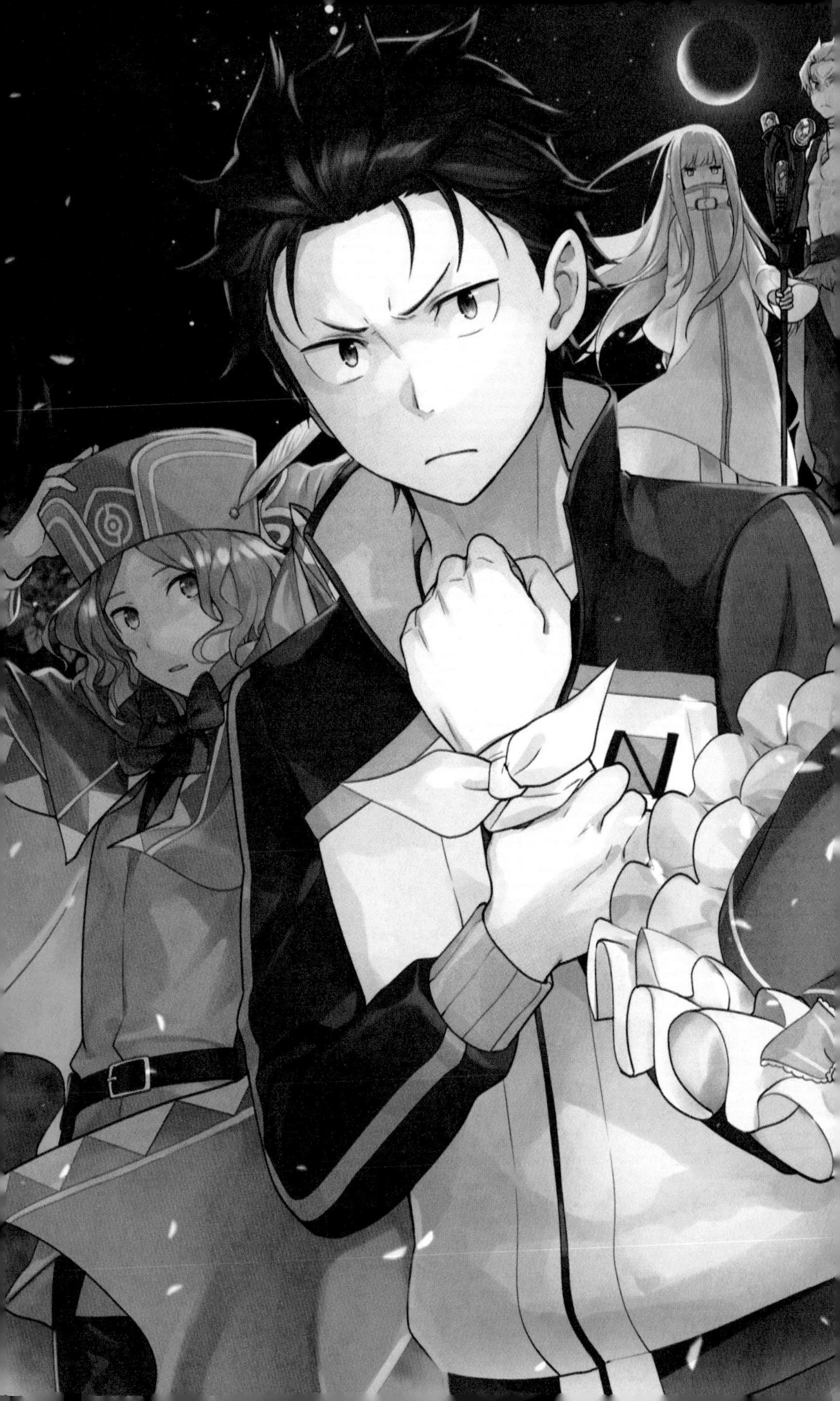

CONTENTS

Re:ZeRo
-Starting Life in Another World-
Chapter 4: The Sanctuary
and the Witch of Greed

APPARENTLY, I'M QUALIFIED TO TAKE THE TRIAL TOO.

YOU SAW THE RUIN SHINING, RIGHT?

Re:ZeRo
-Starting Life in Another World-

SUMMARY

TO BE THIS IS AN SITUATION.

On the way back from a convenience store, high school student Subaru Natsuki was suddenly summoned to another world.

The one ability the powerless boy gains is Return by Death, rewinding time upon his demise.

He strives to use this power for the happiness of those close to him.

TRA...?

WE'VE COME THIS FAR, AND YOU'RE STILL TALKING LIKE THAT, BIG SIS?

Subaru, returning to the Sanctuary after dying from Elsa's raid, succeeds in gaining Ram's aid and races straight to the mansion.

BACK, MASTER

YOU'RE BACK A LOT SOONER THAN EXPECTED.

Subaru is able to assuage his concerns over the safety of Rem and Petra and unravel his suspicions toward Frederica. Yet the very moment he breathes in relief, the Bowel Hunter appears before them once more —

YOU WERE SAFE.

No

...LET U FULFIL THE PROMIS BETWEE US.

Re:ZERO -Starting Life in Another World-
Chapter 4: The Sanctuary and the Witc

CHARACTERS

Re:ZERO -Starting Life in Another World-

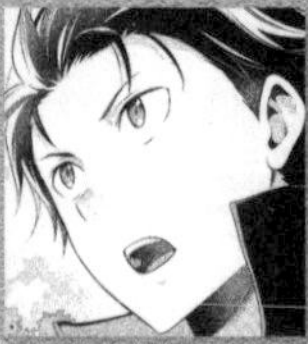

Subaru Natsuki

Modern Japanese boy transported to another world. Strives to use his only power, Return by Death, for the sake of those close to him.

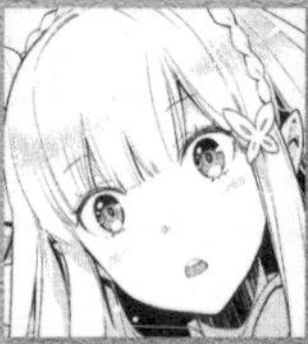

Emilia

Beautiful half-elf girl. Spirit mage served by the cat-form spirit Puck, one of those seeking to become the next Queen of Lugunica.

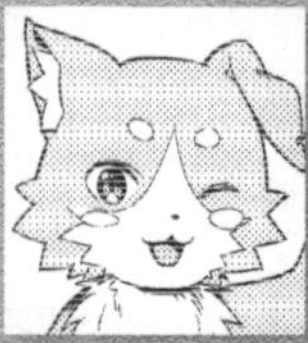

Puck

Spirit in cat form acting in concert with Emilia, who watches over her like a parent. In contrast to his appearance, he wields very powerful magic.

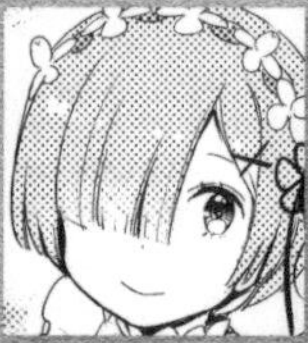

Rem

Demon girl working as a maid at Roswaal Manor where Emilia resides. After the battle with the Witch Cult's Archbishop, she vanished from the memories of others and became a so-called Sleeping Princess.

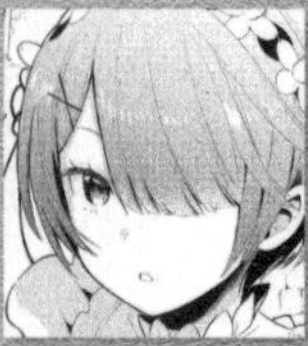

Ram

As a maid of Roswaal Manor, she runs the mansion alongside her twin sister, Rem. She is arrogant and foul-mouthed, but her gentle disposition runs deep.

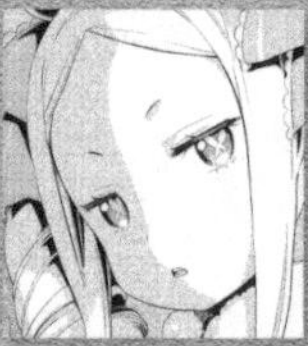

Beatrice

Calls herself the Librarian of the Archive of Forbidden Books at Roswaal Manor. A girl wearing an extravagant dress, she is an exceptionally high-end user of Dark Magic, allowing her to move freely throughout the mansion.

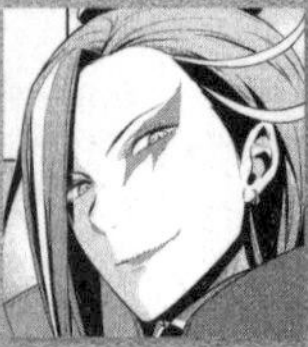

Roswaal L. Mathers

Holds the title of Marquis. Upper-ranking noble of the Kingdom of Lugunica. Sponsor of Emilia in the royal selection. A famous eccentric, he wears clown-like makeup and bizarre outfits.

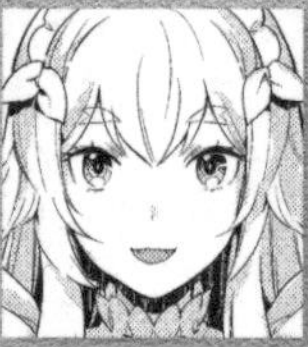

Frederica Baumann

Eldest maid of Roswaal Manor. Formerly on leave for personal reasons, she was summoned back by Ram.

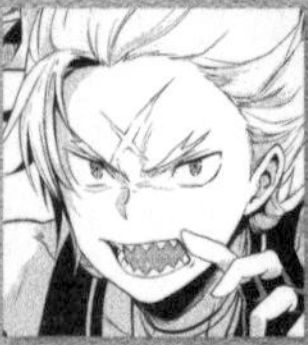

Garfiel Tinzel

A young man with a foul look, sharp fangs, a short temper, and barbaric personality to match. The limit of his combat ability is unknown, but he can easily hurl a land dragon weighing hundreds of kilograms.

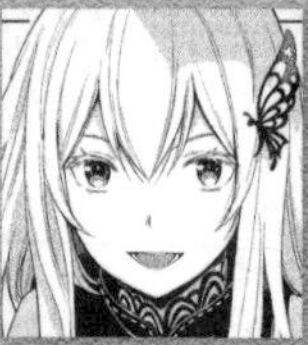

Echidna

One of the seven Witches, dubbed the Witch of Greed for craving all of the knowledge of the world. Destroyed by the Witch of Jealousy, her soul is presently captive in the Sanctuary's tomb.

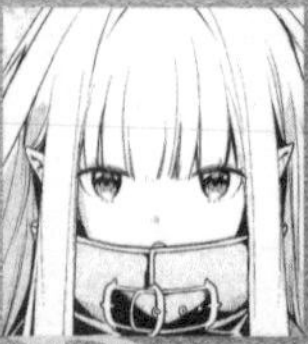

Ryuzu Bilma

Representative of the Sanctuary of Cremaldi. Has long known Garfiel and acts far older than her outward appearance.

Re:ZeRo -Starting Life in Another World-

Chapter 4: The Sanctuary and the Witch of Greed

Episode 14
The Return of Madness

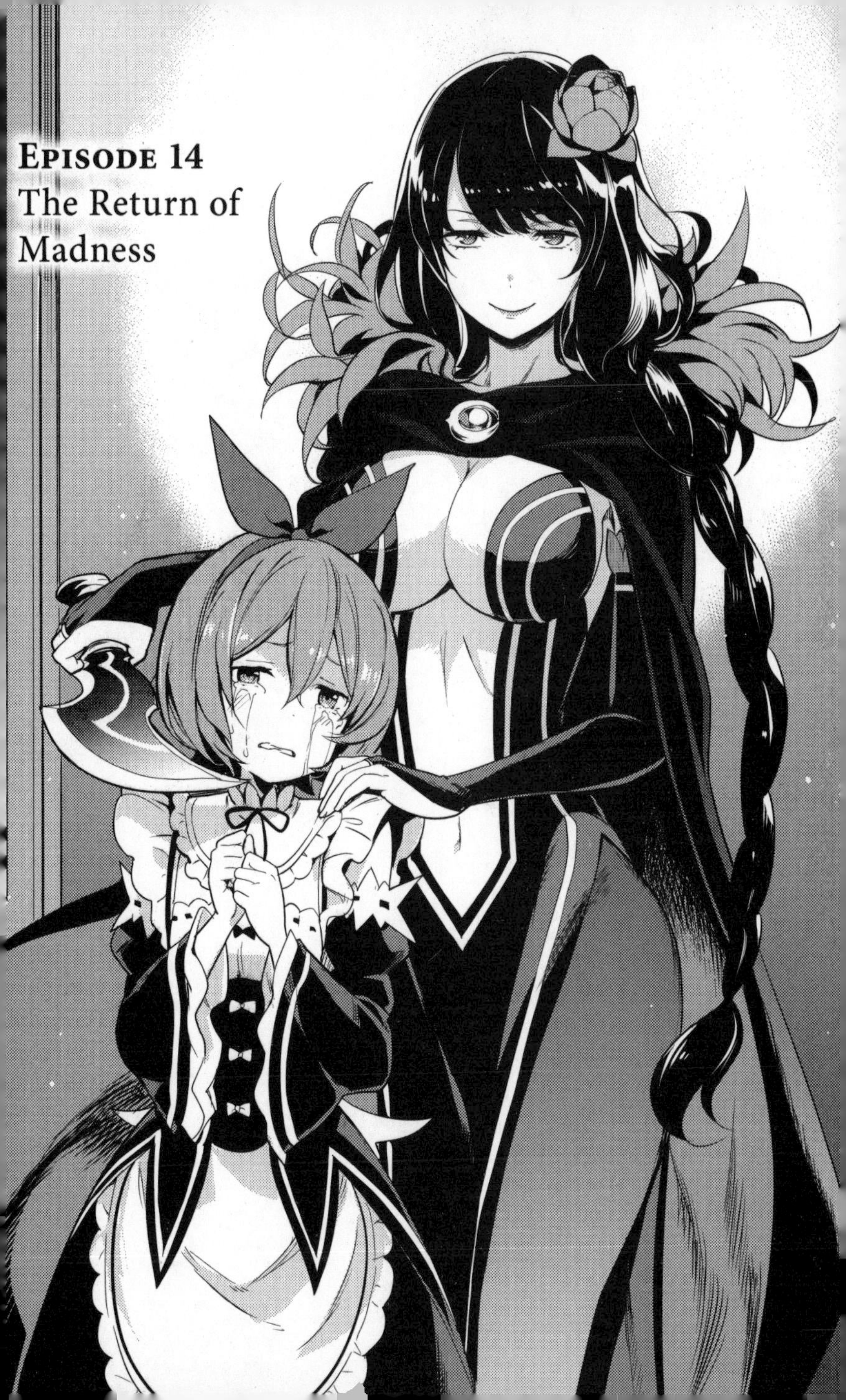

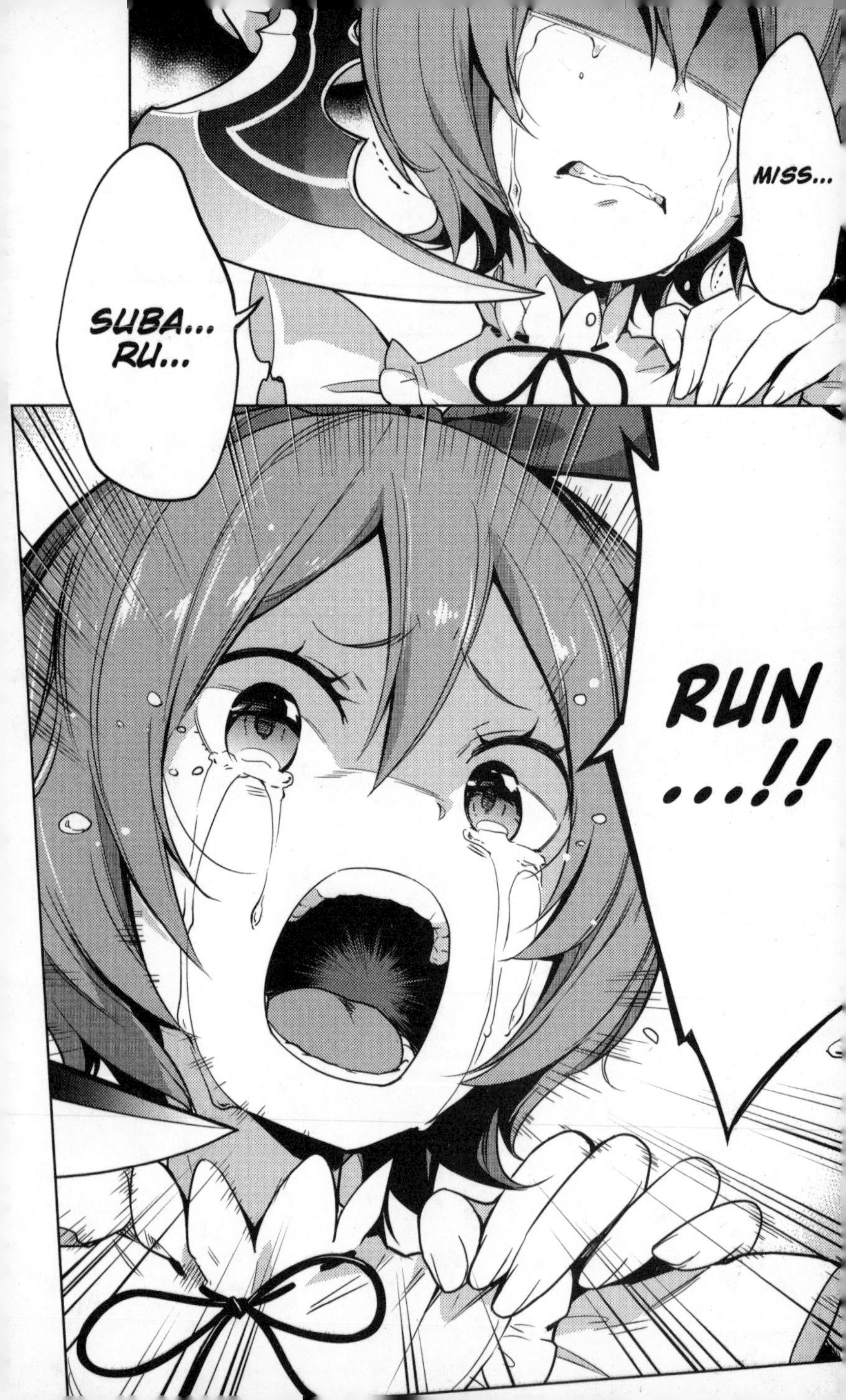
MISS...
SUBA... RU...
RUN ...!!

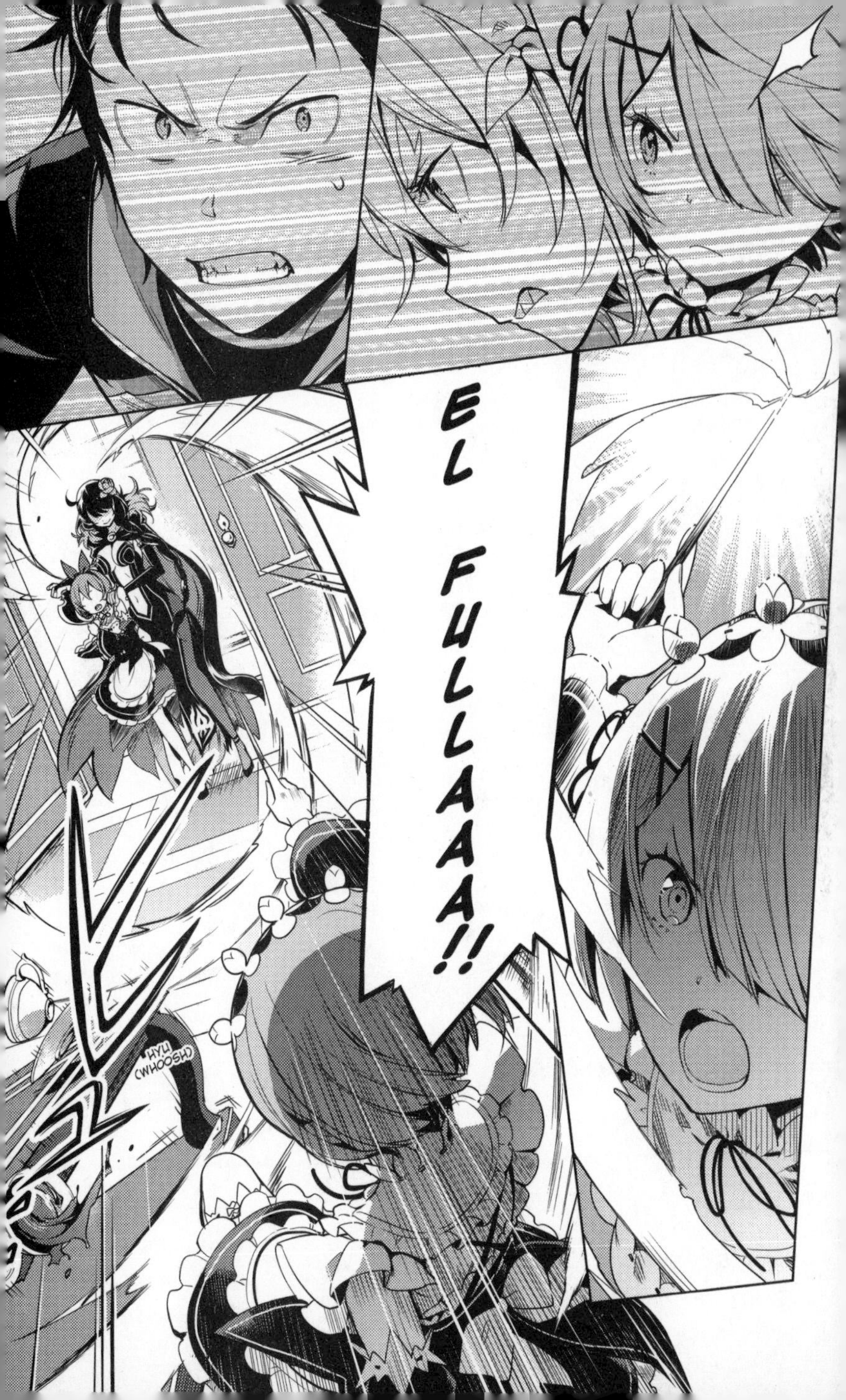
EL FULLAAA!!
HYU (WHOOSH)

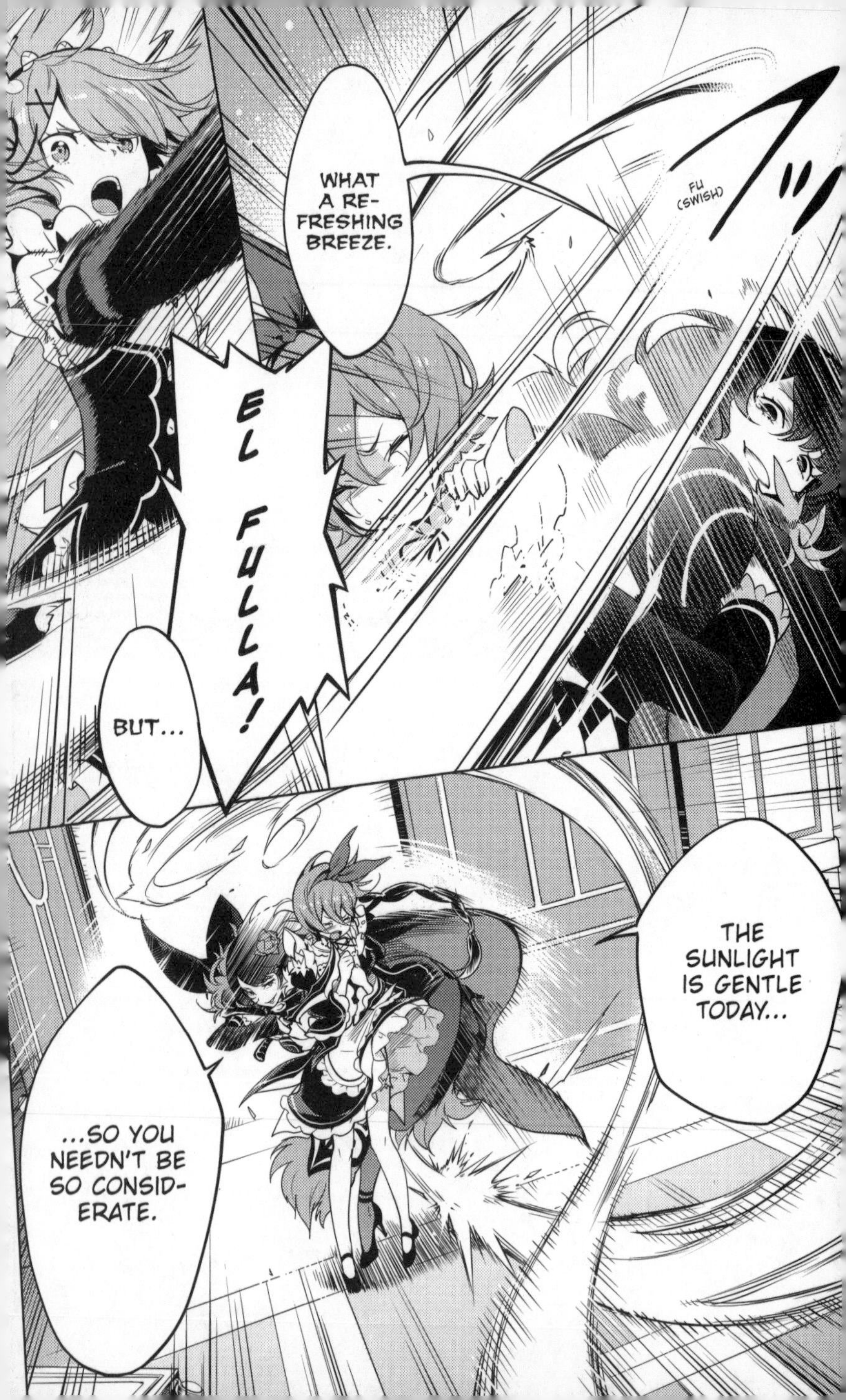
FU (SWISH)
WHAT A REFRESHING BREEZE.
EL FULLA!
BUT...
THE SUNLIGHT IS GENTLE TODAY...
...SO YOU NEEDN'T BE SO CONSIDERATE.

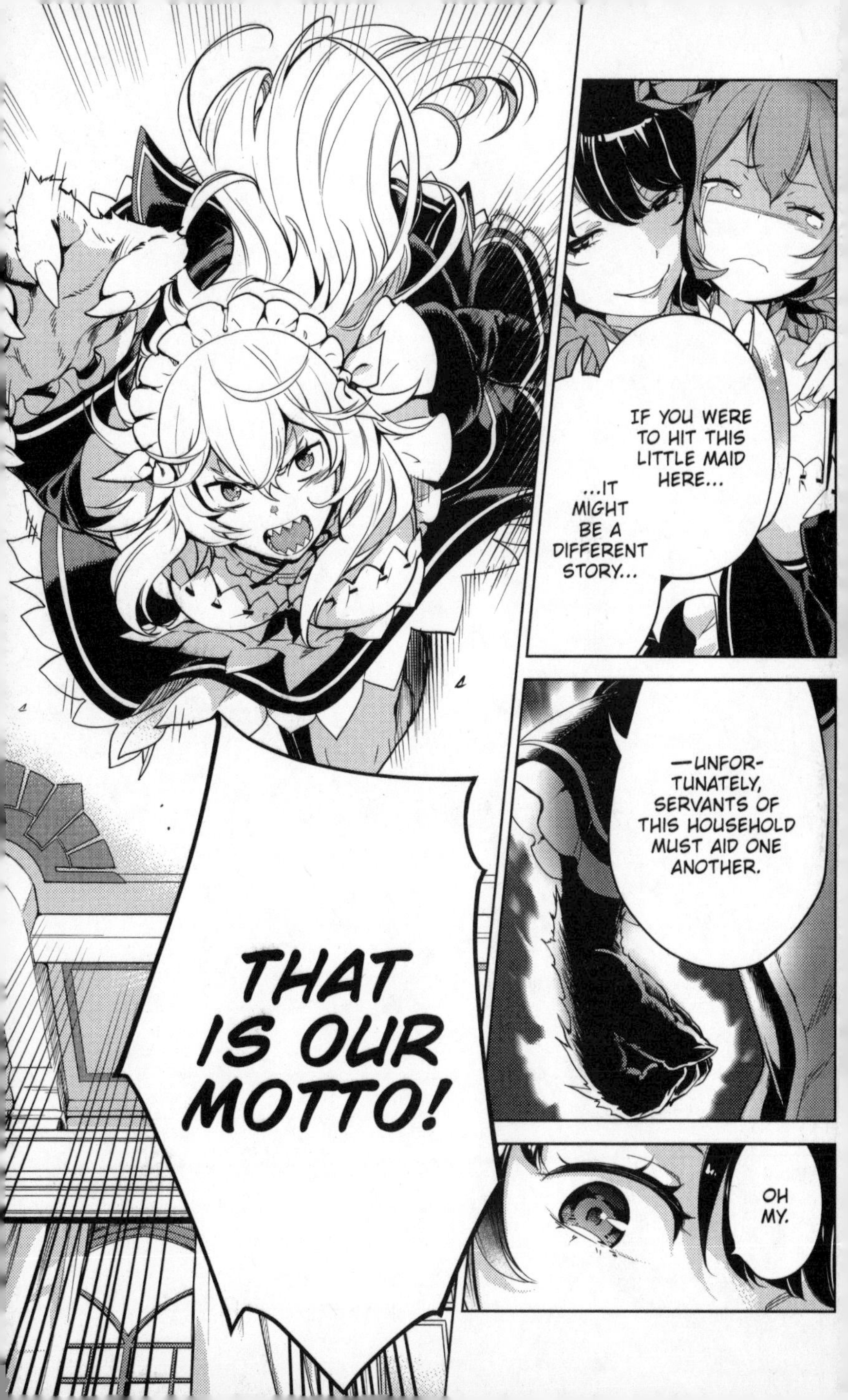
IF YOU WERE TO HIT THIS LITTLE MAID HERE...
...IT MIGHT BE A DIFFERENT STORY...
—UNFOR-TUNATELY, SERVANTS OF THIS HOUSEHOLD MUST AID ONE ANOTHER.
OH MY.
THAT IS OUR MOTTO!

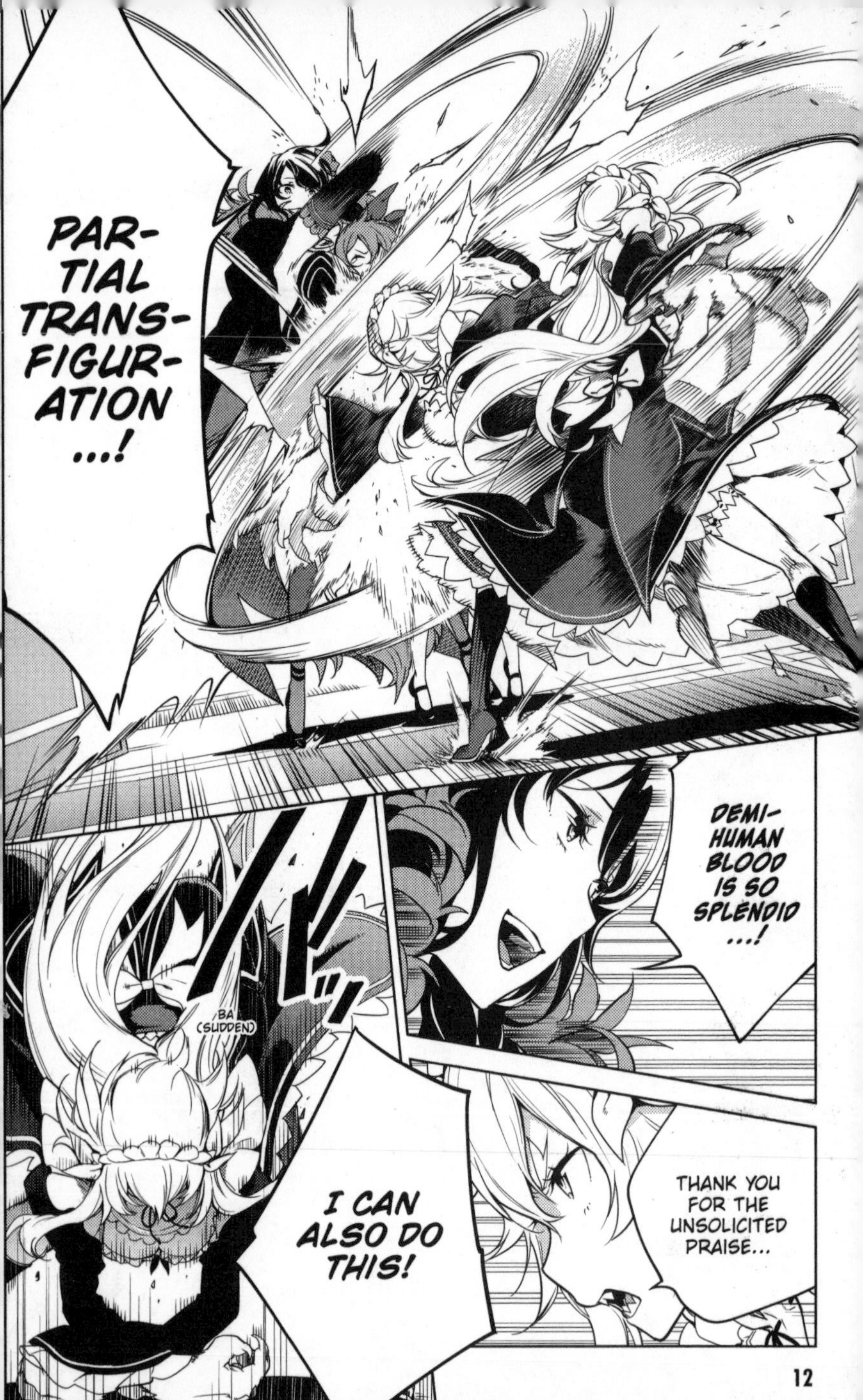
PAR-TIAL TRANS-FIGUR-ATION ...!
DEMI-HUMAN BLOOD IS SO SPLENDID ...!
THANK YOU FOR THE UNSOLICITED PRAISE...
BA (SUDDEN)
I CAN ALSO DO THIS!

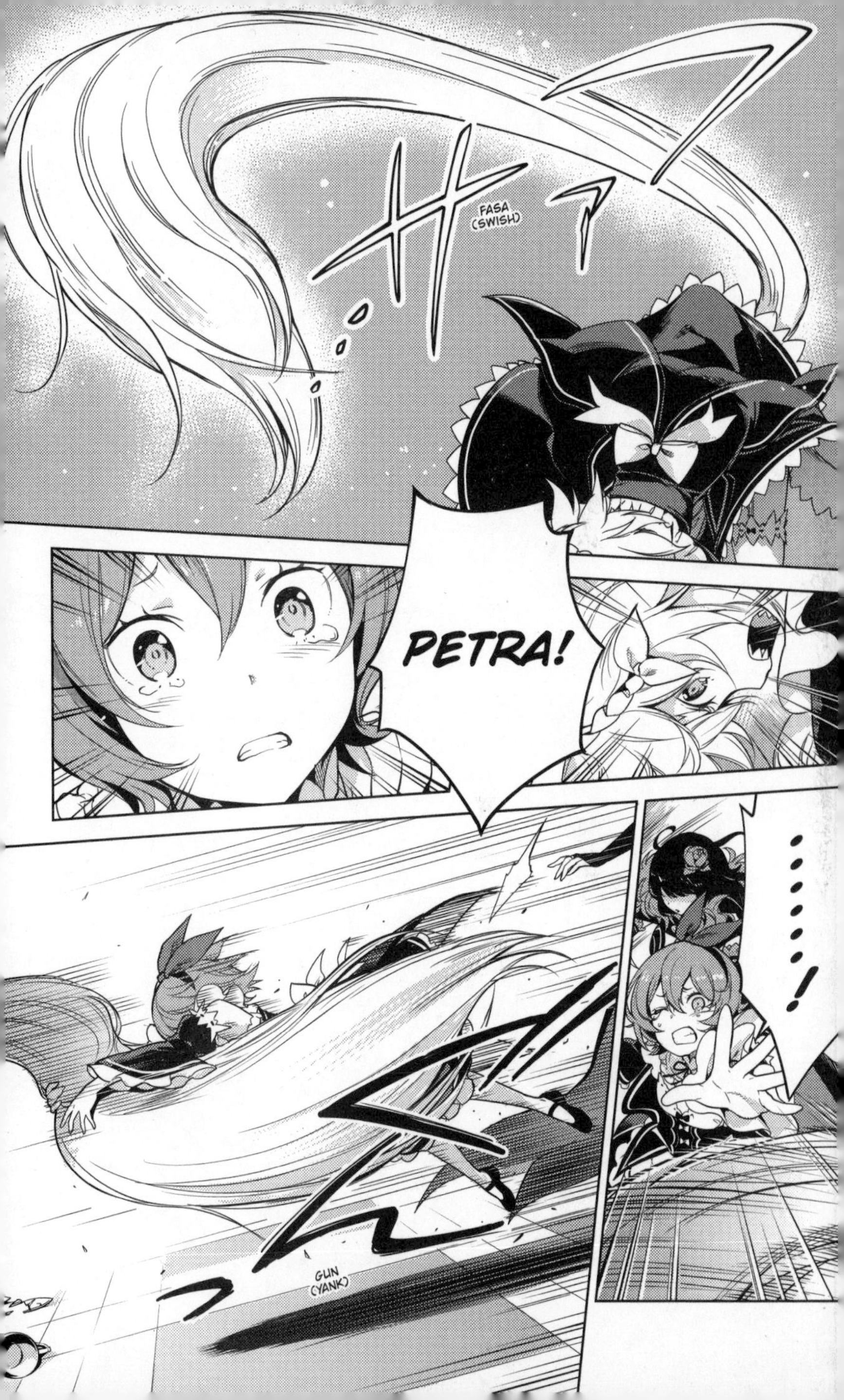
FASA (SWISH)
PETRA!
......!
GUN (YANK)

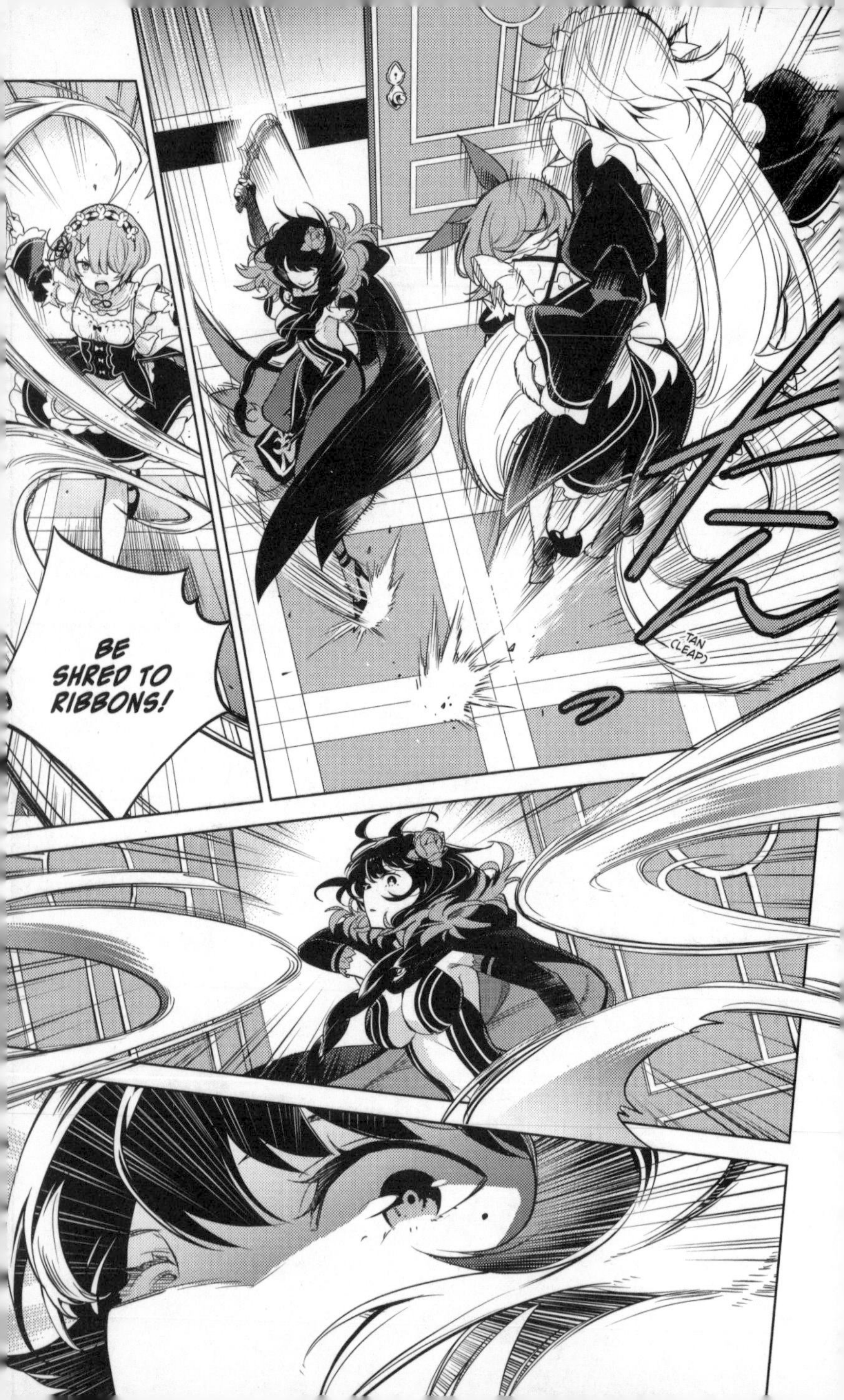
TAN (LEAP)
BE SHRED TO RIBBONS!

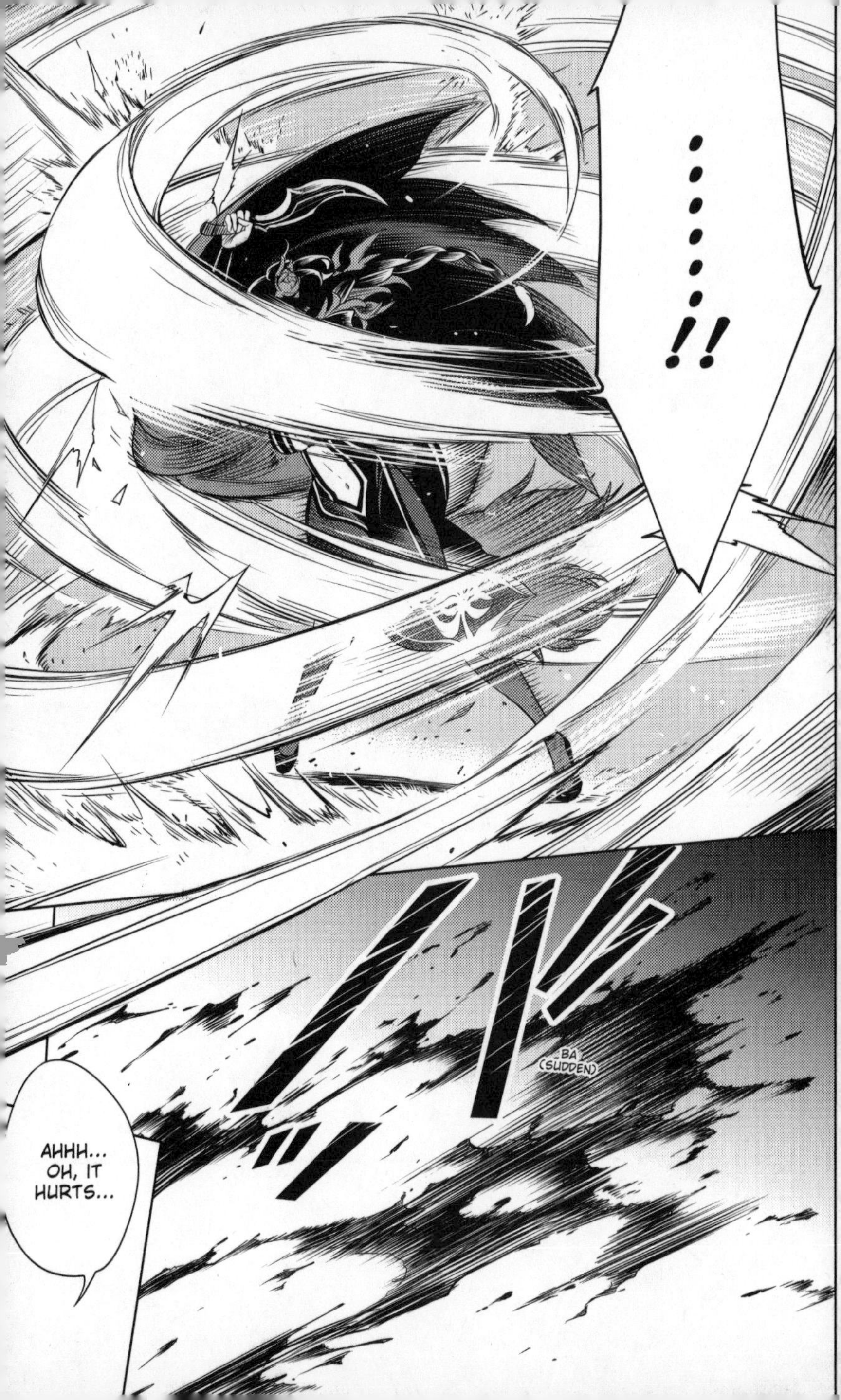

......!!
BA (SUDDEN)
AHHH... OH, IT HURTS...

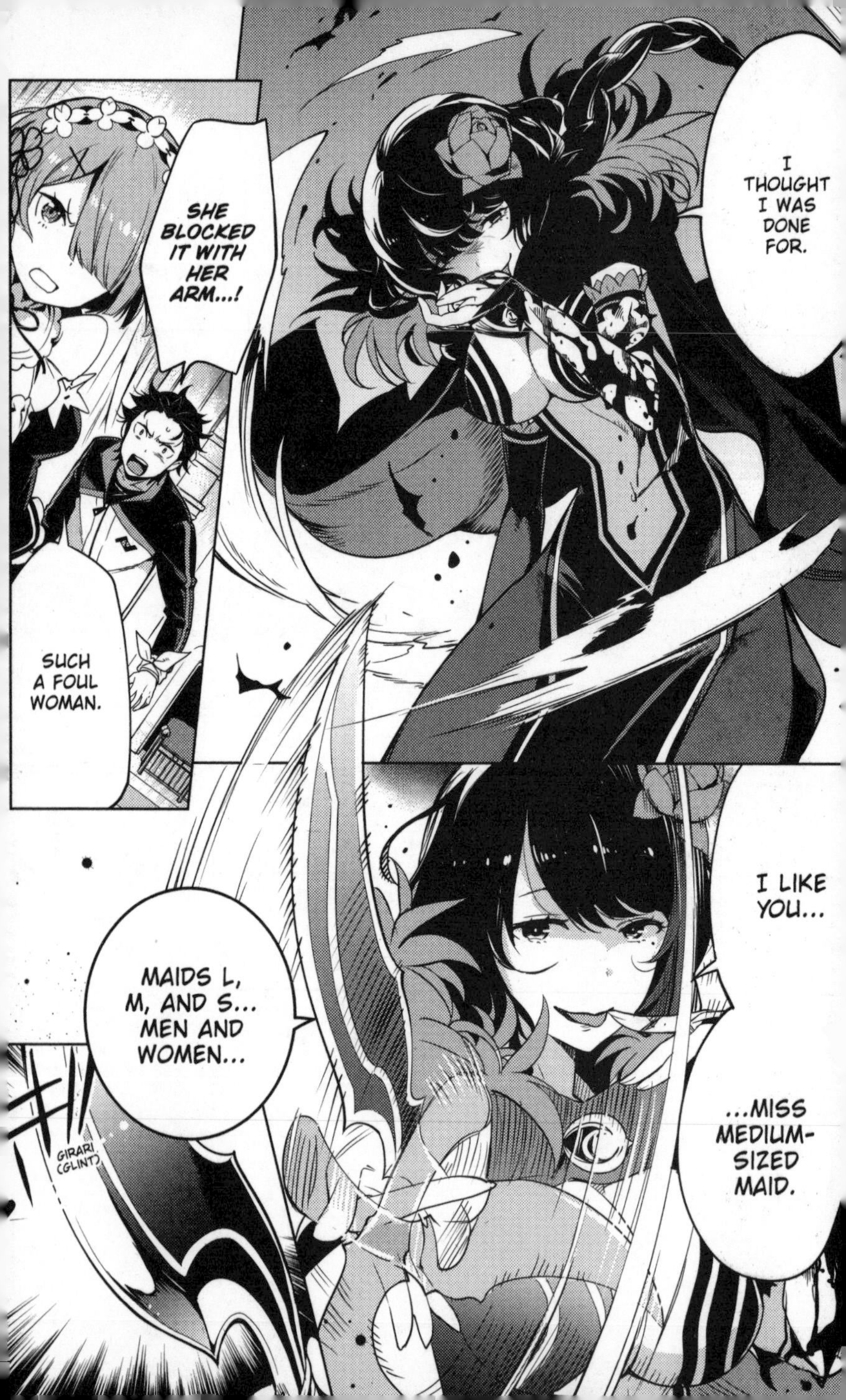
I THOUGHT I WAS DONE FOR.
SHE BLOCKED IT WITH HER ARM...!
SUCH A FOUL WOMAN.
I LIKE YOU...
MAIDS L, M, AND S... MEN AND WOMEN...
...MISS MEDIUM-SIZED MAID.
GIRARI (GLINT)

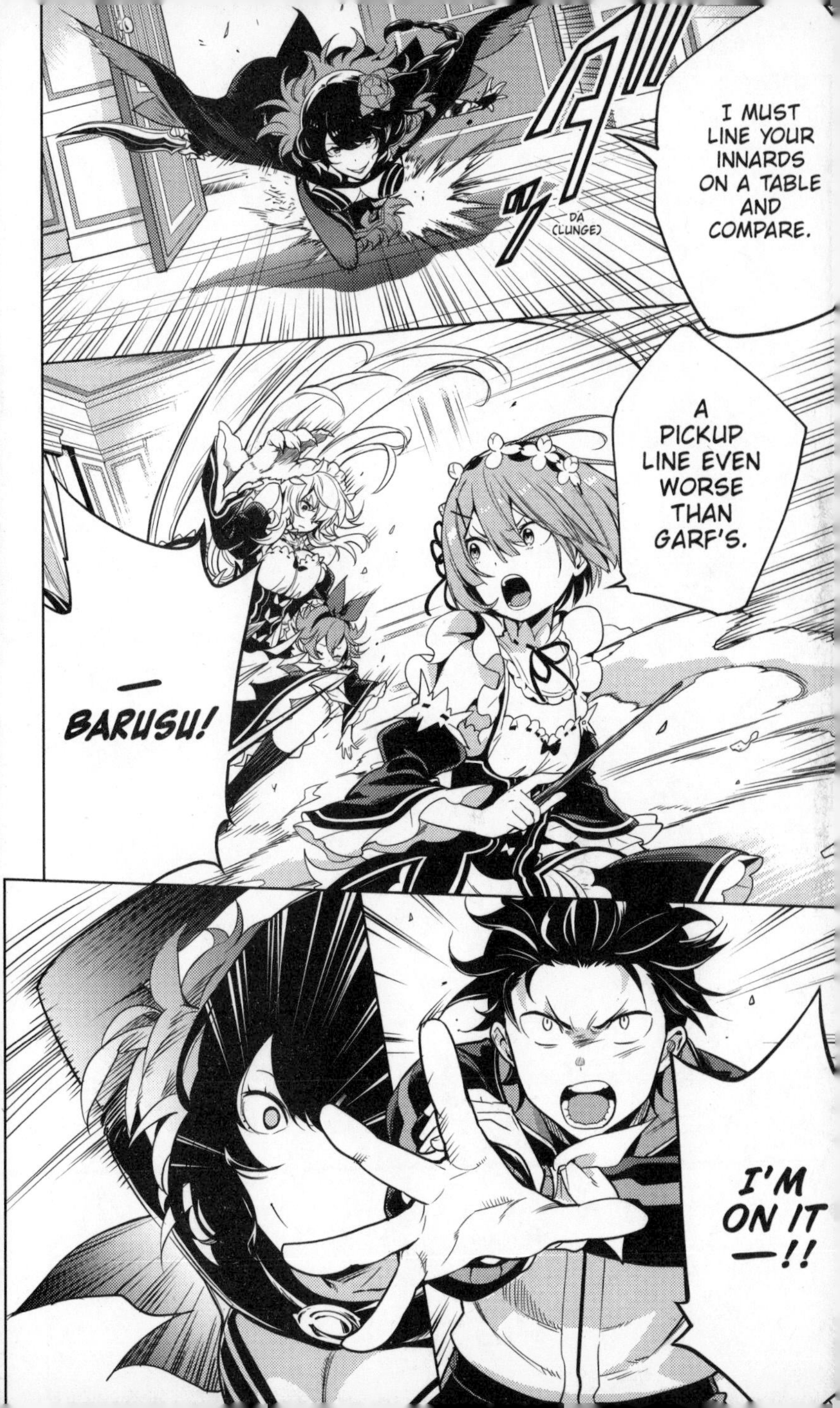
I MUST LINE YOUR INNARDS ON A TABLE AND COMPARE.
DA (LUNGE)
A PICKUP LINE EVEN WORSE THAN GARF'S.
—BARUSU!
I'M ON IT—!!

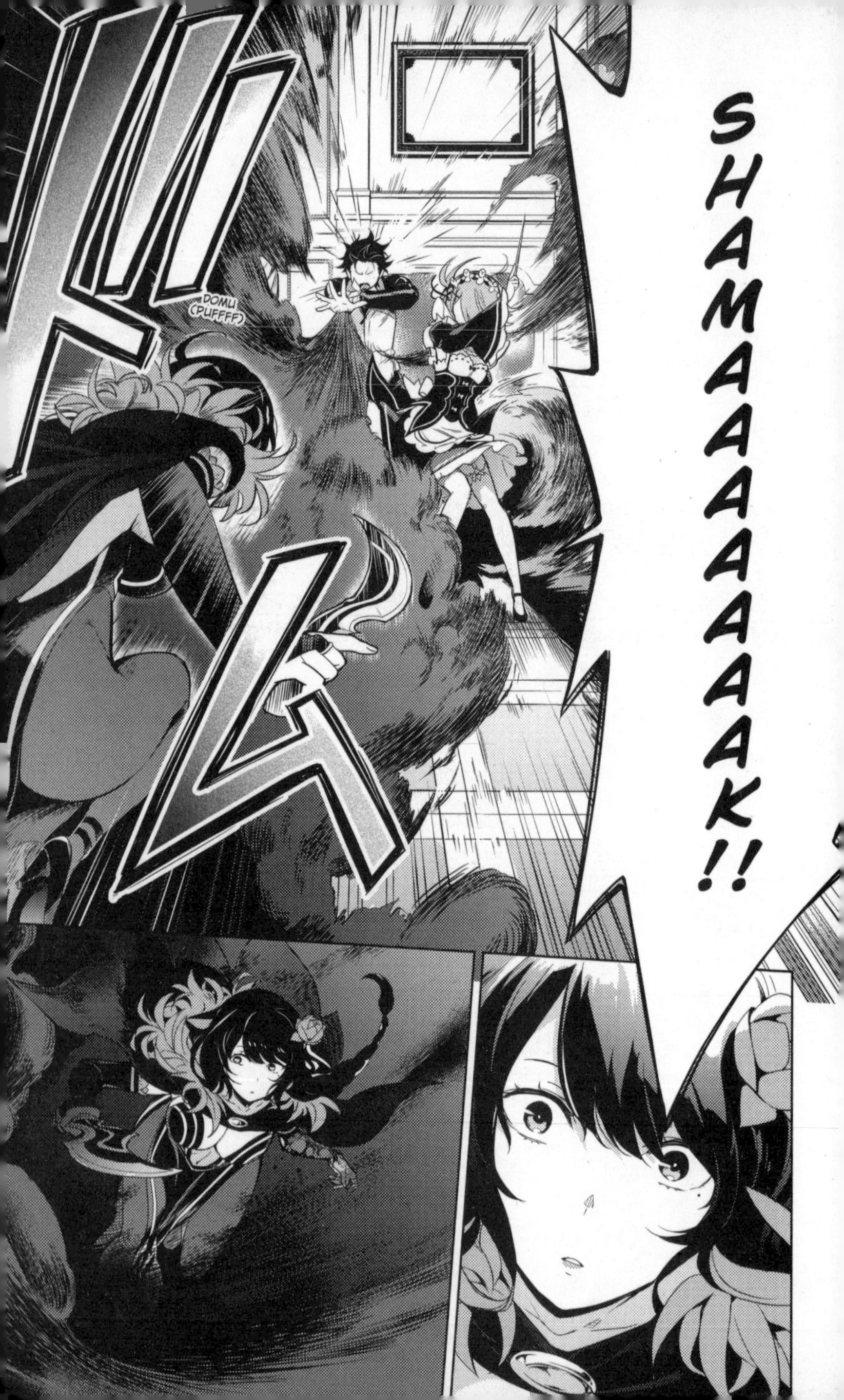
SHAMAAAAAAAAK!!
DOMU (PUFFFF)

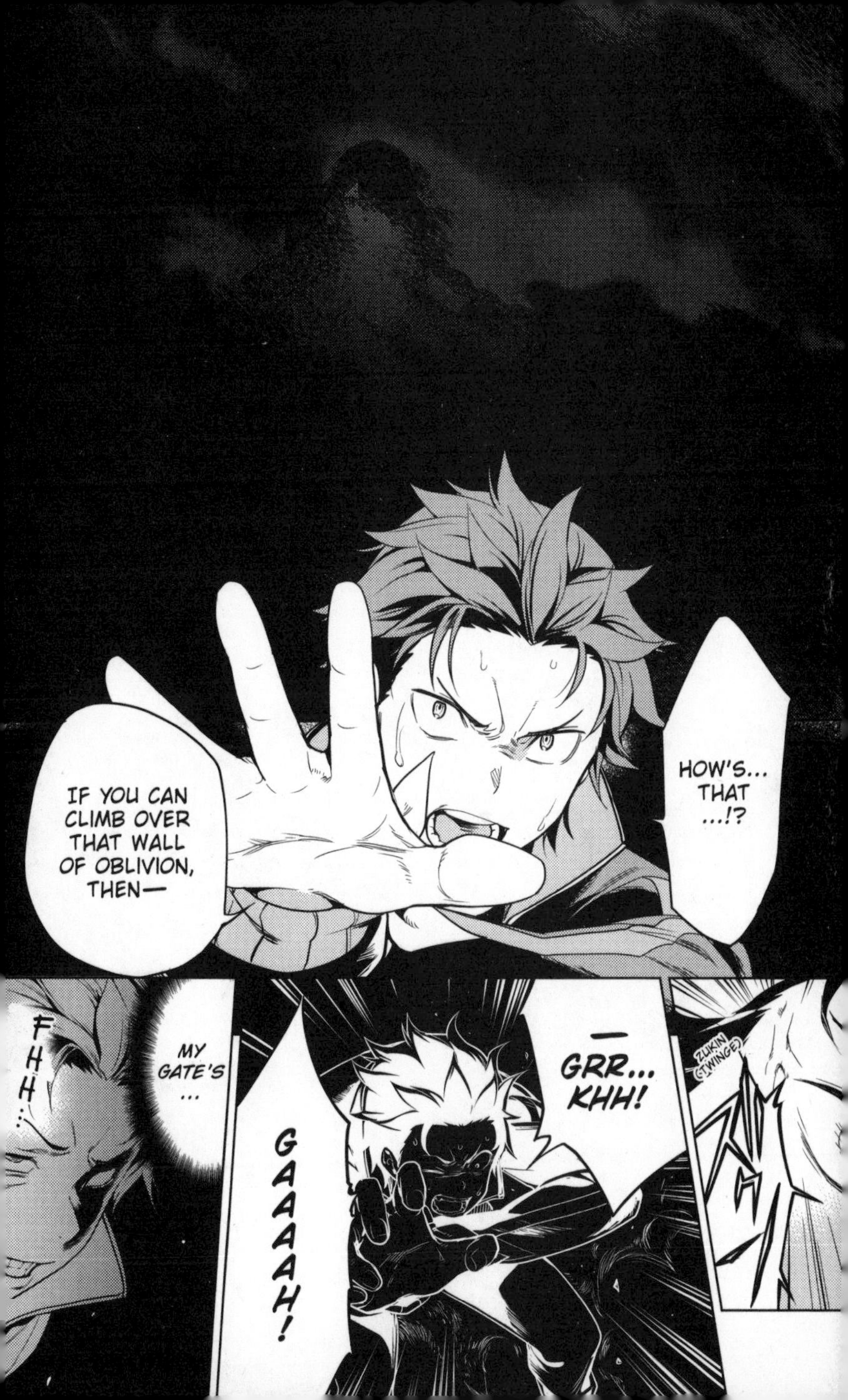
HOW'S... THAT ...!?
IF YOU CAN CLIMB OVER THAT WALL OF OBLIVION, THEN—
ZUKIN (TWINGE)
—GRR... KHH!
GAAAAAH!
MY GATE'S ...
FHH...

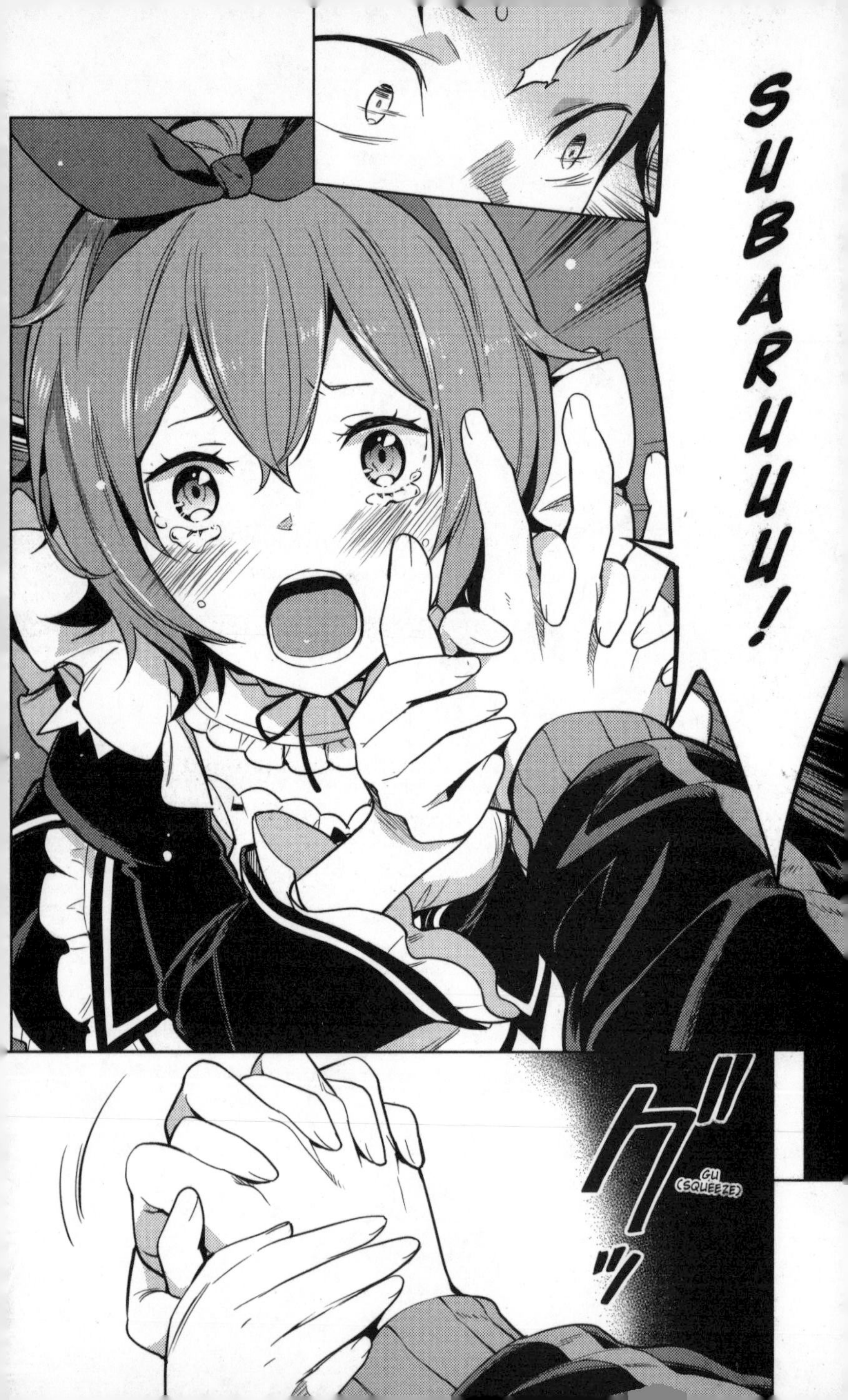
SUBARUUUU!
GU (SQUEEZE)

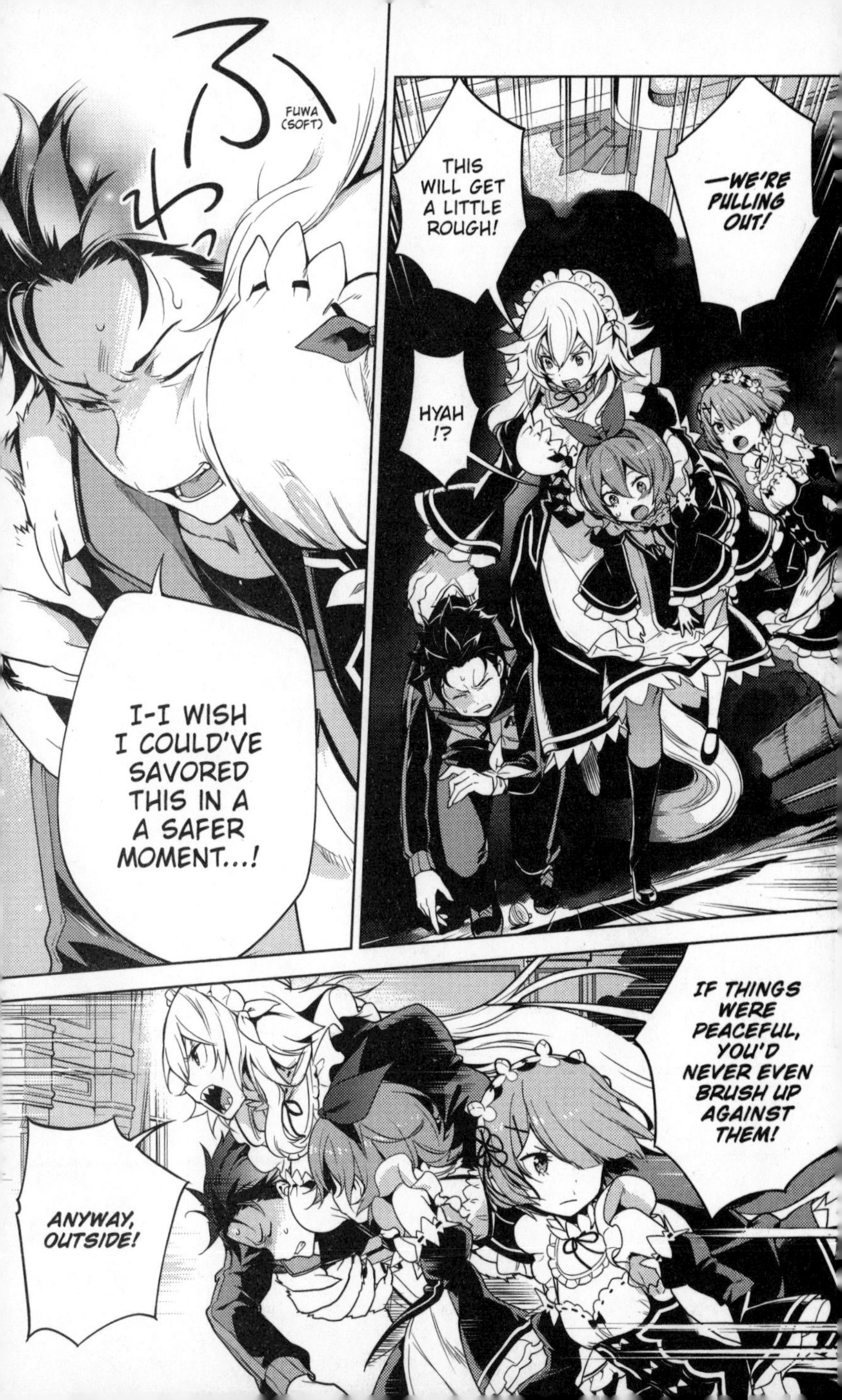
—WE'RE PULLING OUT!
THIS WILL GET A LITTLE ROUGH!
HYAH!?
ふわっ
FUWA (SOFT)
I-I WISH I COULD'VE SAVORED THIS IN A A SAFER MOMENT...!
IF THINGS WERE PEACEFUL, YOU'D NEVER EVEN BRUSH UP AGAINST THEM!
ANYWAY, OUTSIDE!

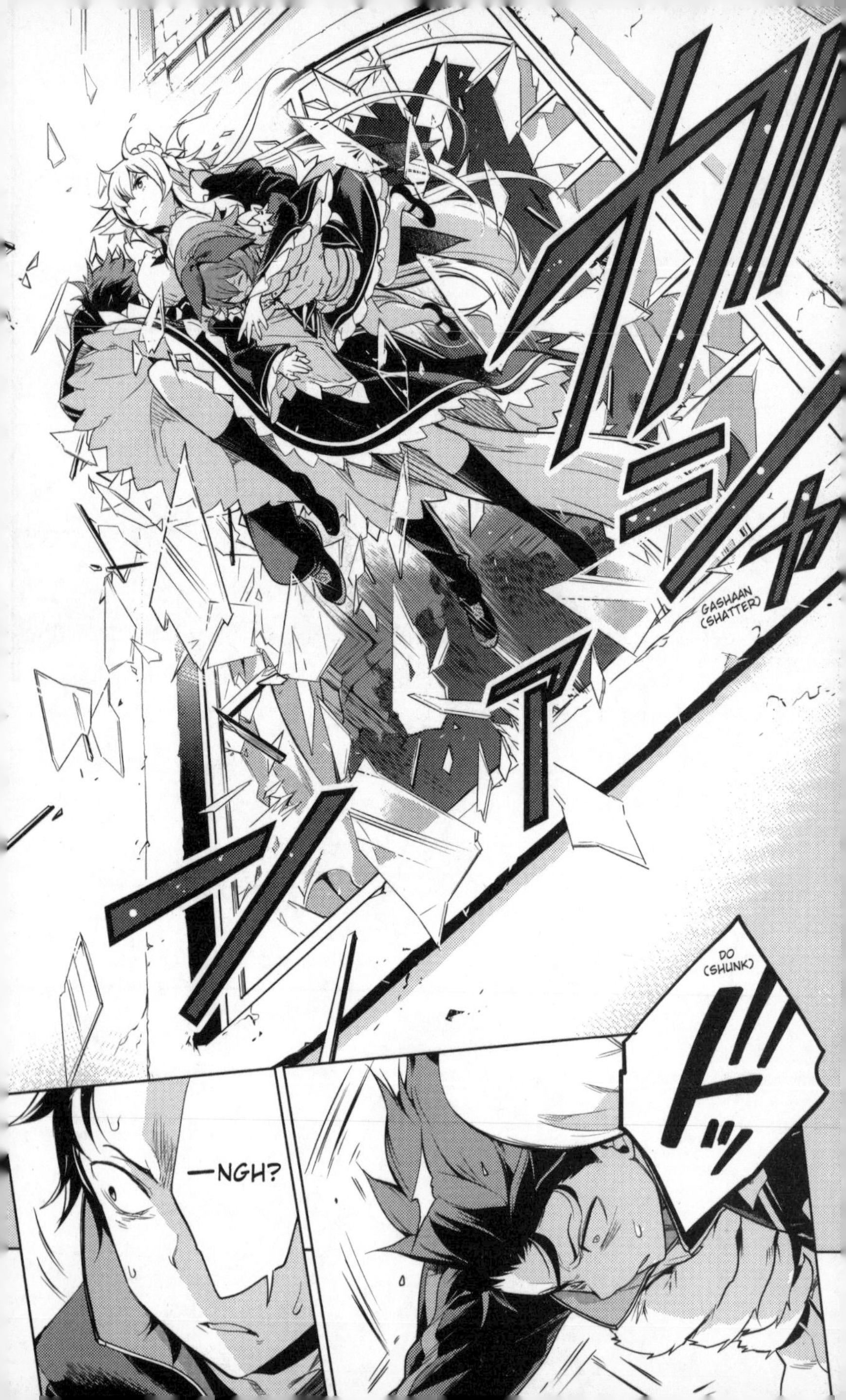
GASHAAN
(SHATTER)
DO
(SHUNK)
—NGH?

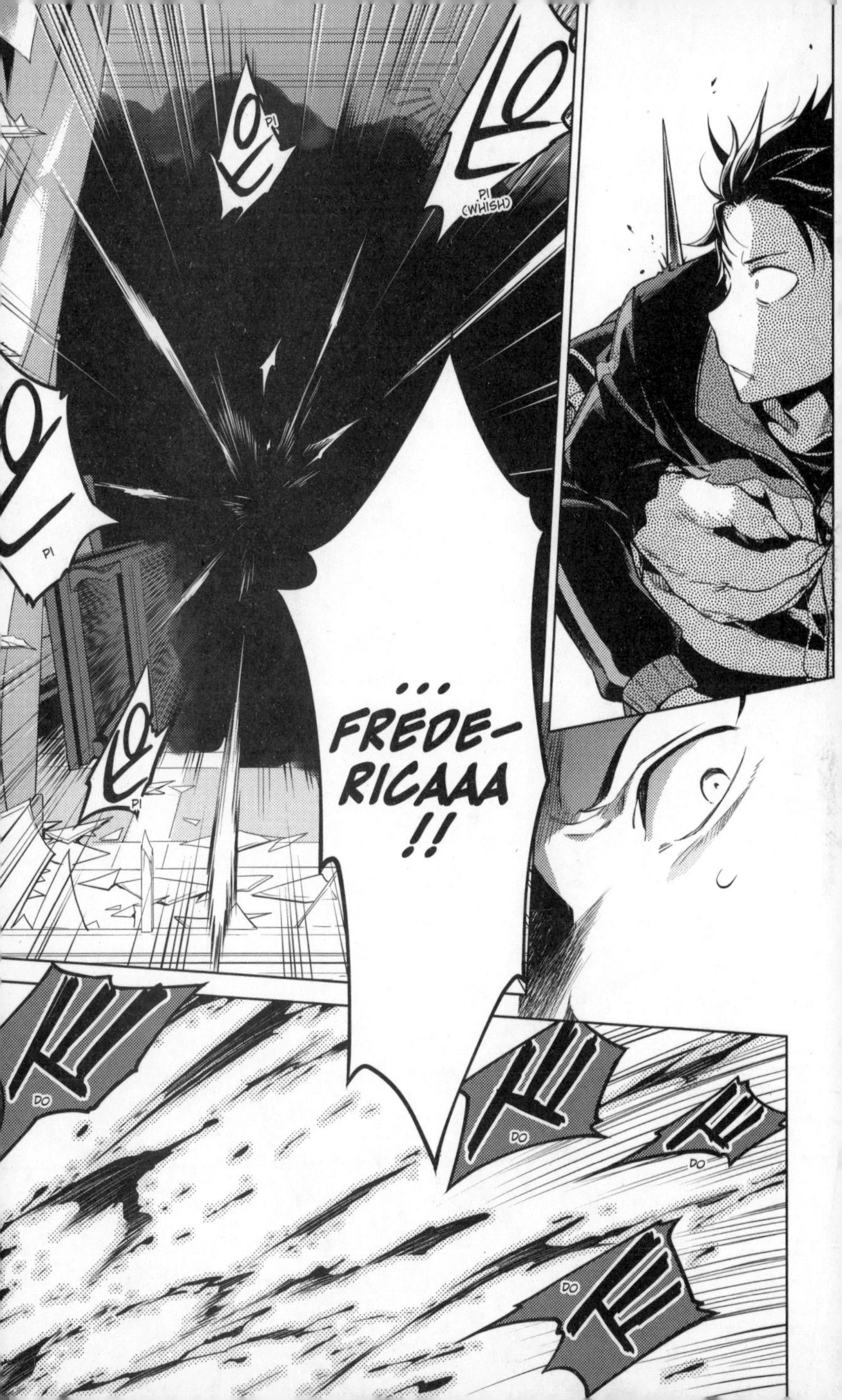
PI
PI (WHISH)
PI
PI
...FREDE-RICAAA!!
DO
DO
DO
DO

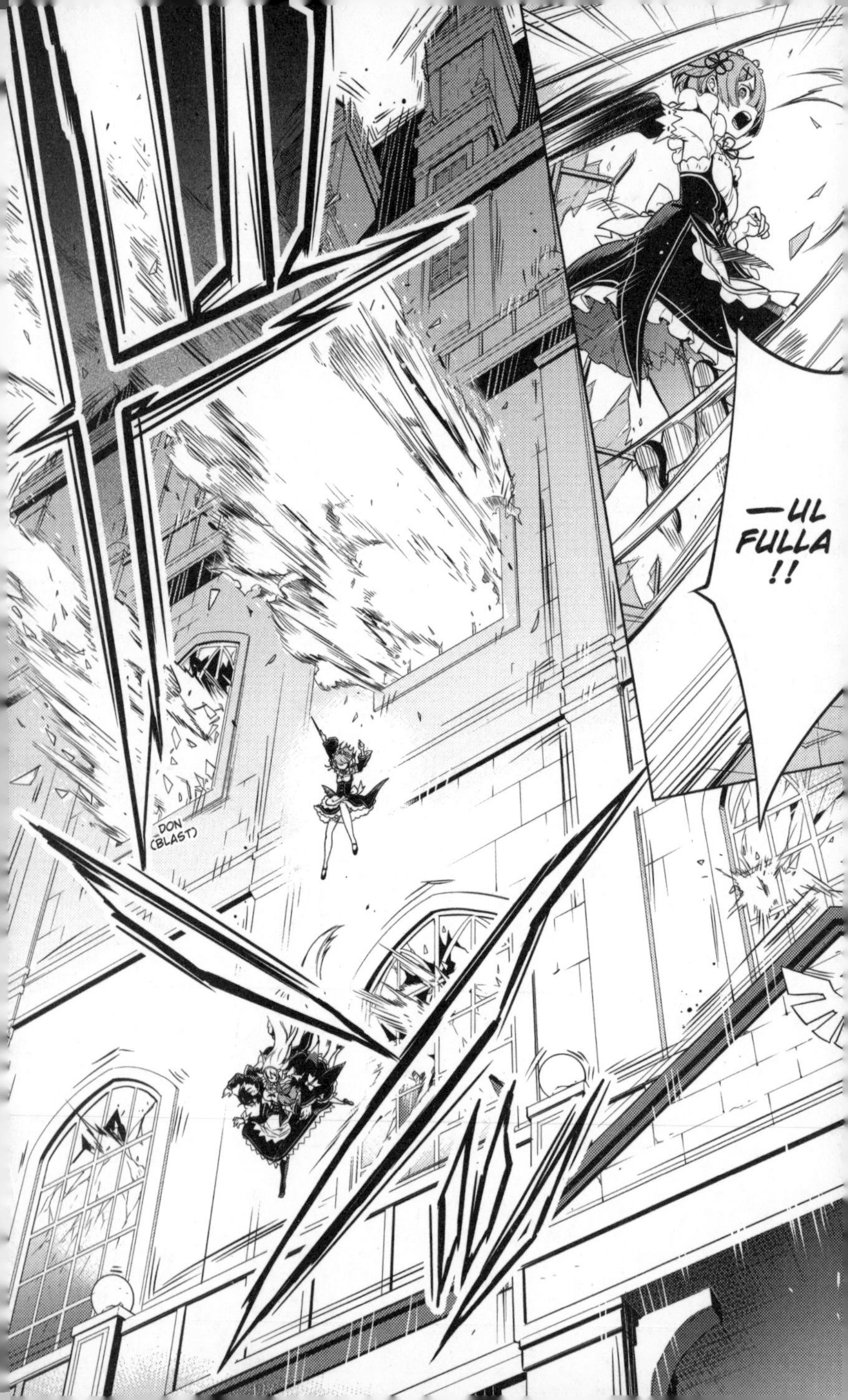
—UL FULLA!!
DON (BLAST)

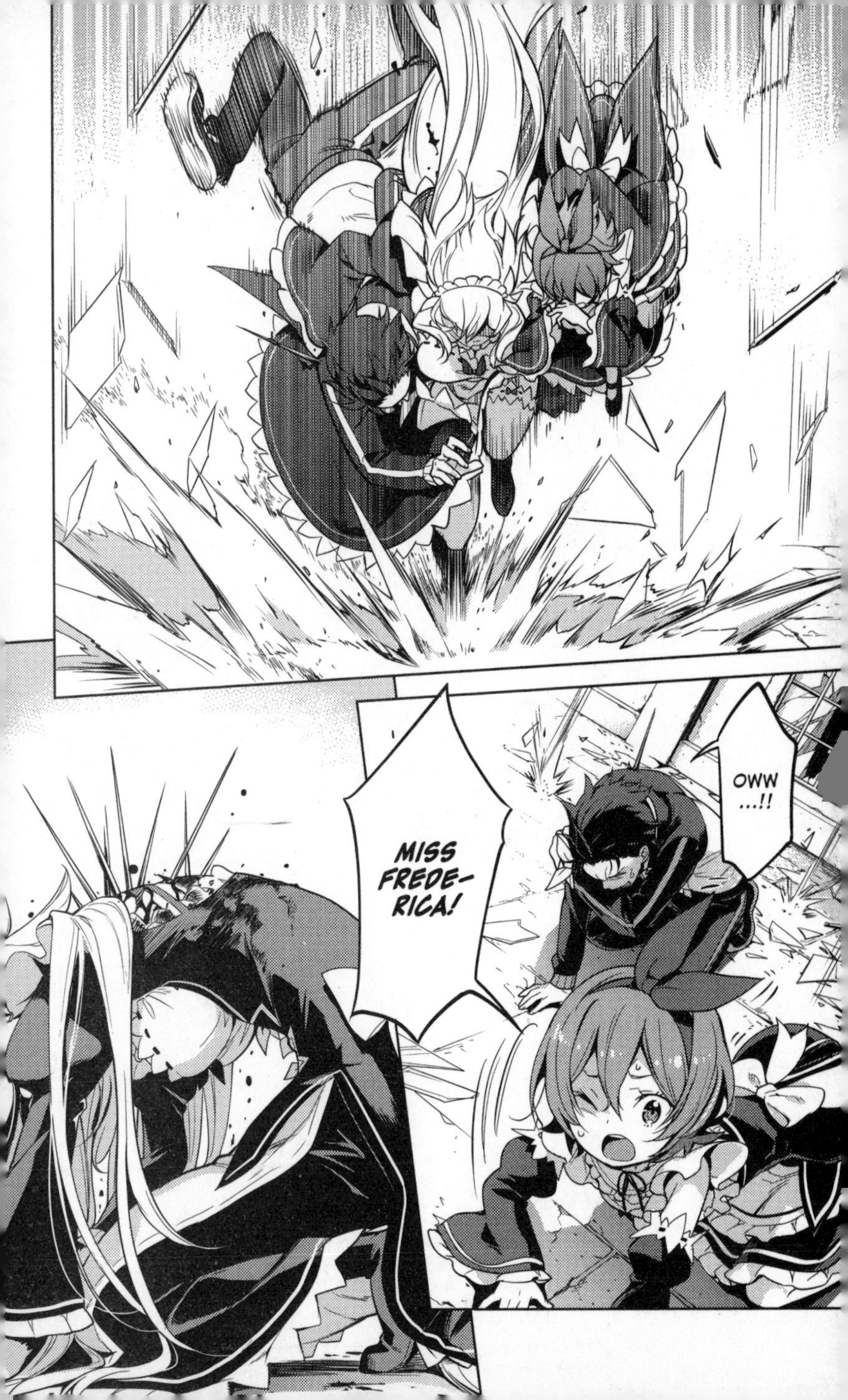
OWW ...!!
MISS FREDE-RICA!

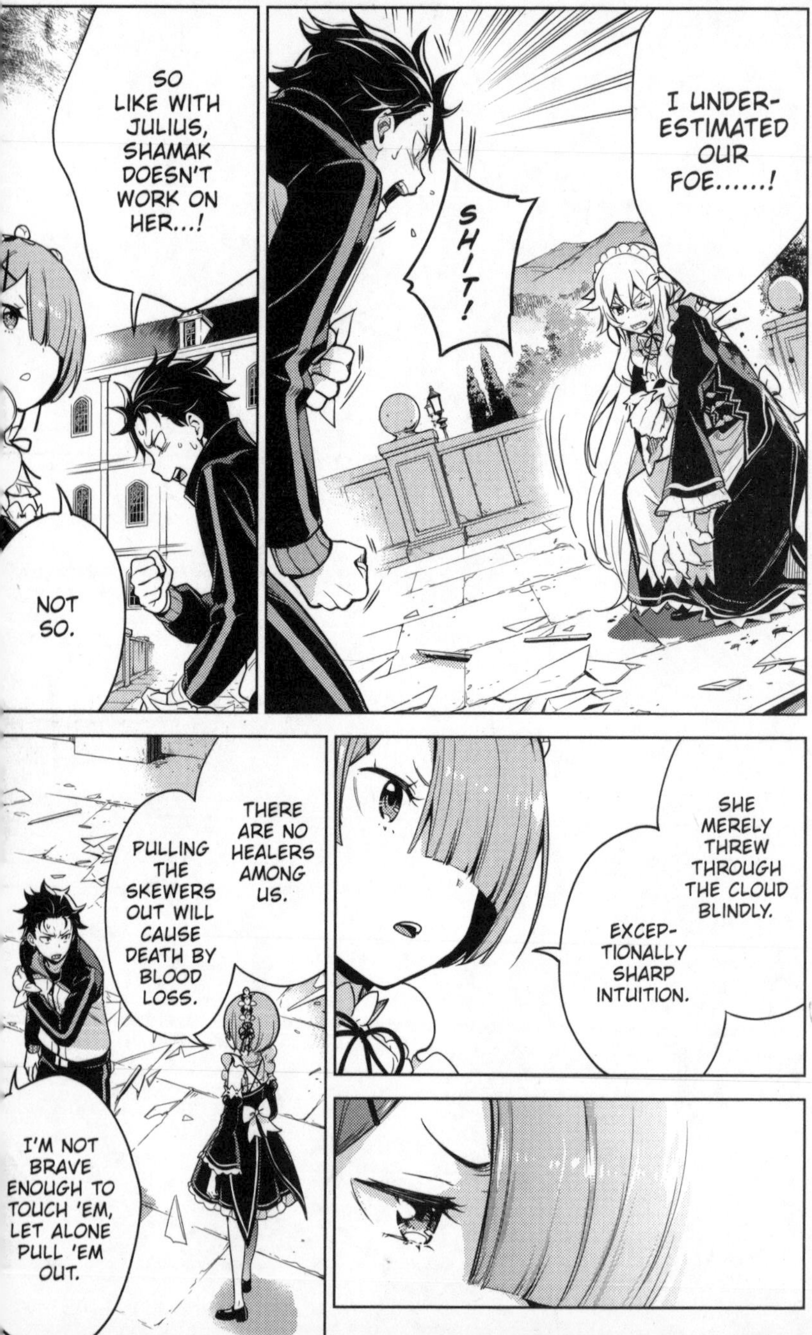
I UNDER-ESTIMATED OUR FOE......!
SHIT!
SO LIKE WITH JULIUS, SHAMAK DOESN'T WORK ON HER...!
NOT SO.
SHE MERELY THREW THROUGH THE CLOUD BLINDLY.
EXCEPTIONALLY SHARP INTUITION.
THERE ARE NO HEALERS AMONG US.
PULLING THE SKEWERS OUT WILL CAUSE DEATH BY BLOOD LOSS.
I'M NOT BRAVE ENOUGH TO TOUCH 'EM, LET ALONE PULL 'EM OUT.

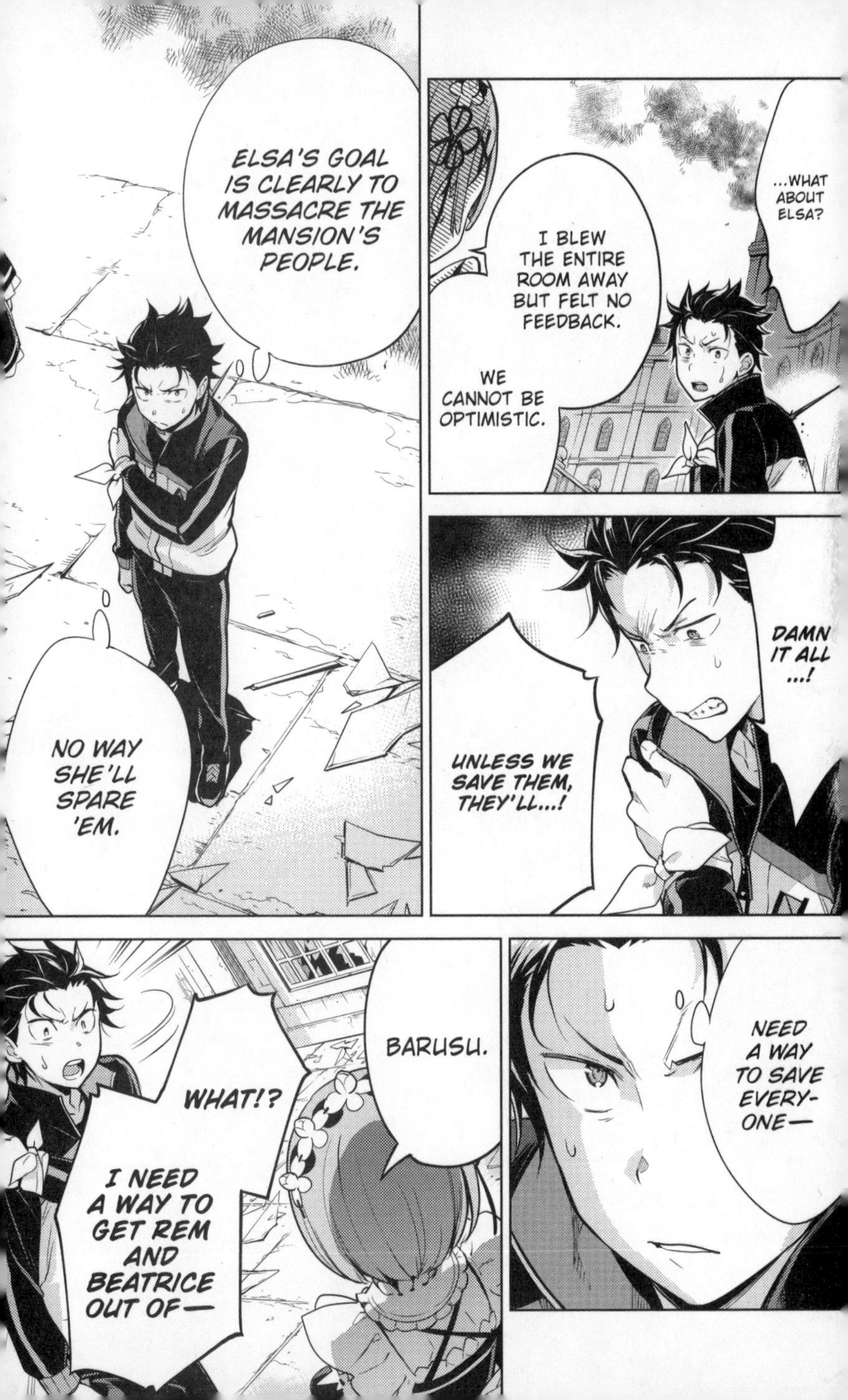
...WHAT ABOUT ELSA?
I BLEW THE ENTIRE ROOM AWAY BUT FELT NO FEEDBACK.
WE CANNOT BE OPTIMISTIC.
DAMN IT ALL ...!
UNLESS WE SAVE THEM, THEY'LL...!
ELSA'S GOAL IS CLEARLY TO MASSACRE THE MANSION'S PEOPLE.
NO WAY SHE'LL SPARE 'EM.
NEED A WAY TO SAVE EVERY-ONE—
BARUSU.
WHAT!?
I NEED A WAY TO GET REM AND BEATRICE OUT OF—

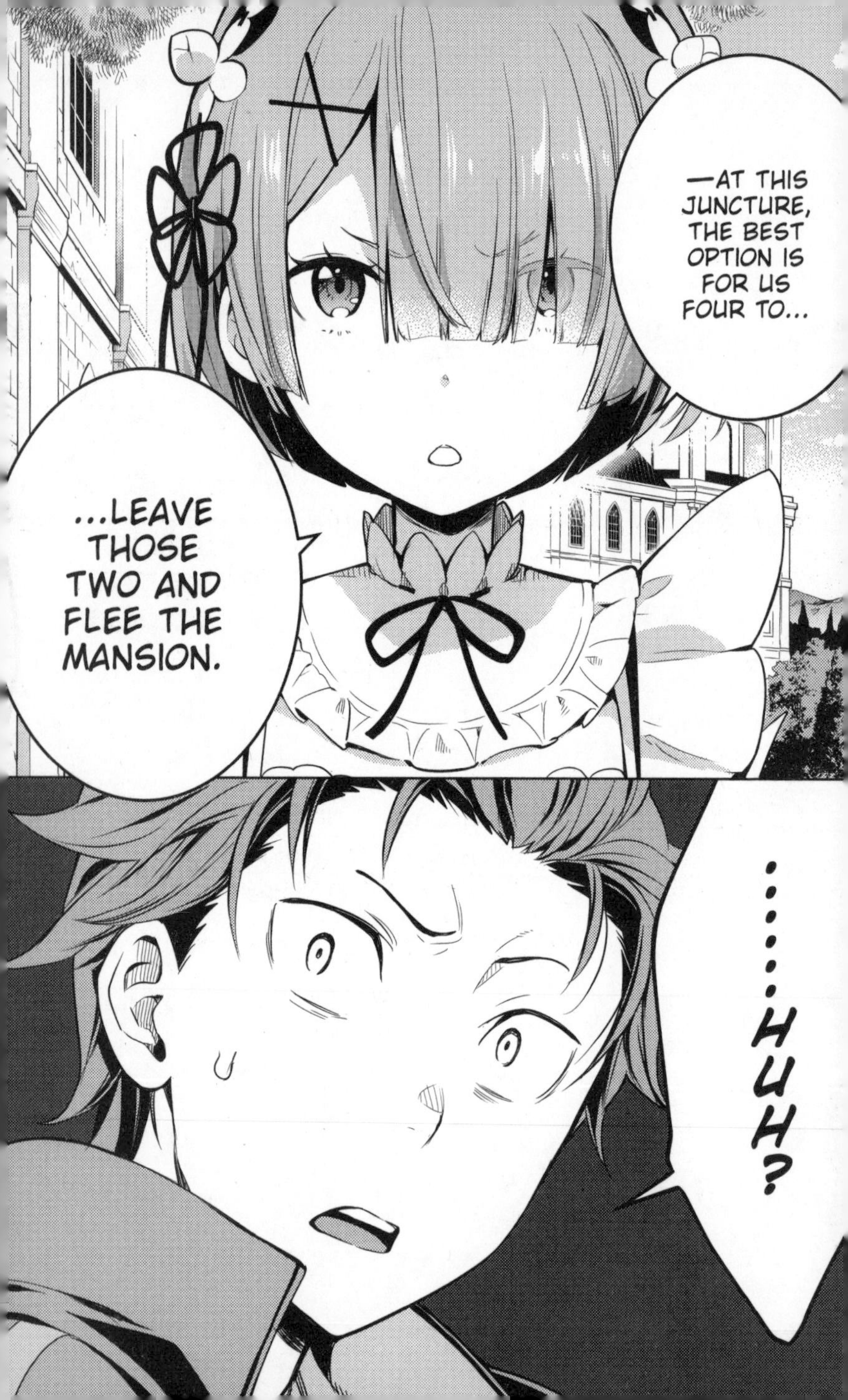
—AT THIS JUNCTURE, THE BEST OPTION IS FOR US FOUR TO...
...LEAVE THOSE TWO AND FLEE THE MANSION.
......HUH?

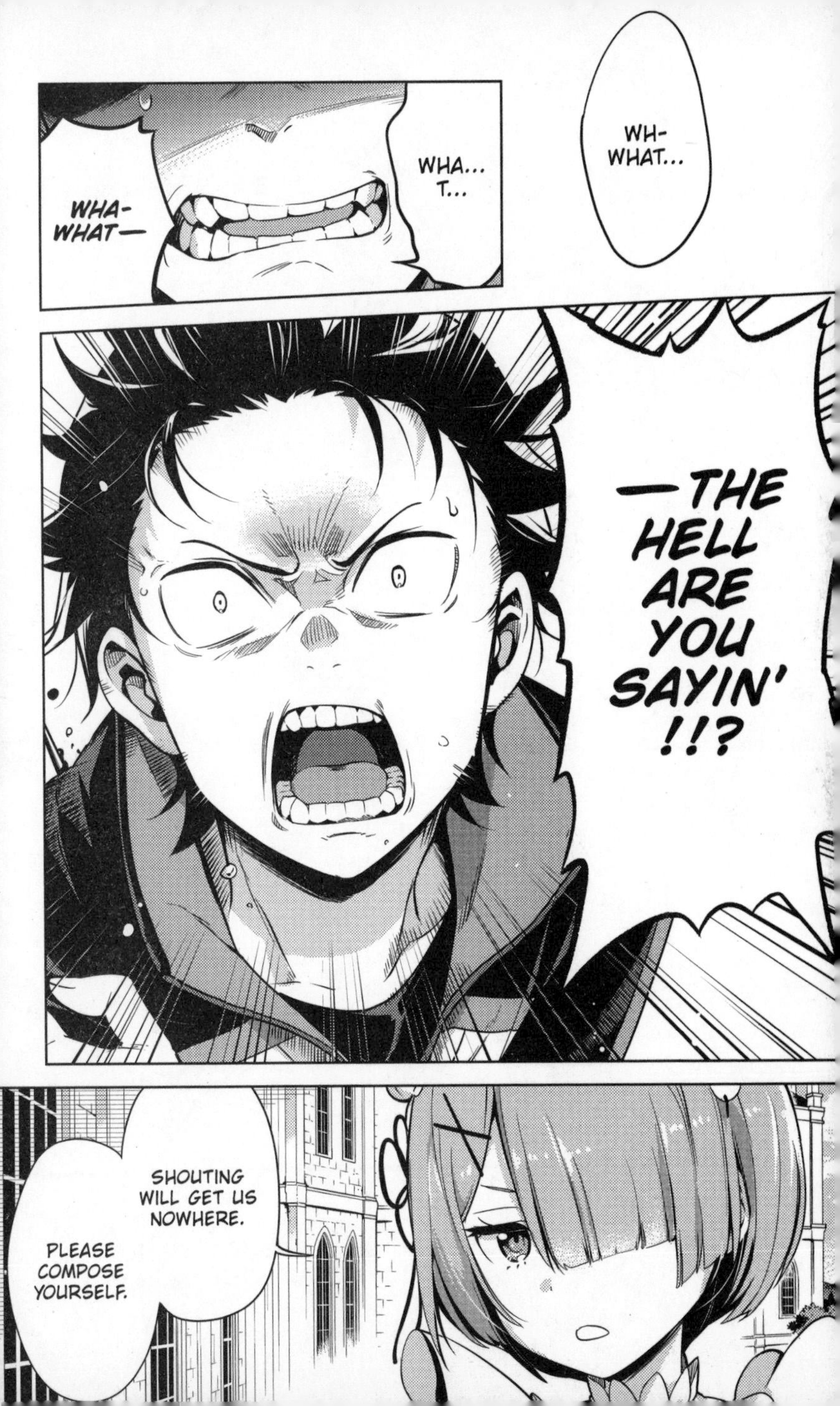
WH- WHAT...
WHA... T...
WHA- WHAT—
—THE HELL ARE YOU SAYIN' !!?
SHOUTING WILL GET US NOWHERE.
PLEASE COMPOSE YOURSELF.

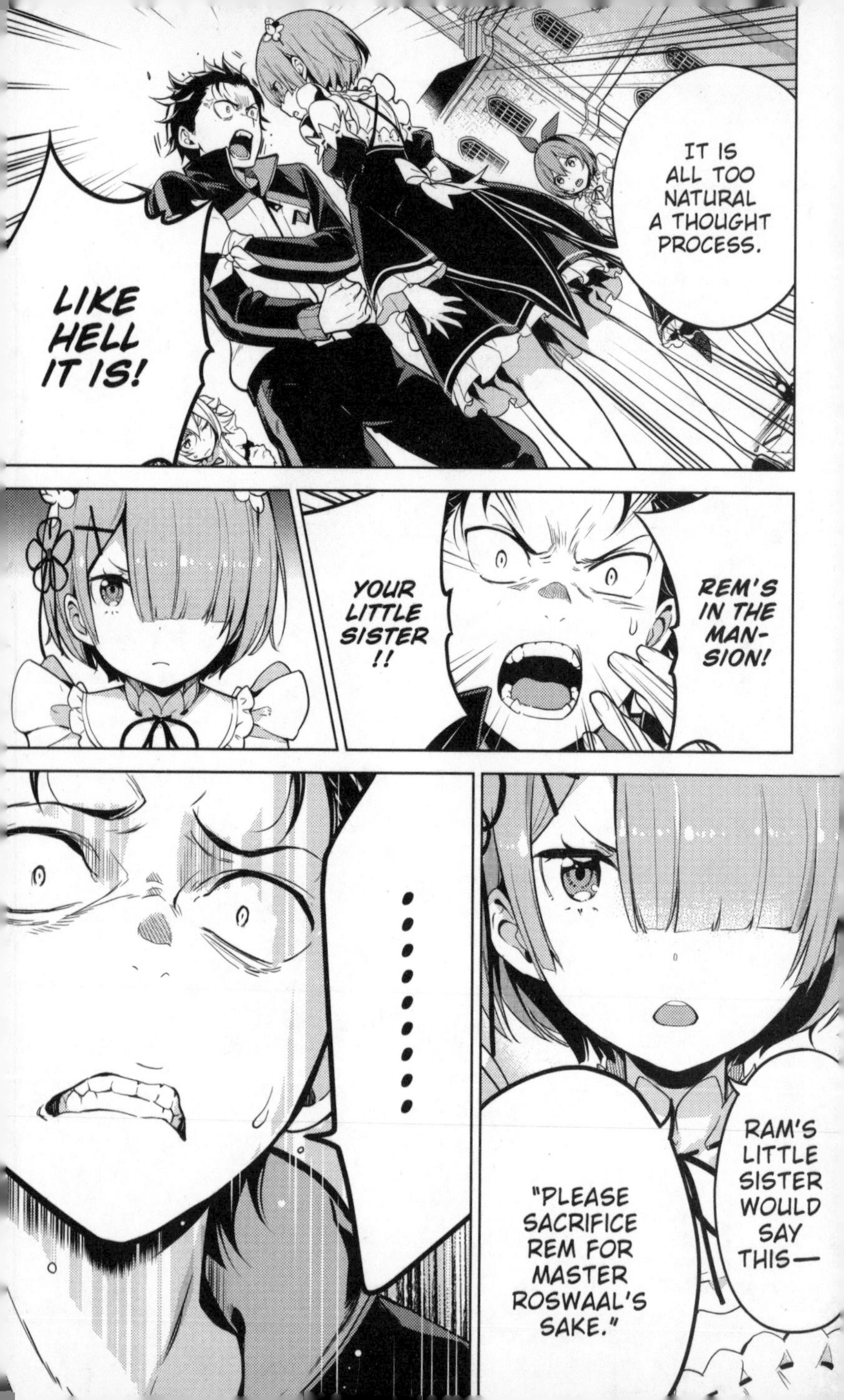
IT IS ALL TOO NATURAL A THOUGHT PROCESS.
LIKE HELL IT IS!
REM'S IN THE MAN-SION!
YOUR LITTLE SISTER !!
RAM'S LITTLE SISTER WOULD SAY THIS—
"PLEASE SACRIFICE REM FOR MASTER ROSWAAL'S SAKE."
....

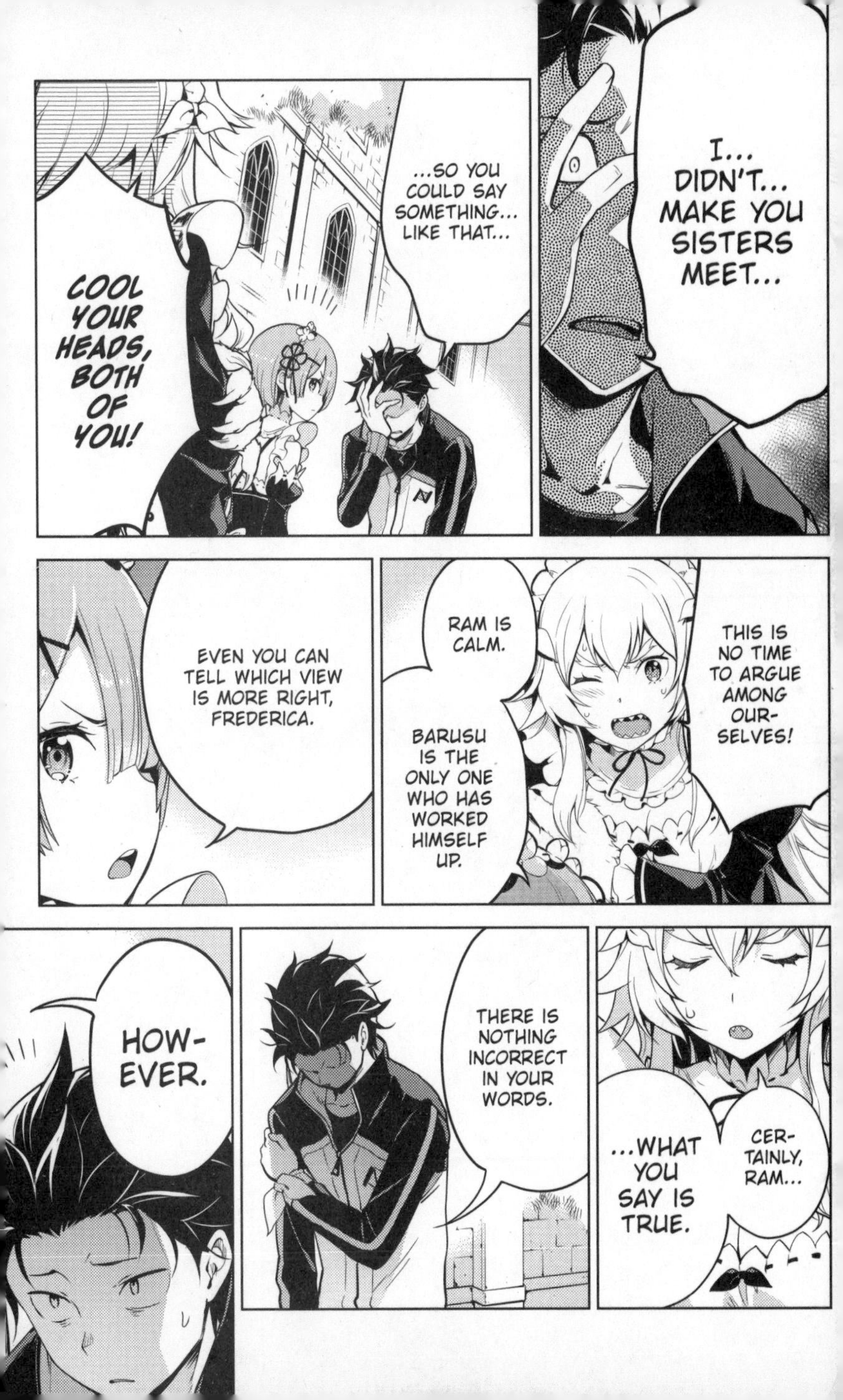
I... DIDN'T... MAKE YOU SISTERS MEET...
...SO YOU COULD SAY SOMETHING... LIKE THAT...
COOL YOUR HEADS, BOTH OF YOU!
THIS IS NO TIME TO ARGUE AMONG OUR-SELVES!
RAM IS CALM.
BARUSU IS THE ONLY ONE WHO HAS WORKED HIMSELF UP.
EVEN YOU CAN TELL WHICH VIEW IS MORE RIGHT, FREDERICA.
CER-TAINLY, RAM...
...WHAT YOU SAY IS TRUE.
THERE IS NOTHING INCORRECT IN YOUR WORDS.
HOW-EVER.

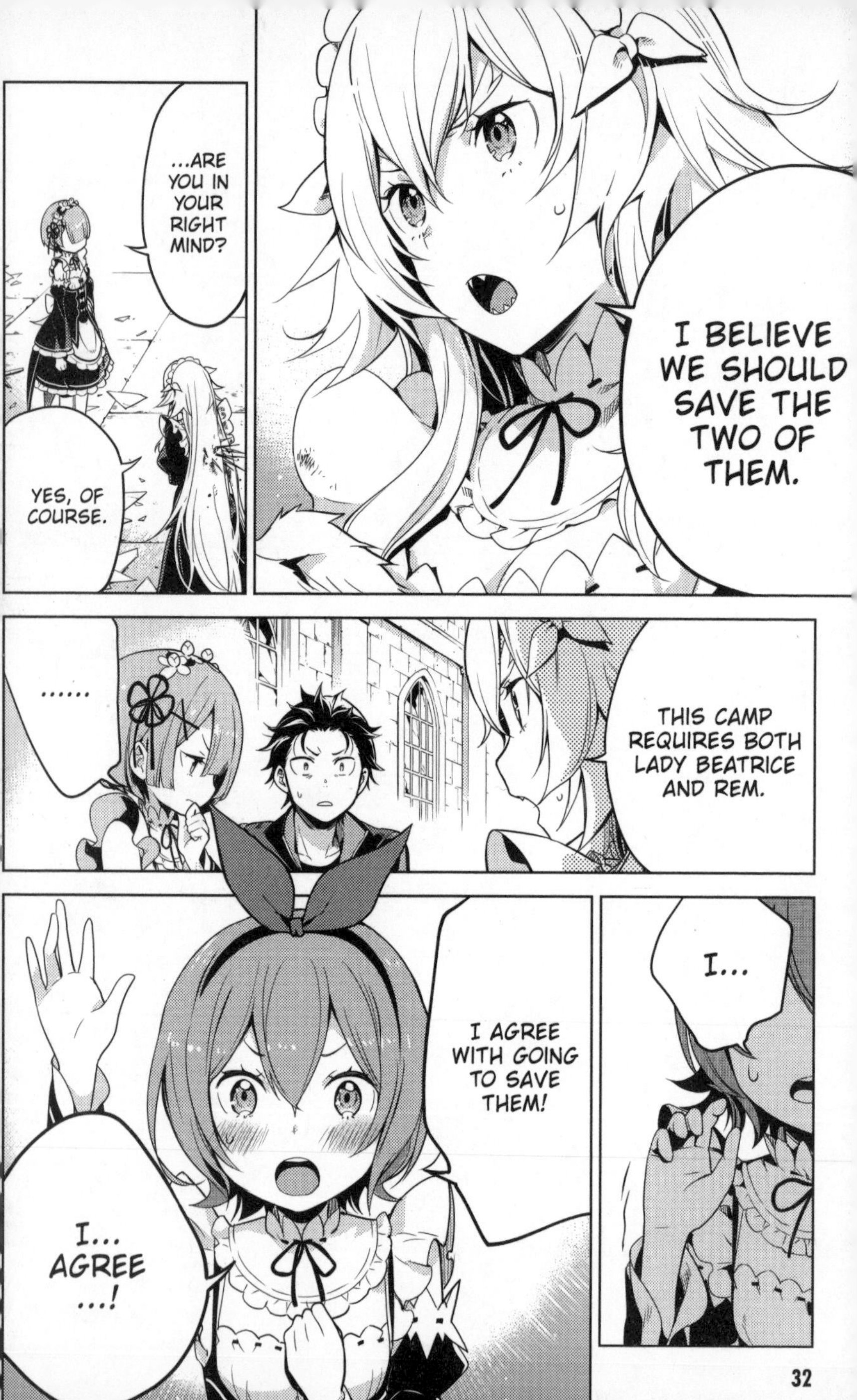
I BELIEVE WE SHOULD SAVE THE TWO OF THEM.
...ARE YOU IN YOUR RIGHT MIND?
YES, OF COURSE.
THIS CAMP REQUIRES BOTH LADY BEATRICE AND REM.
......
I...
I AGREE WITH GOING TO SAVE THEM!
I... AGREE ...!

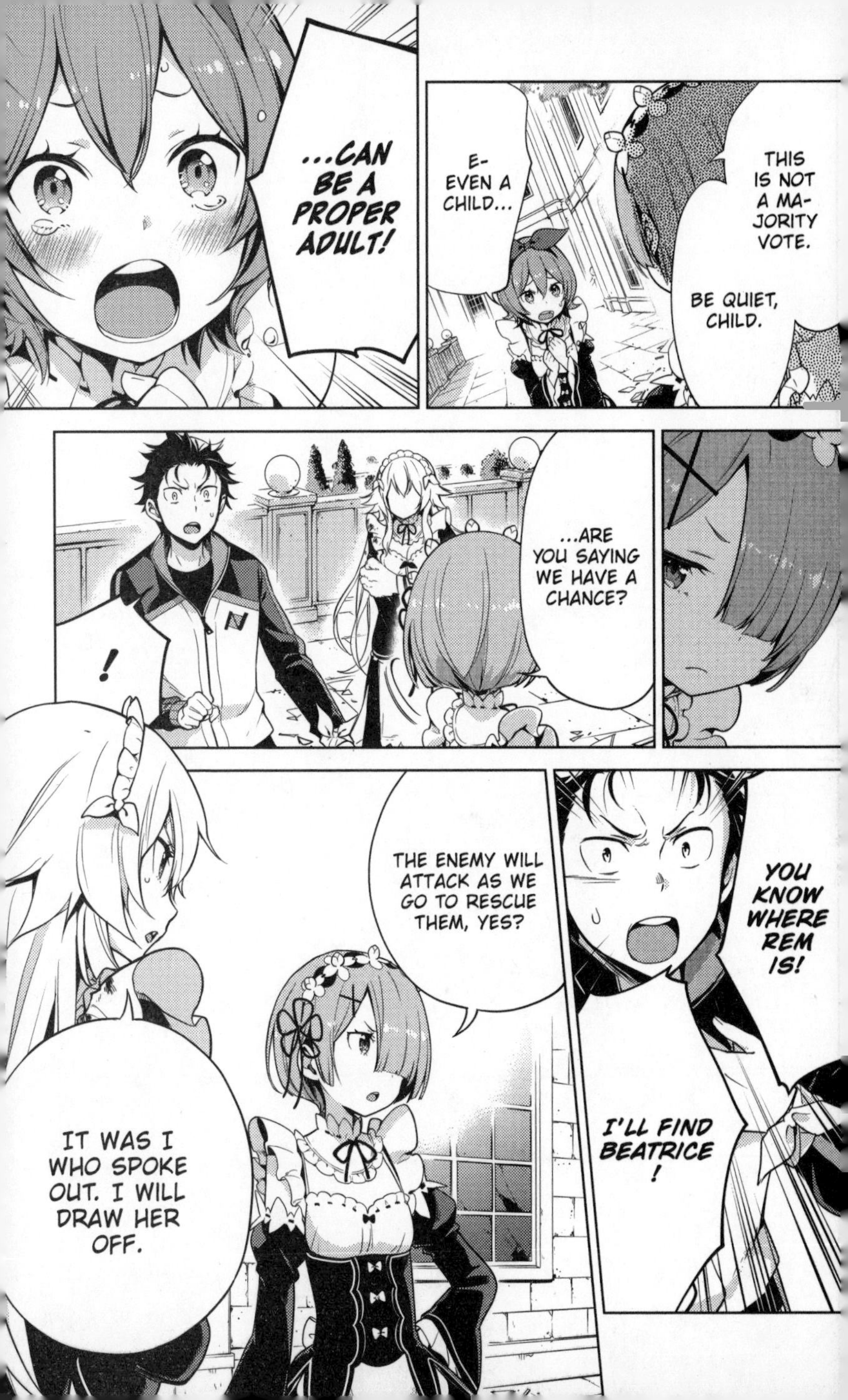
THIS IS NOT A MAJORITY VOTE.
BE QUIET, CHILD.
E-EVEN A CHILD...
...CAN BE A PROPER ADULT!
...ARE YOU SAYING WE HAVE A CHANCE?
!
YOU KNOW WHERE REM IS!
I'LL FIND BEATRICE!
THE ENEMY WILL ATTACK AS WE GO TO RESCUE THEM, YES?
IT WAS I WHO SPOKE OUT. I WILL DRAW HER OFF.

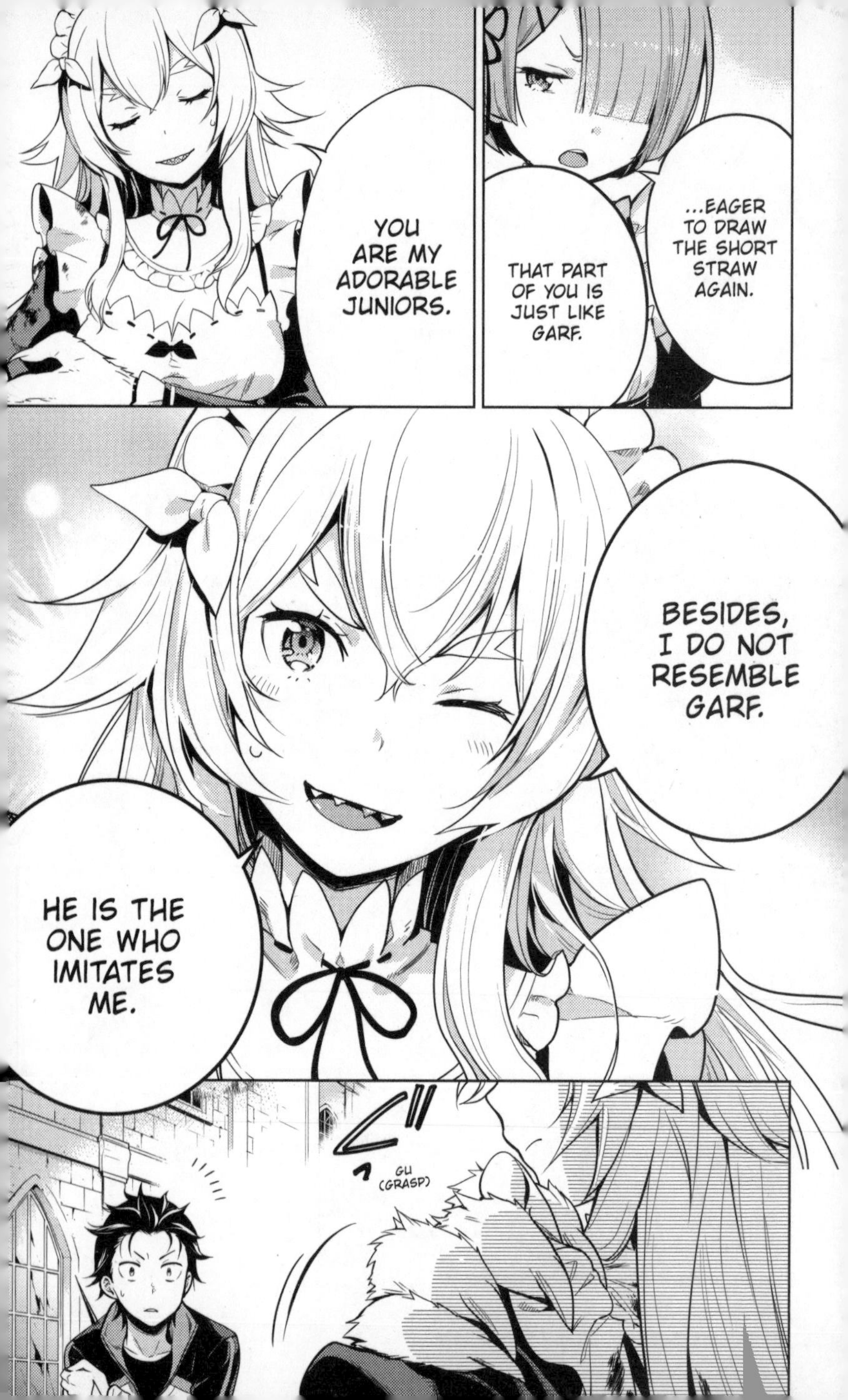
...EAGER TO DRAW THE SHORT STRAW AGAIN.
THAT PART OF YOU IS JUST LIKE GARF.
YOU ARE MY ADORABLE JUNIORS.
BESIDES, I DO NOT RESEMBLE GARF.
HE IS THE ONE WHO IMITATES ME.
GU (GRASP)

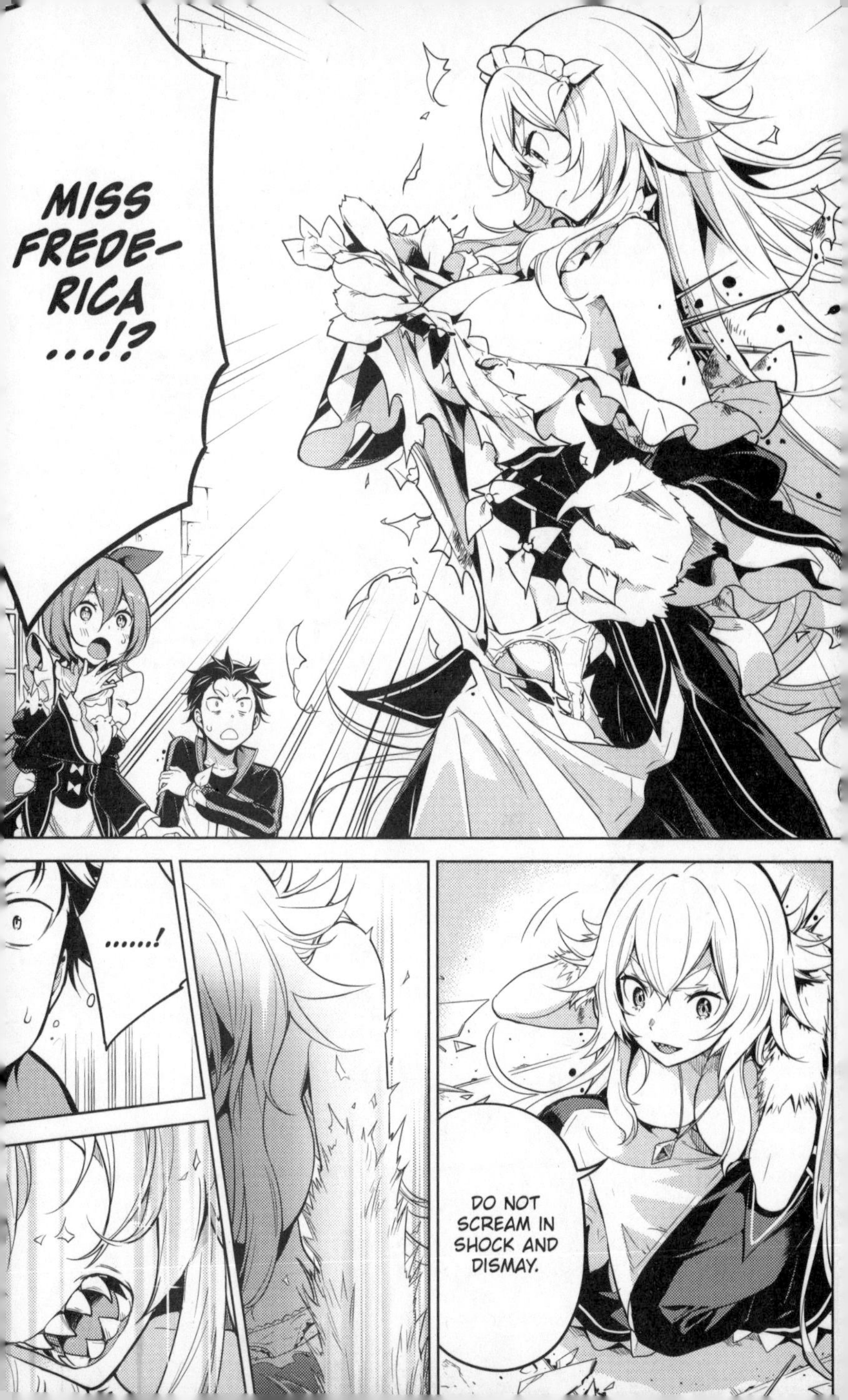
MISS FREDE-RICA ...!?
DO NOT SCREAM IN SHOCK AND DISMAY.
......!

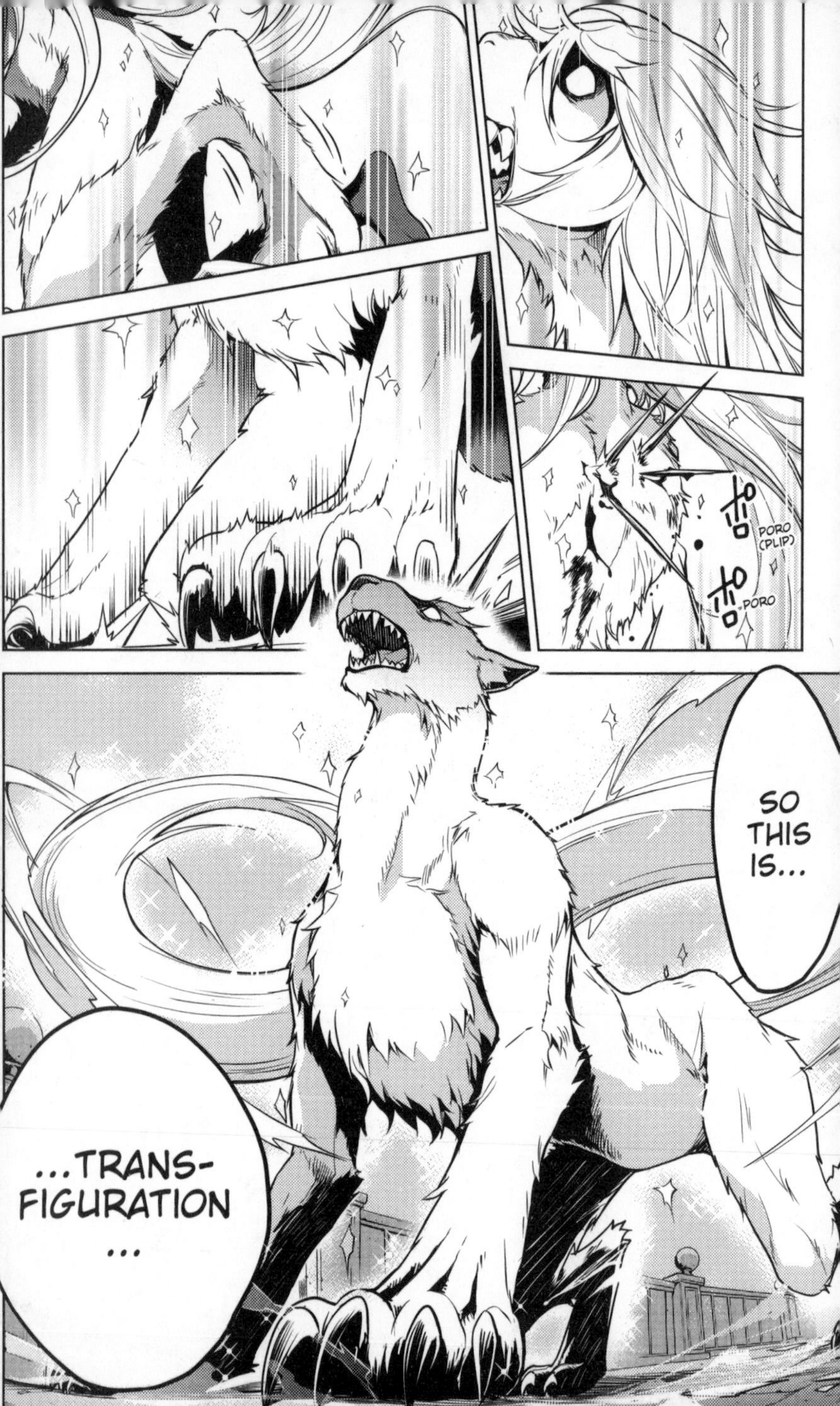
포로
PORO (PLIP)
포로
PORO
SO THIS IS...
...TRANS-FIGURATION ...

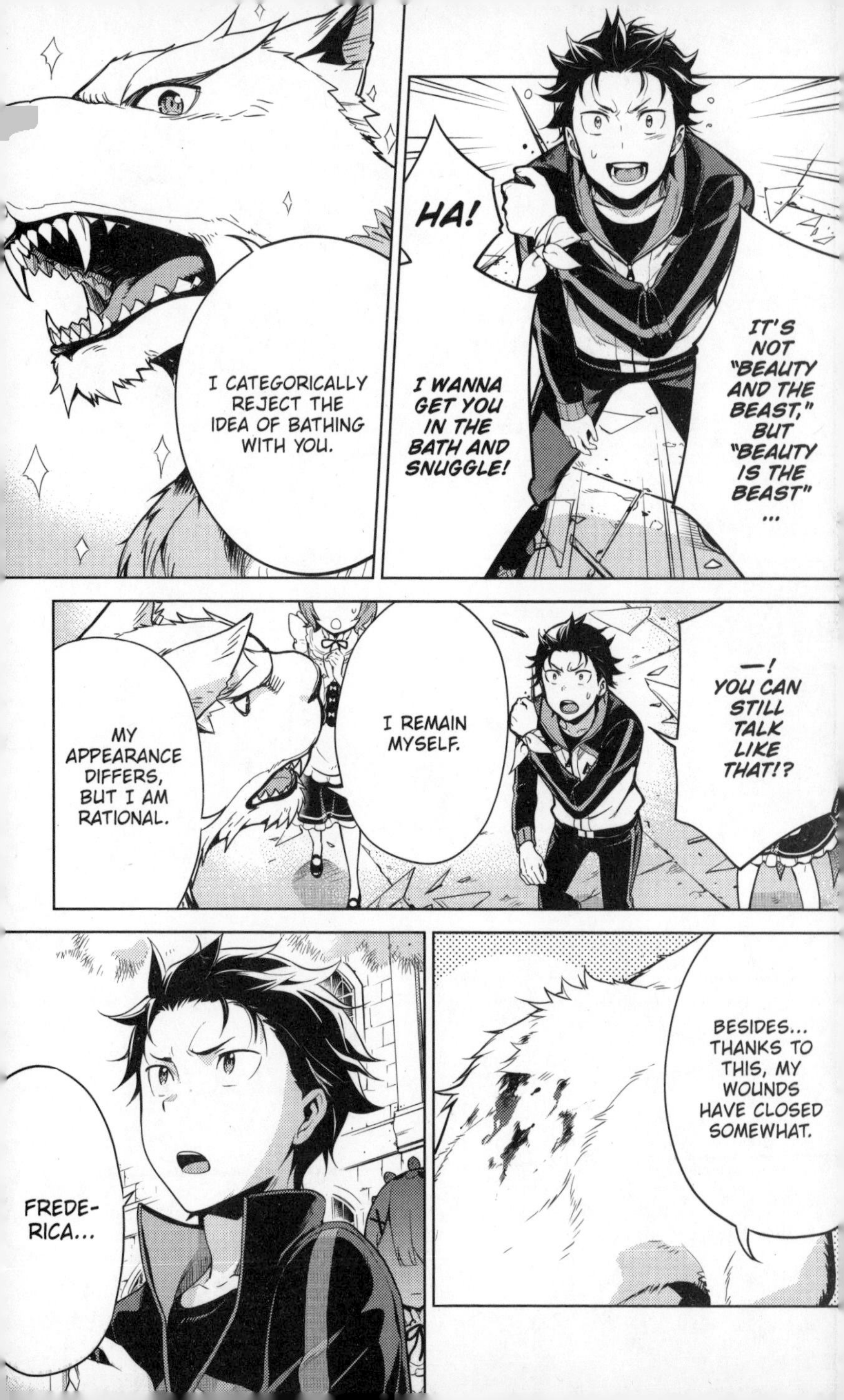
HA!
I WANNA GET YOU IN THE BATH AND SNUGGLE!
IT'S NOT "BEAUTY AND THE BEAST," BUT "BEAUTY IS THE BEAST"...
I CATEGORICALLY REJECT THE IDEA OF BATHING WITH YOU.
—! YOU CAN STILL TALK LIKE THAT!?
I REMAIN MYSELF.
MY APPEARANCE DIFFERS, BUT I AM RATIONAL.
BESIDES... THANKS TO THIS, MY WOUNDS HAVE CLOSED SOMEWHAT.
FREDE-RICA...

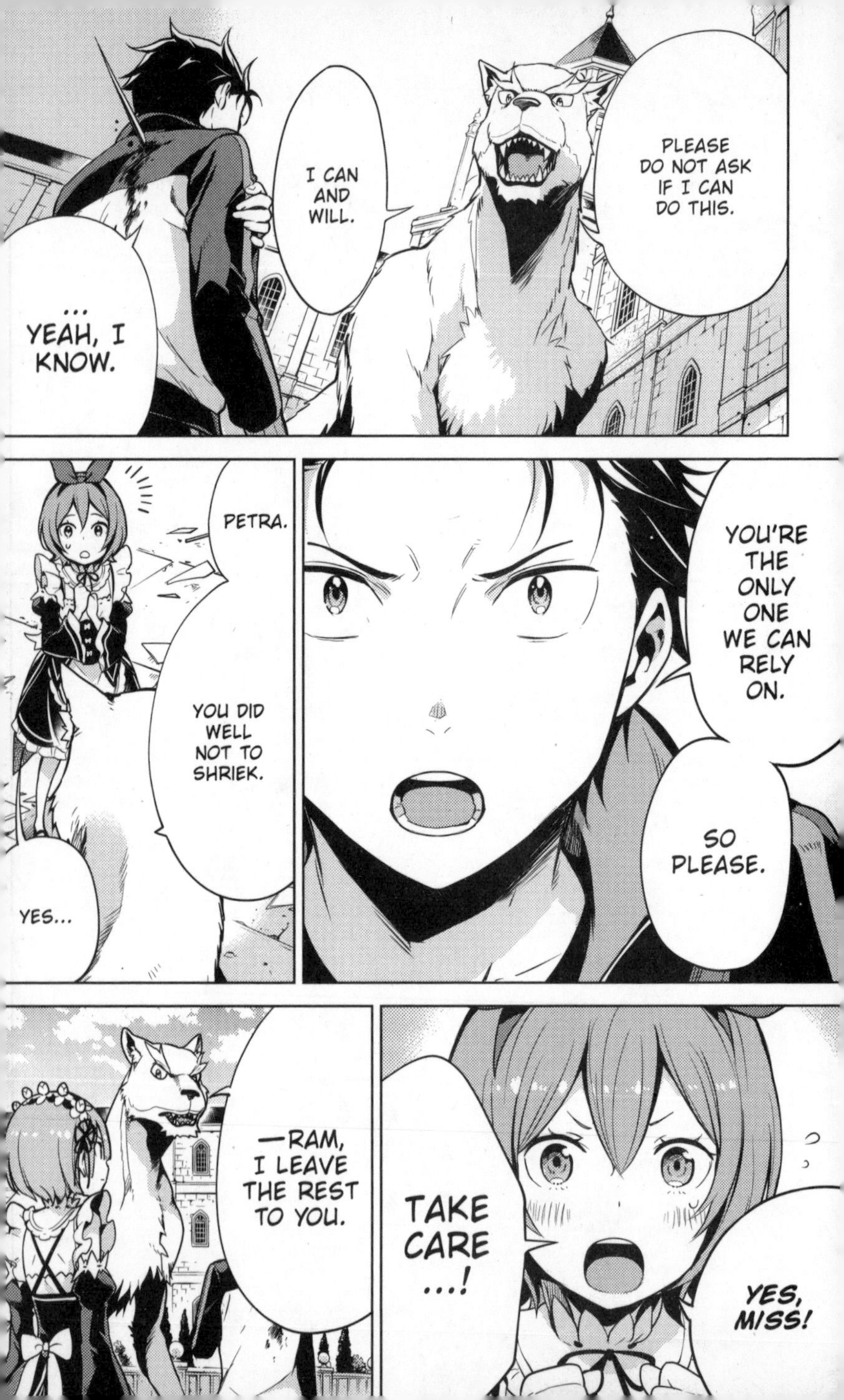

PLEASE DO NOT ASK IF I CAN DO THIS.
I CAN AND WILL.
... YEAH, I KNOW.
YOU'RE THE ONLY ONE WE CAN RELY ON.
SO PLEASE.
PETRA.
YOU DID WELL NOT TO SHRIEK.
YES...
TAKE CARE ...!
YES, MISS!
—RAM, I LEAVE THE REST TO YOU.

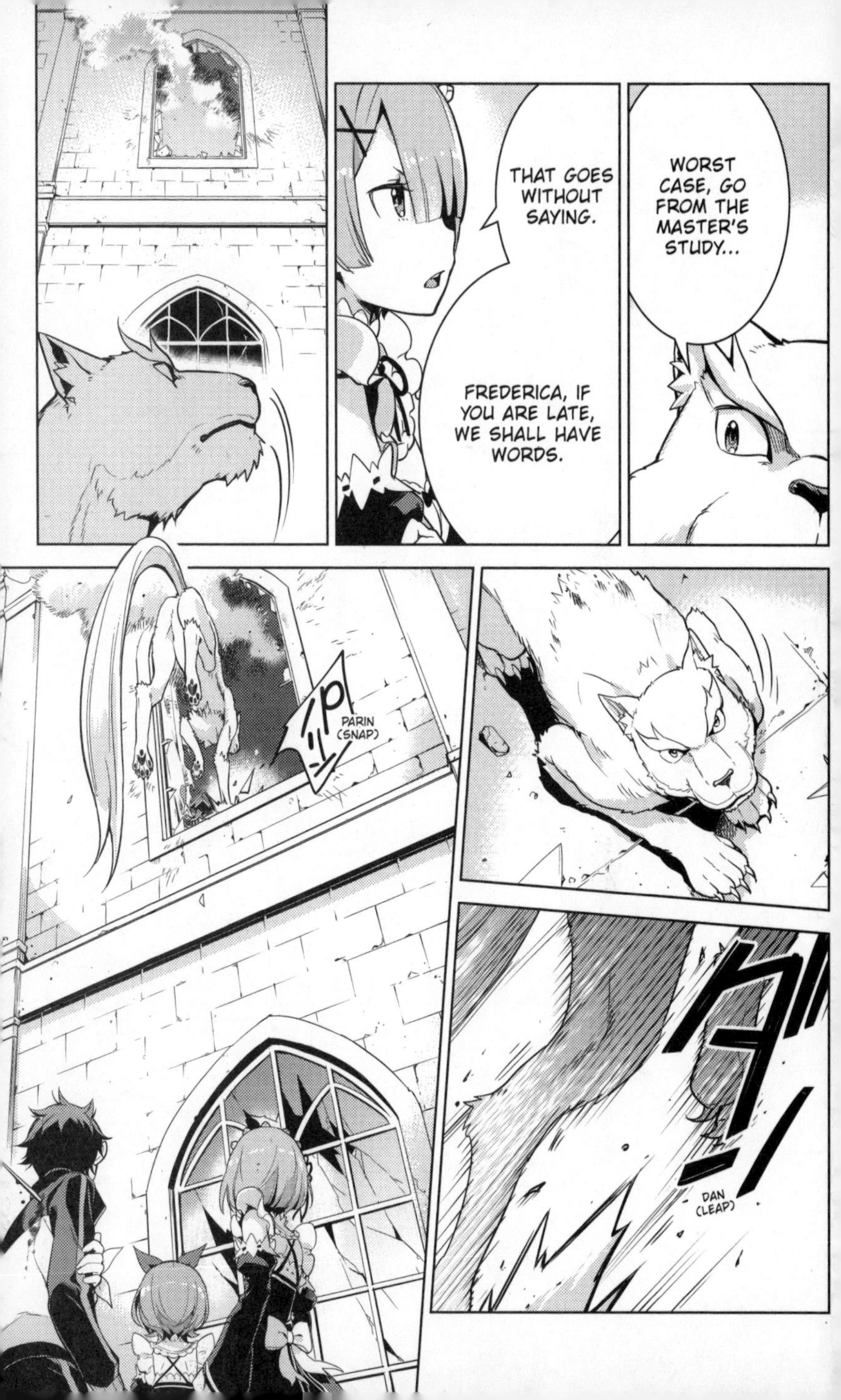
WORST CASE, GO FROM THE MASTER'S STUDY...
THAT GOES WITHOUT SAYING.
FREDERICA, IF YOU ARE LATE, WE SHALL HAVE WORDS.
DAN (LEAP)
PARIN (SNAP)

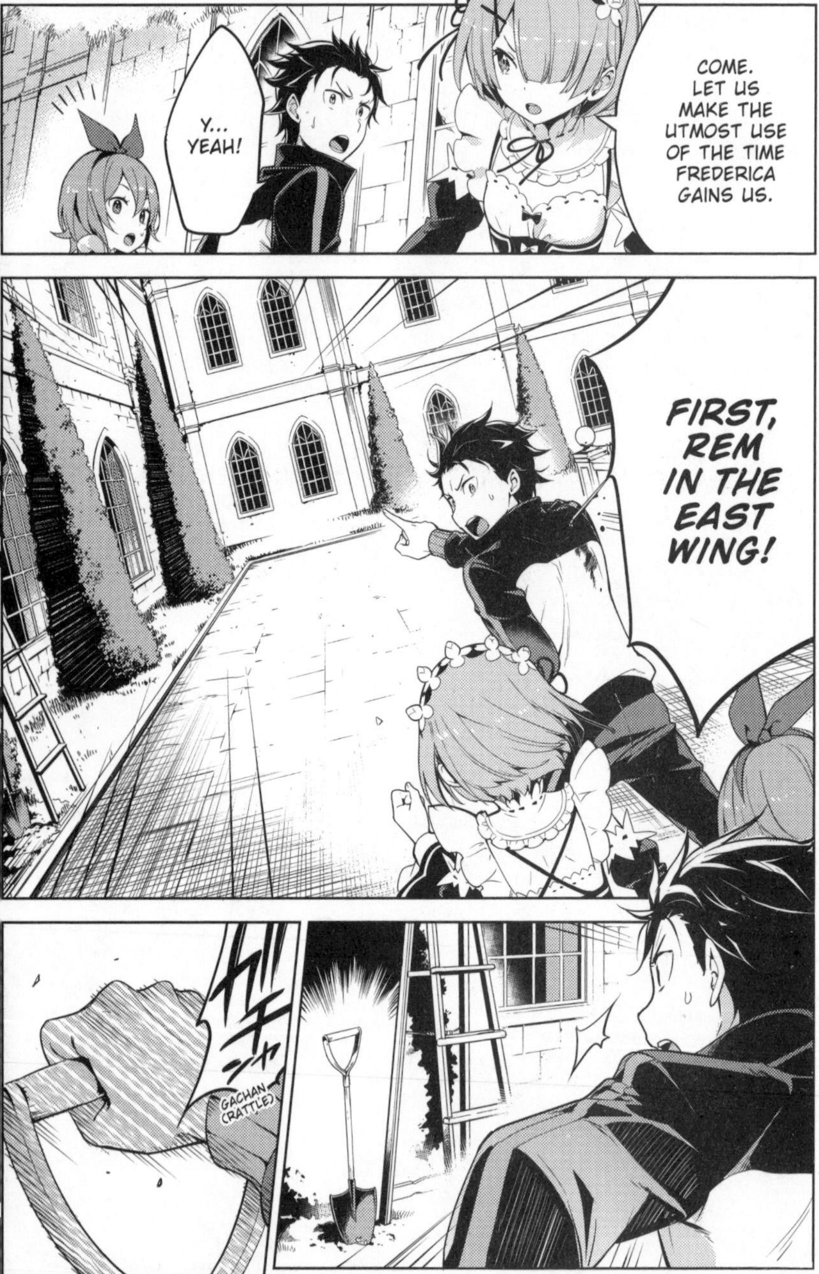
COME. LET US MAKE THE UTMOST USE OF THE TIME FREDERICA GAINS US.
Y... YEAH!
FIRST, REM IN THE EAST WING!
GACHAN (RATTLE)

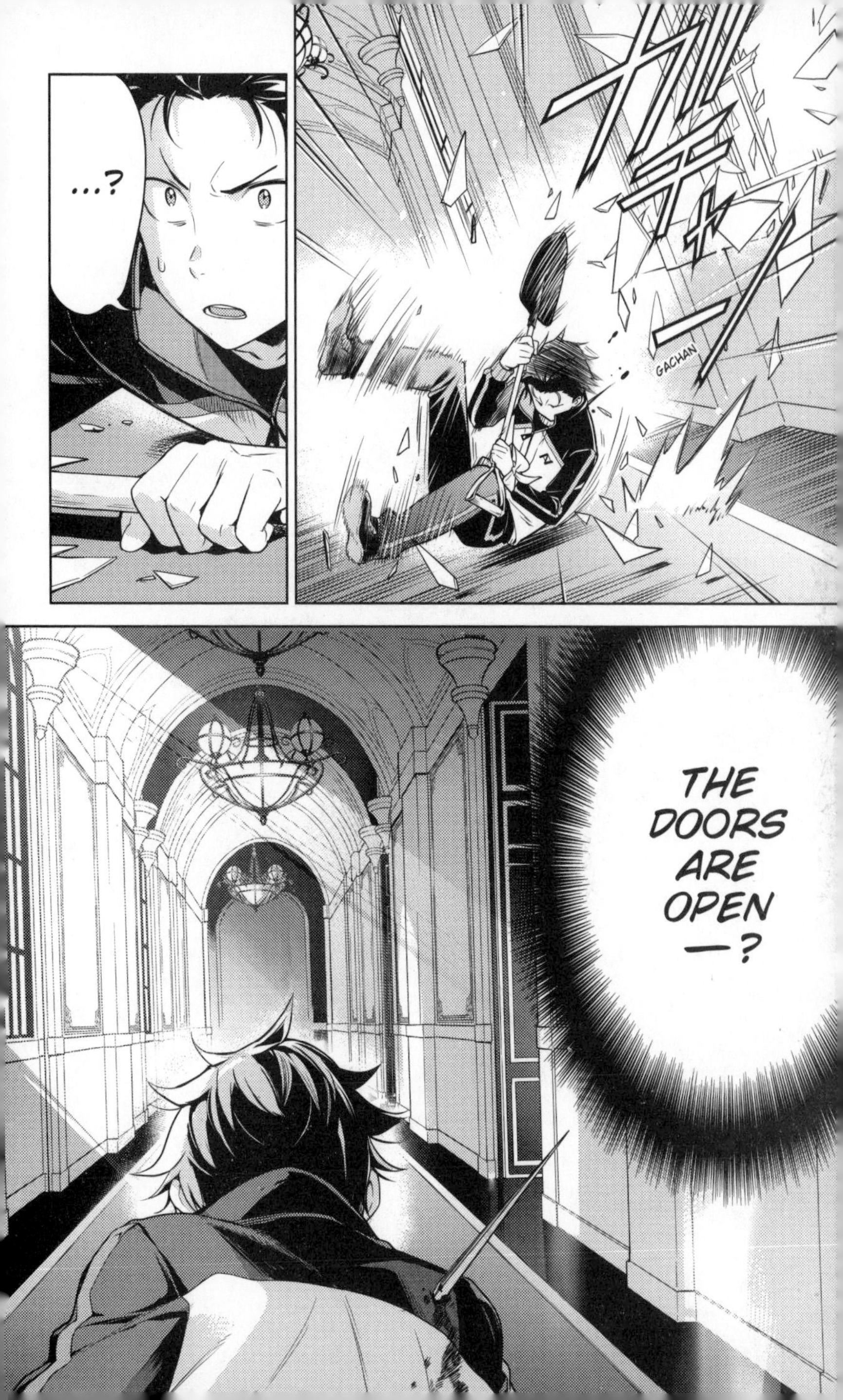
GACHAN
...?
THE DOORS ARE OPEN—?

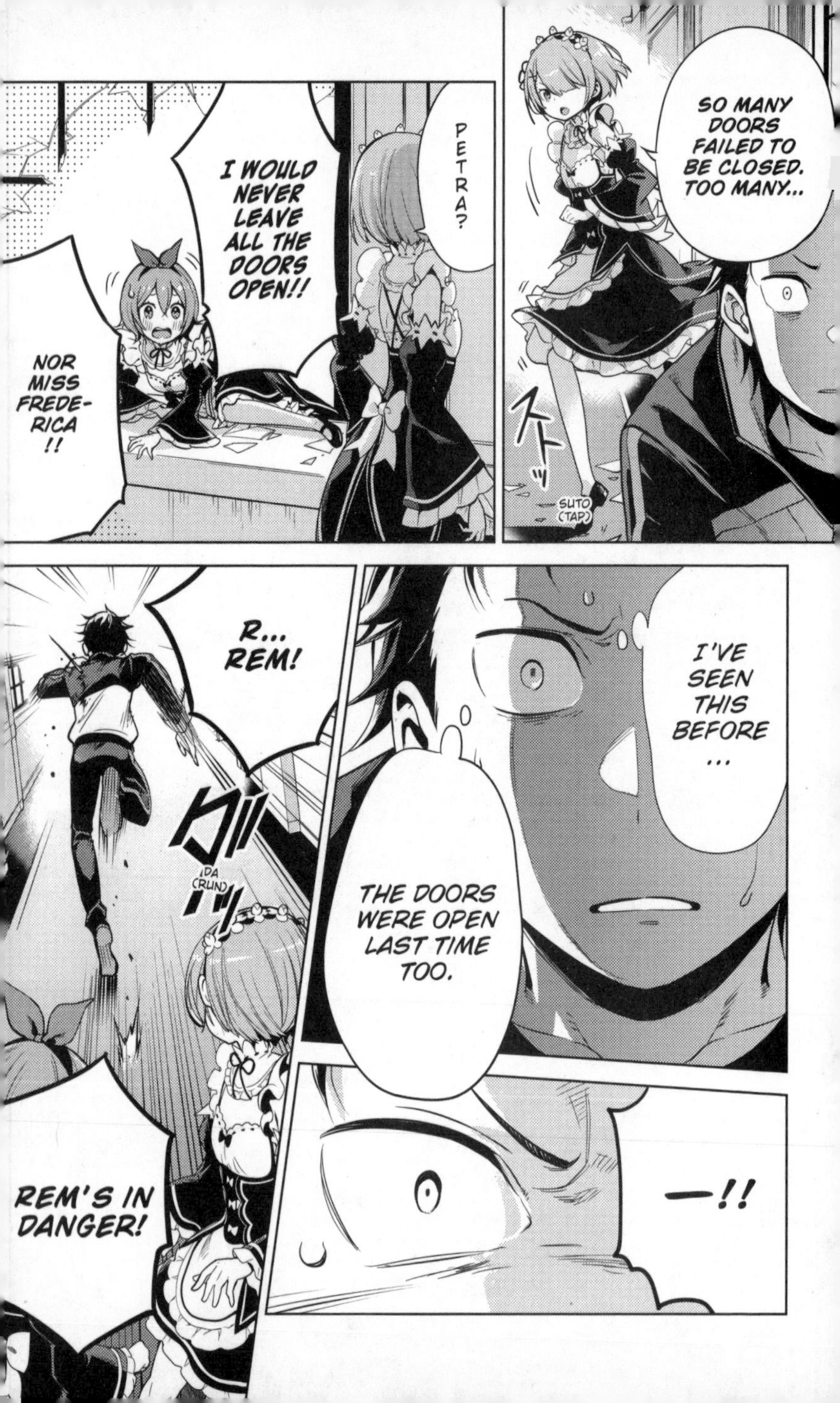
SO MANY DOORS FAILED TO BE CLOSED. TOO MANY...
SUTO (TAP)
PETRA?
I WOULD NEVER LEAVE ALL THE DOORS OPEN!!
NOR MISS FREDERICA!!
I'VE SEEN THIS BEFORE...
THE DOORS WERE OPEN LAST TIME TOO.
—!!
R... REM!
DA (RUN)
REM'S IN DANGER!

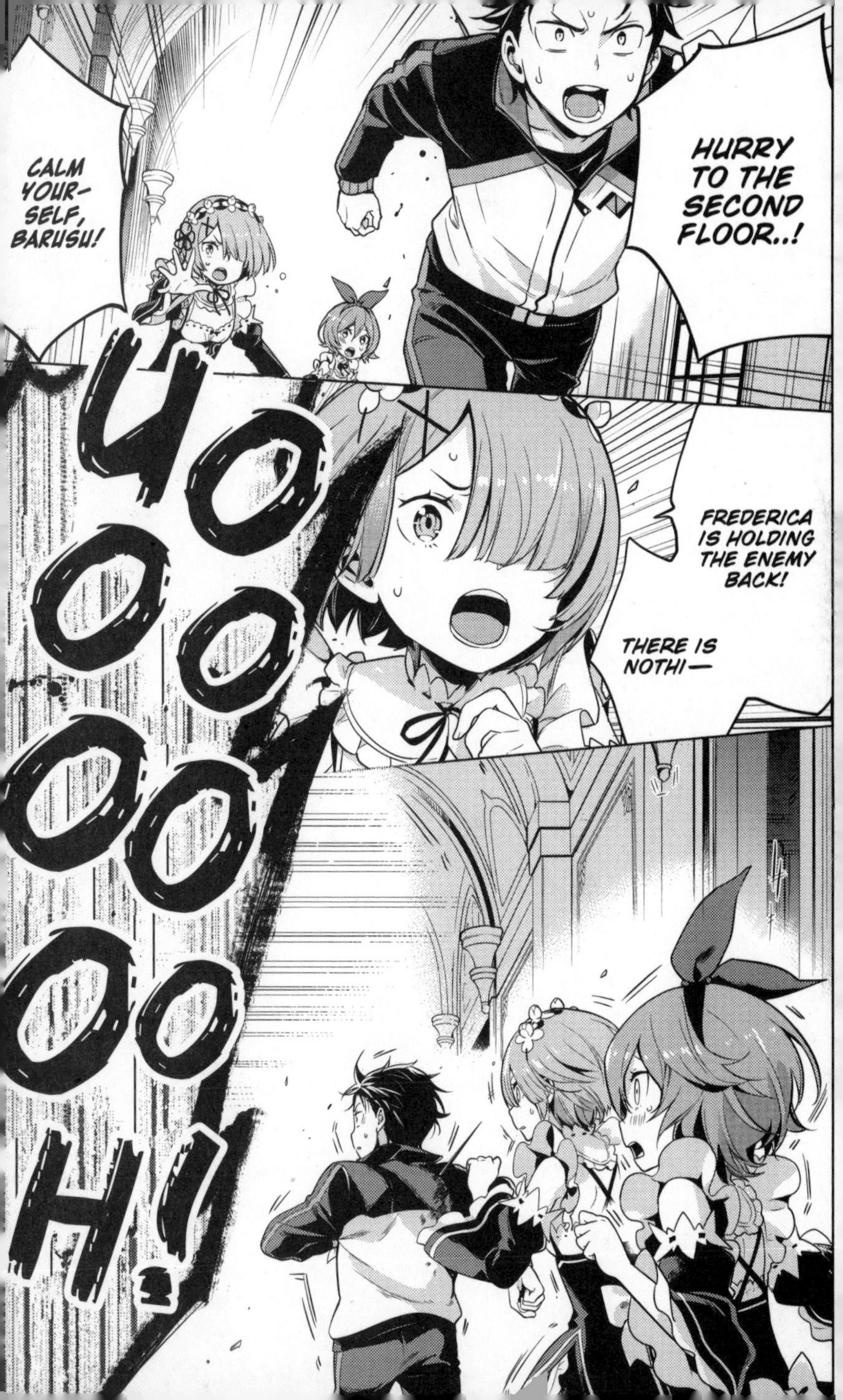
HURRY TO THE SECOND FLOOR..!
CALM YOURSELF, BARUSU!
FREDERICA IS HOLDING THE ENEMY BACK!
THERE IS NOTHI—
UOOOOOOOOOH!

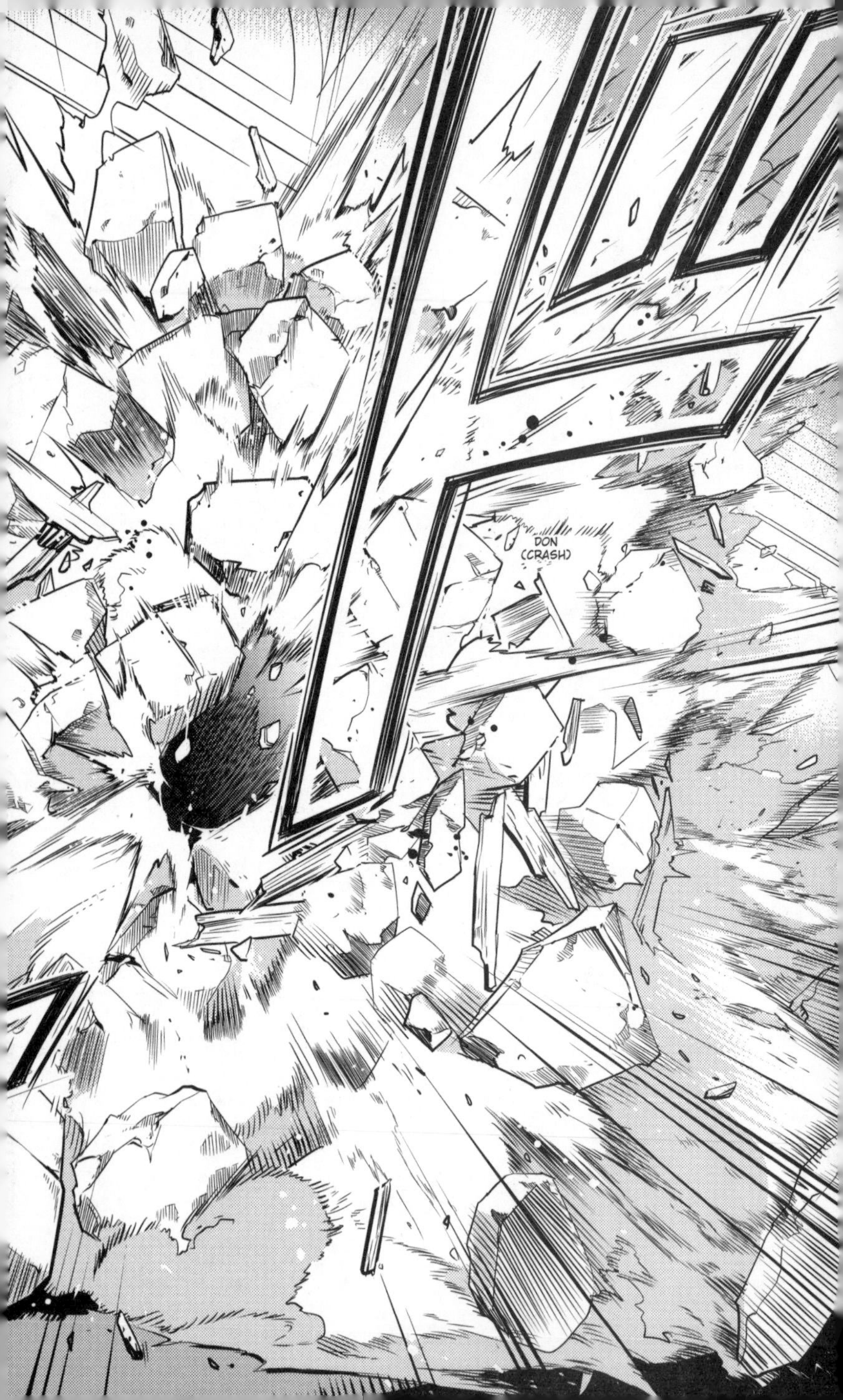
DON
(CRASH)

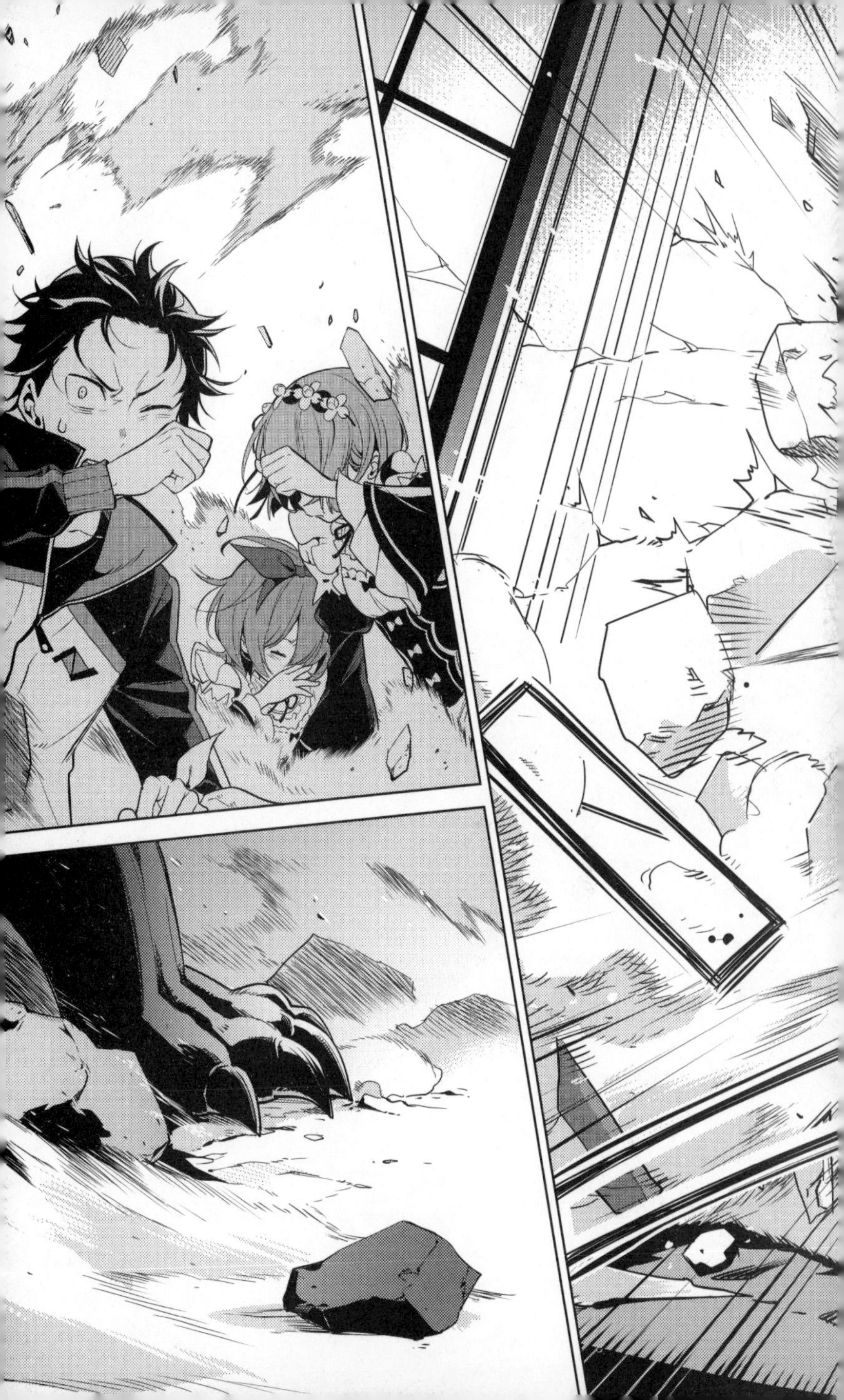

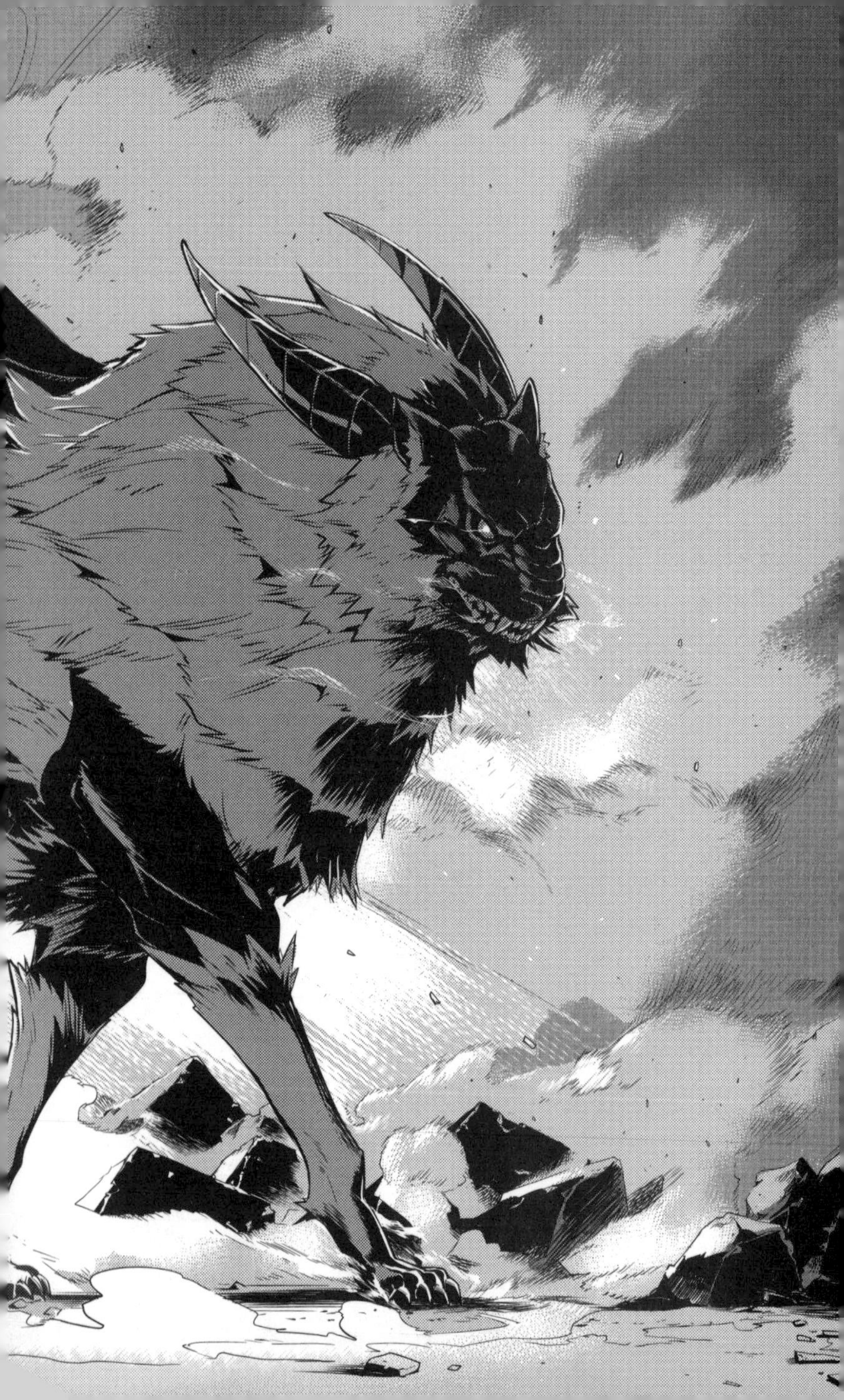

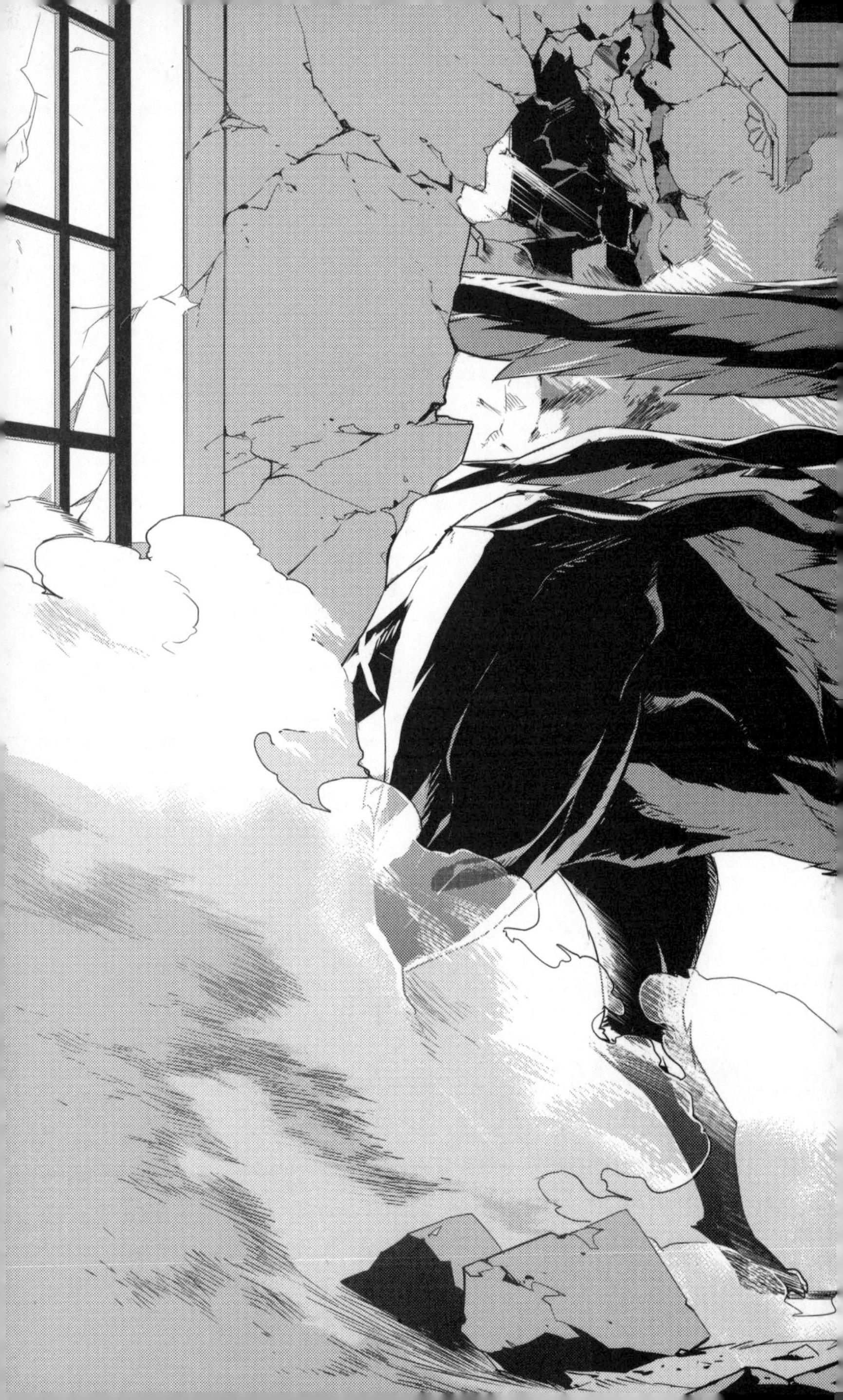

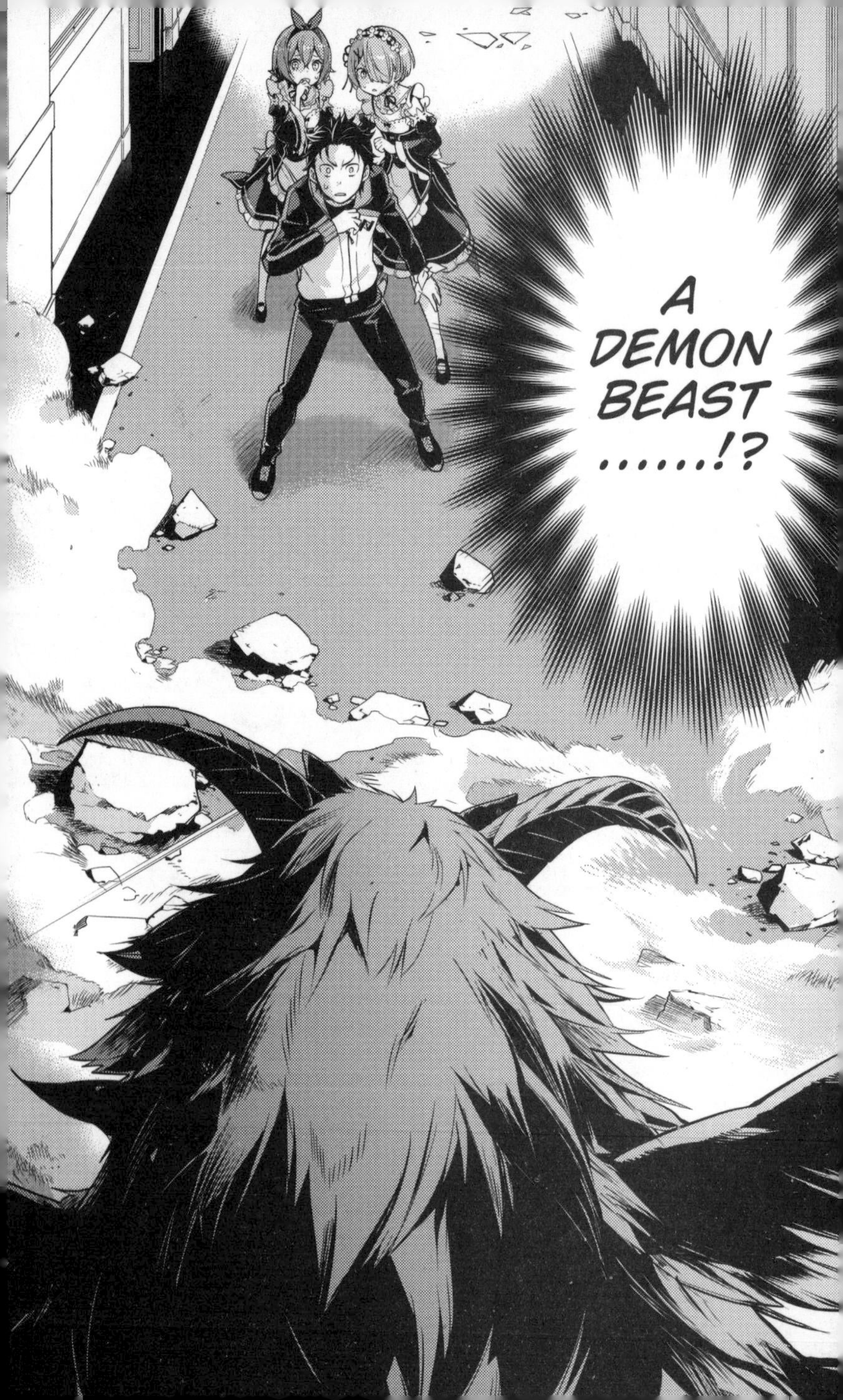
A DEMON BEAST ......!?

Episode 15
A Doomed World

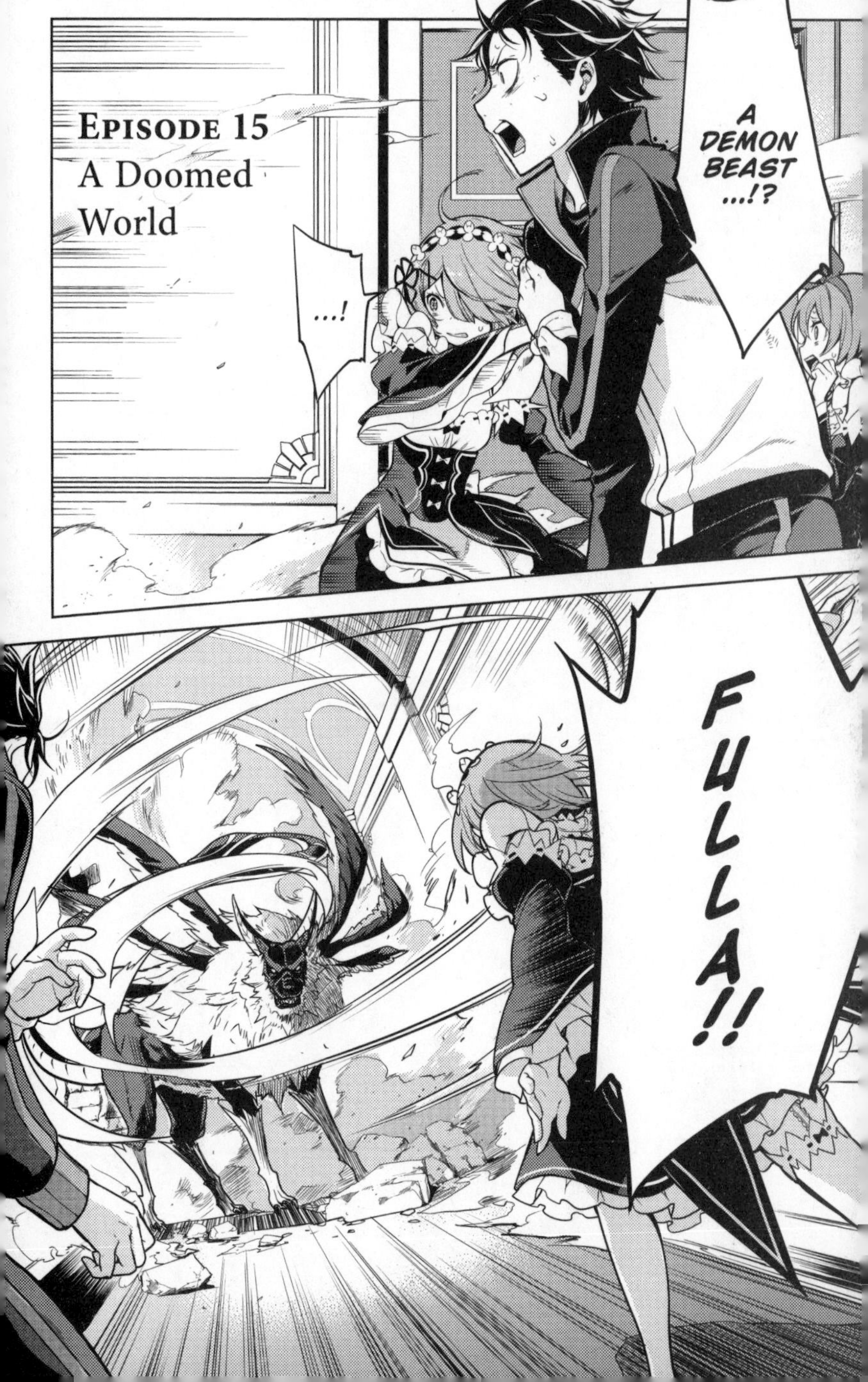
A DEMON BEAST ...!?
...!
FULLA!!

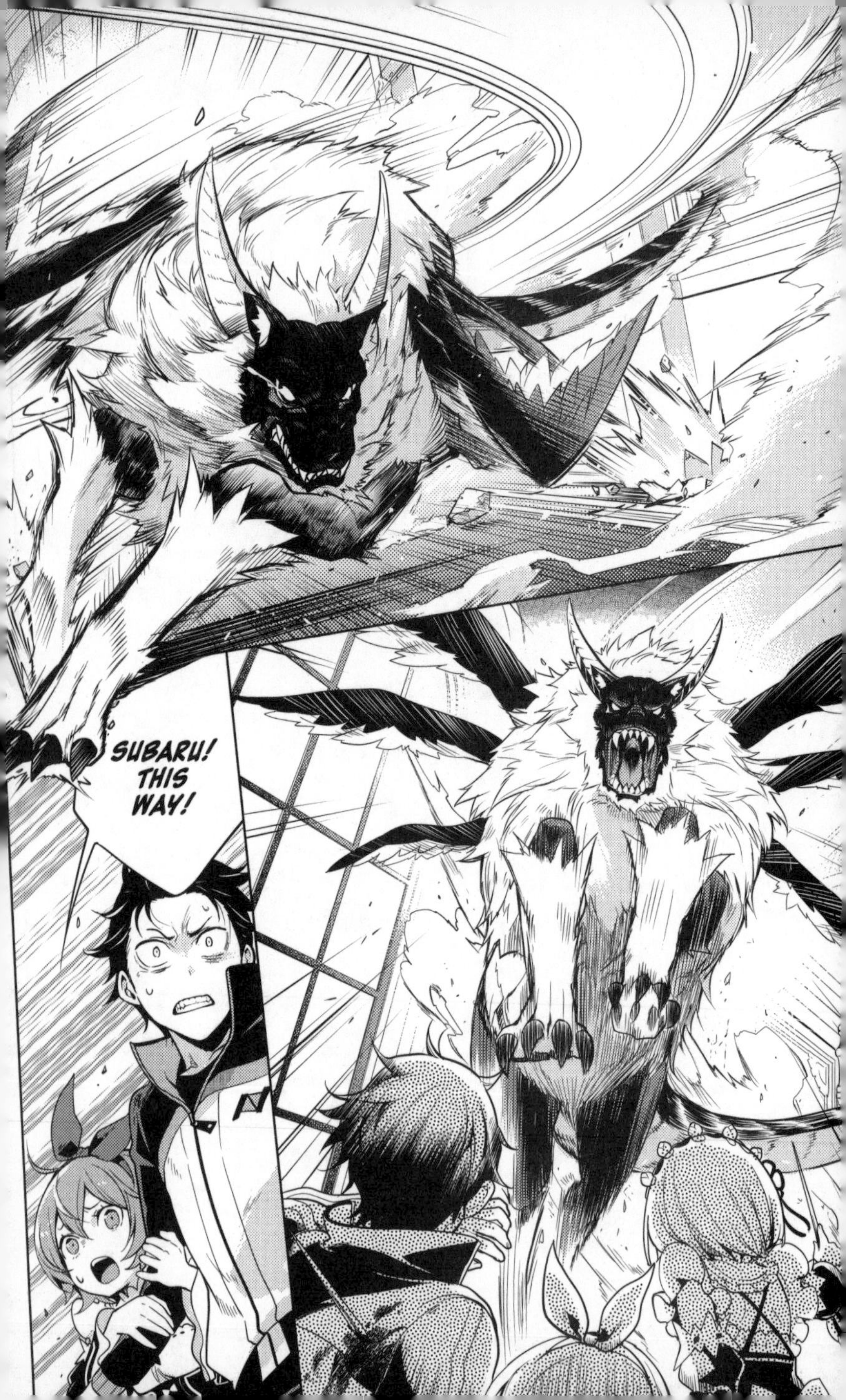
SUBARU! THIS WAY!

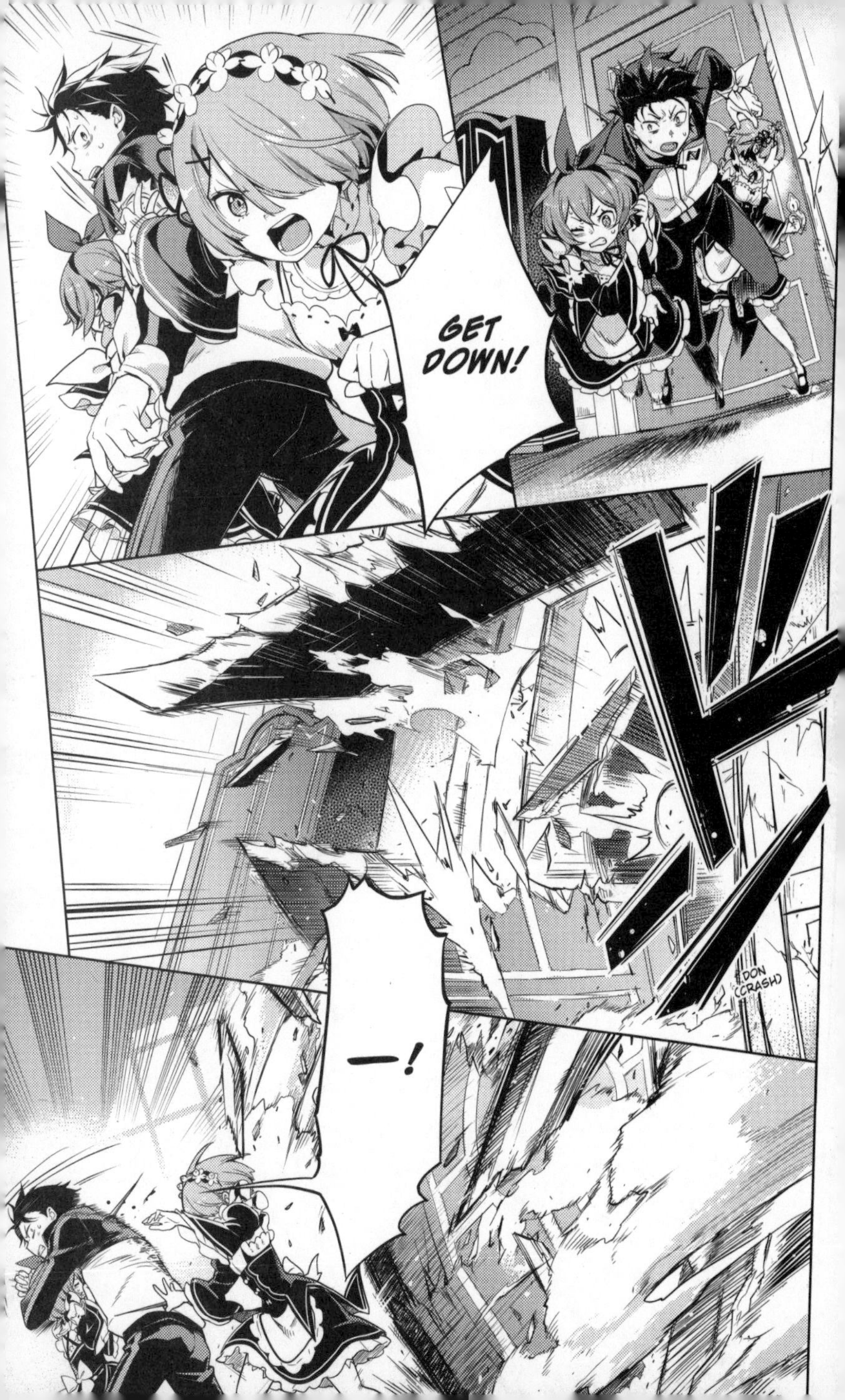
GET DOWN!
DON (CRASH)
—!

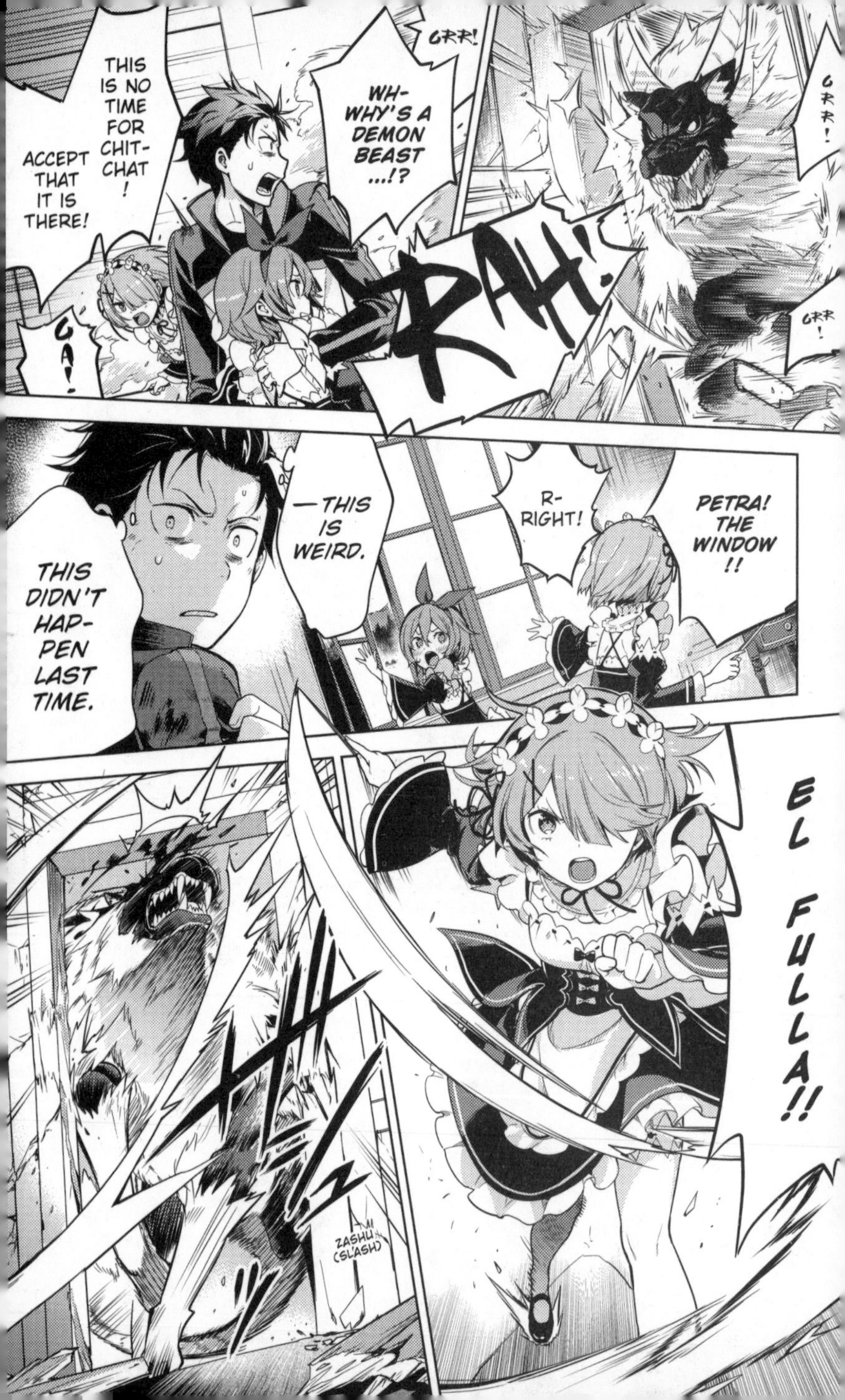
GRR!
GRR!
GRR!
WH-WHY'S A DEMON BEAST ...!?
THIS IS NO TIME FOR CHIT-CHAT!
ACCEPT THAT IT IS THERE!
RAH!
GA!
PETRA! THE WINDOW!!
R-RIGHT!
—THIS IS WEIRD.
THIS DIDN'T HAP-PEN LAST TIME.
EL FULLA!!
ZASHU (SLASH)

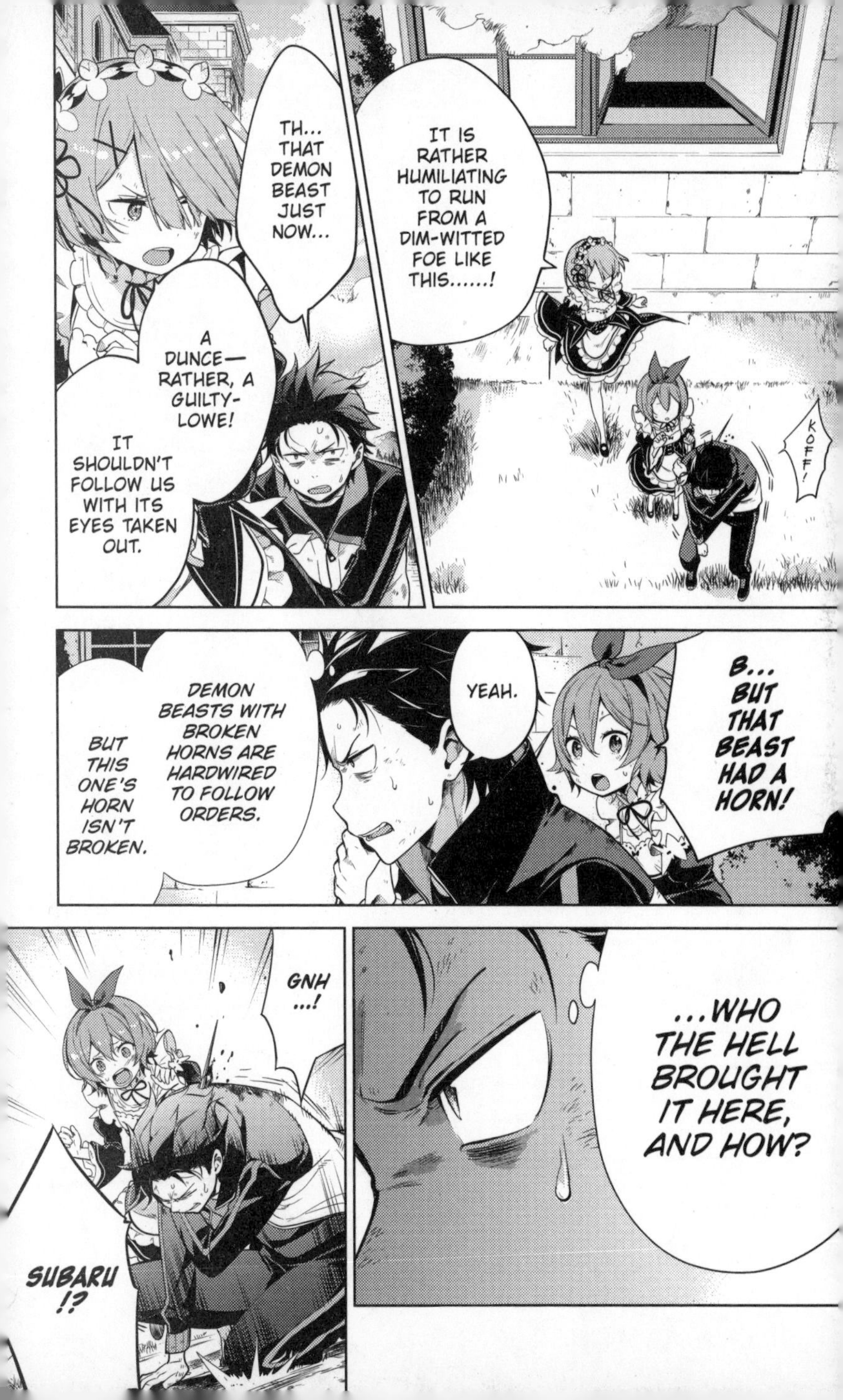
IT IS RATHER HUMILIATING TO RUN FROM A DIM-WITTED FOE LIKE THIS......!
KOFF!
TH... THAT DEMON BEAST JUST NOW...
A DUNCE—RATHER, A GUILTY-LOWE!
IT SHOULDN'T FOLLOW US WITH ITS EYES TAKEN OUT.
B... BUT THAT BEAST HAD A HORN!
YEAH.
DEMON BEASTS WITH BROKEN HORNS ARE HARDWIRED TO FOLLOW ORDERS.
BUT THIS ONE'S HORN ISN'T BROKEN.
...WHO THE HELL BROUGHT IT HERE, AND HOW?
GNH ...!
SUBARU !?

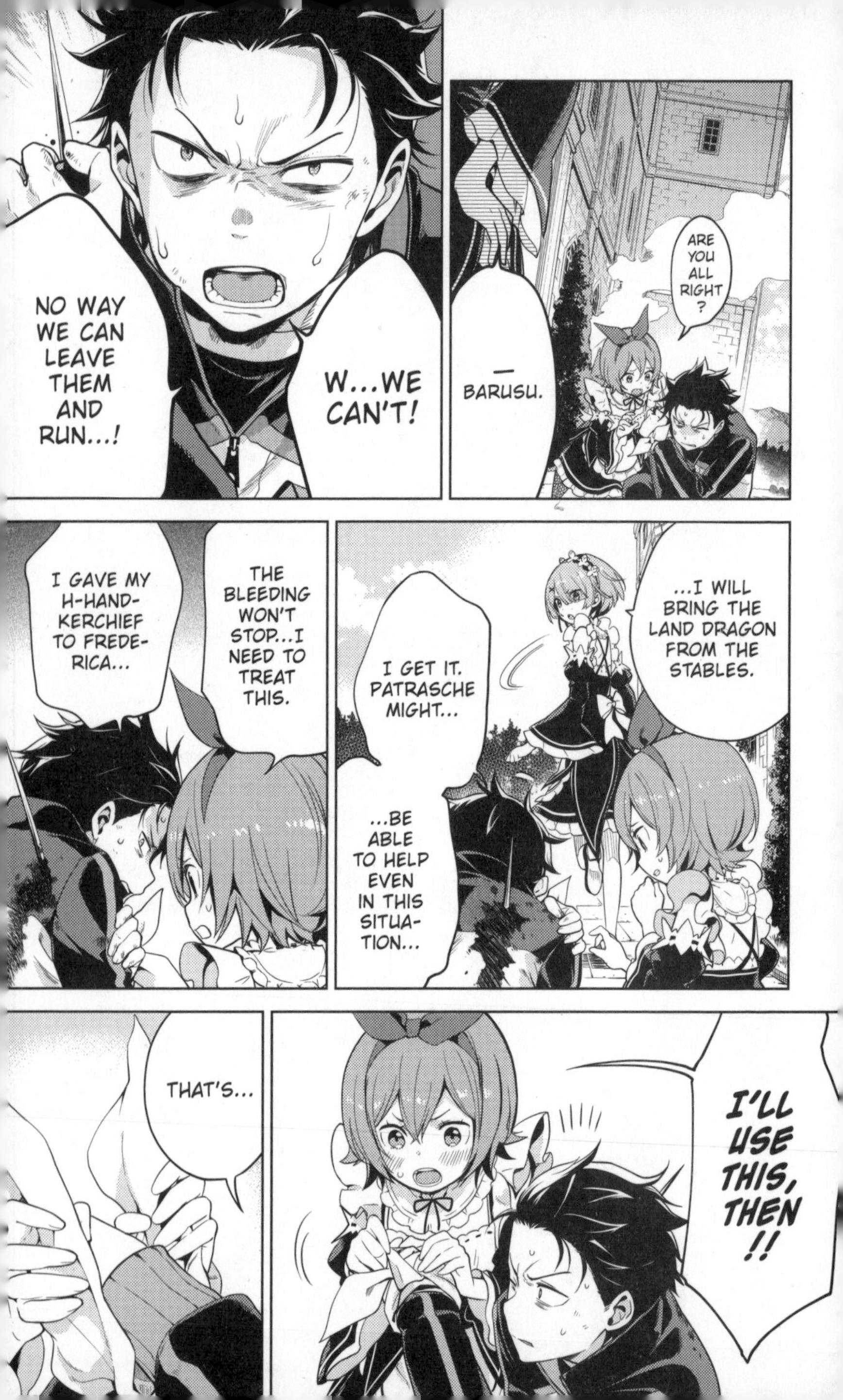
ARE YOU ALL RIGHT?
—BARUSU.
W...WE CAN'T!
NO WAY WE CAN LEAVE THEM AND RUN...!
...I WILL BRING THE LAND DRAGON FROM THE STABLES.
I GET IT. PATRASCHE MIGHT...
...BE ABLE TO HELP EVEN IN THIS SITUATION...
THE BLEEDING WON'T STOP...I NEED TO TREAT THIS.
I GAVE MY H-HANDKERCHIEF TO FREDERICA...
I'LL USE THIS, THEN!!
THAT'S...

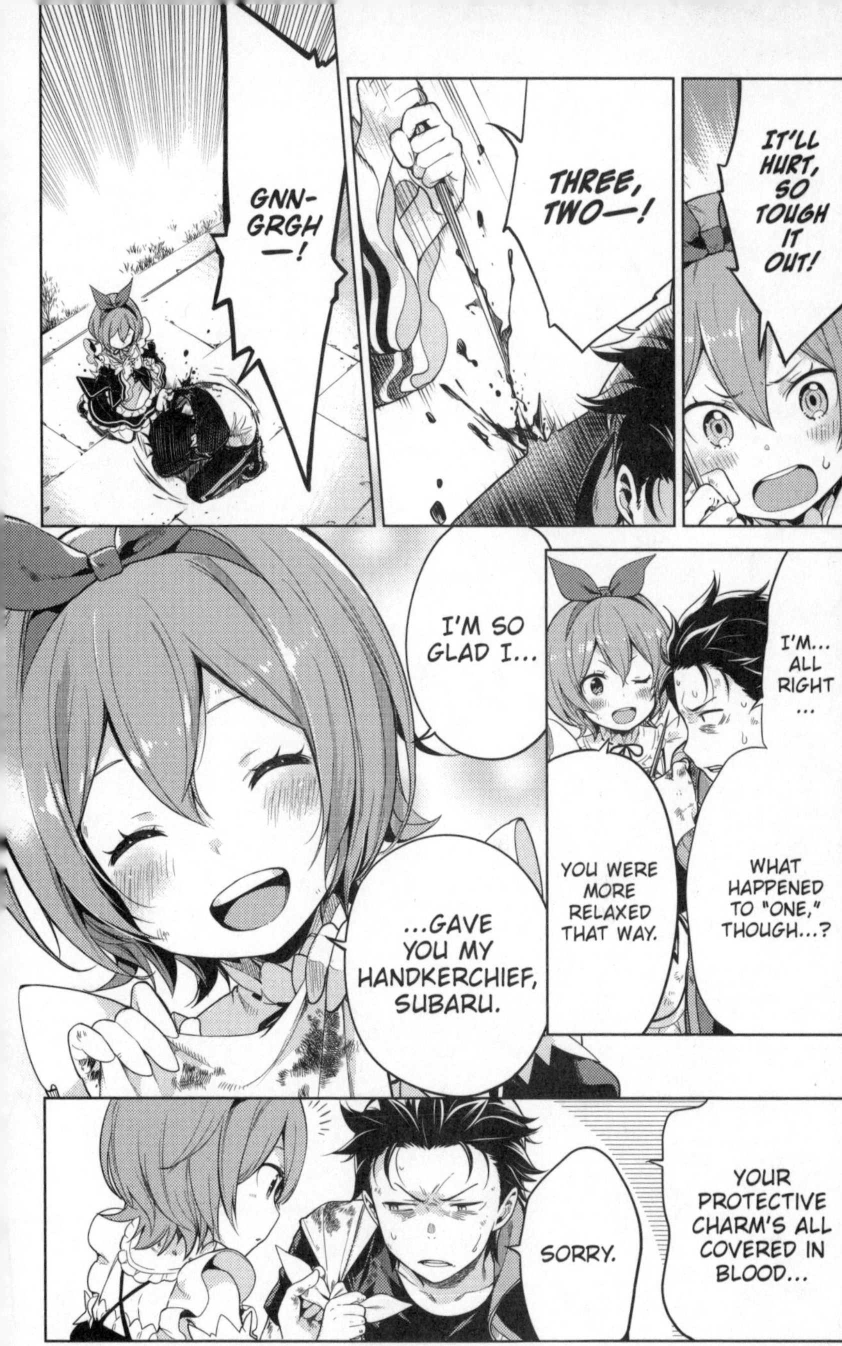
IT'LL HURT, SO TOUGH IT OUT!
THREE, TWO—!
GNN-GRGH—!
I'M... ALL RIGHT...
WHAT HAPPENED TO "ONE," THOUGH...?
YOU WERE MORE RELAXED THAT WAY.
I'M SO GLAD I...
...GAVE YOU MY HANDKERCHIEF, SUBARU.
YOUR PROTECTIVE CHARM'S ALL COVERED IN BLOOD...
SORRY.

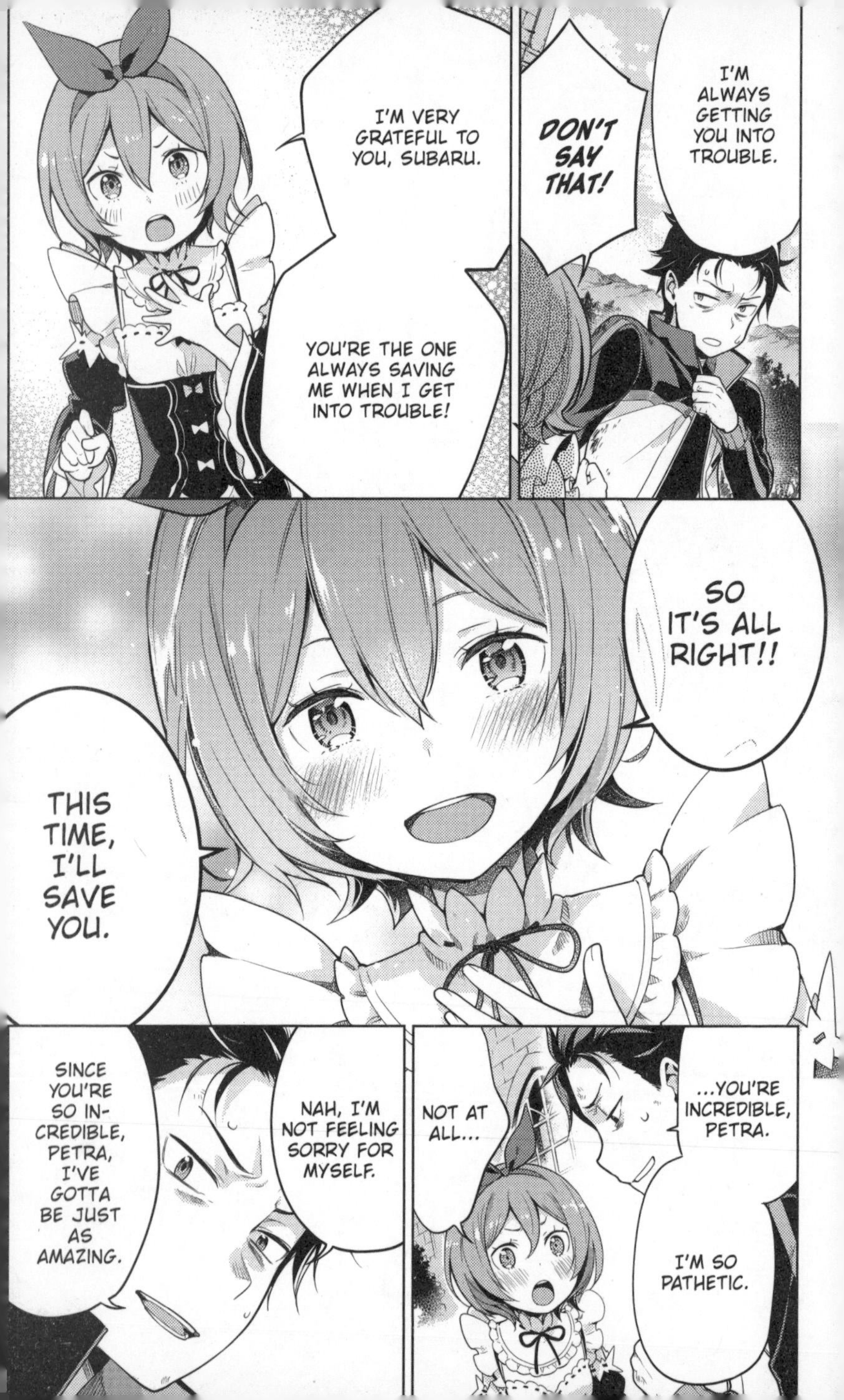
I'M ALWAYS GETTING YOU INTO TROUBLE.
DON'T SAY THAT!
I'M VERY GRATEFUL TO YOU, SUBARU.
YOU'RE THE ONE ALWAYS SAVING ME WHEN I GET INTO TROUBLE!
SO IT'S ALL RIGHT!!
THIS TIME, I'LL SAVE YOU.
...YOU'RE INCREDIBLE, PETRA.
I'M SO PATHETIC.
NOT AT ALL...
NAH, I'M NOT FEELING SORRY FOR MYSELF.
SINCE YOU'RE SO IN-CREDIBLE, PETRA, I'VE GOTTA BE JUST AS AMAZING.

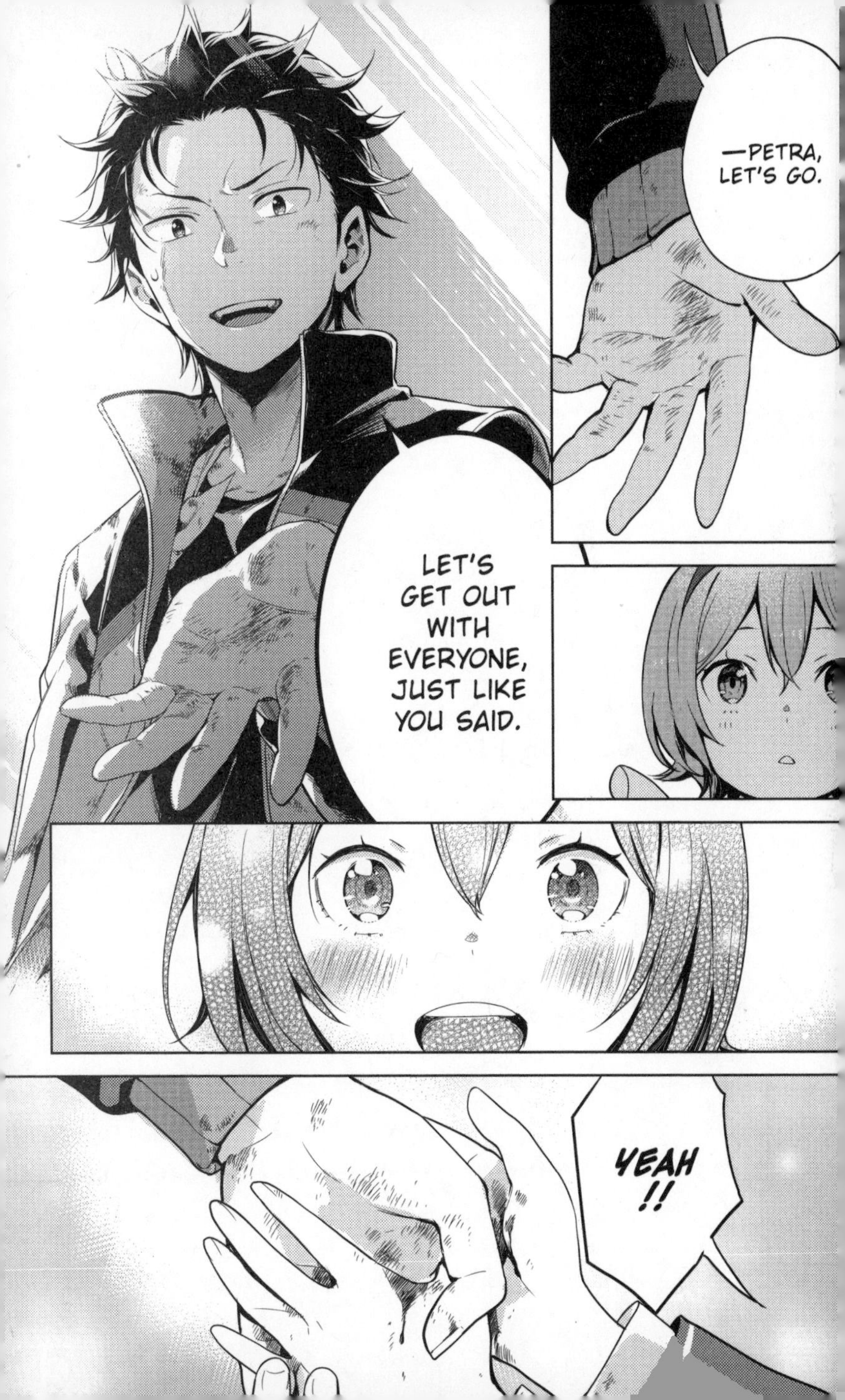
—PETRA, LET'S GO.
LET'S GET OUT WITH EVERYONE, JUST LIKE YOU SAID.
YEAH !!

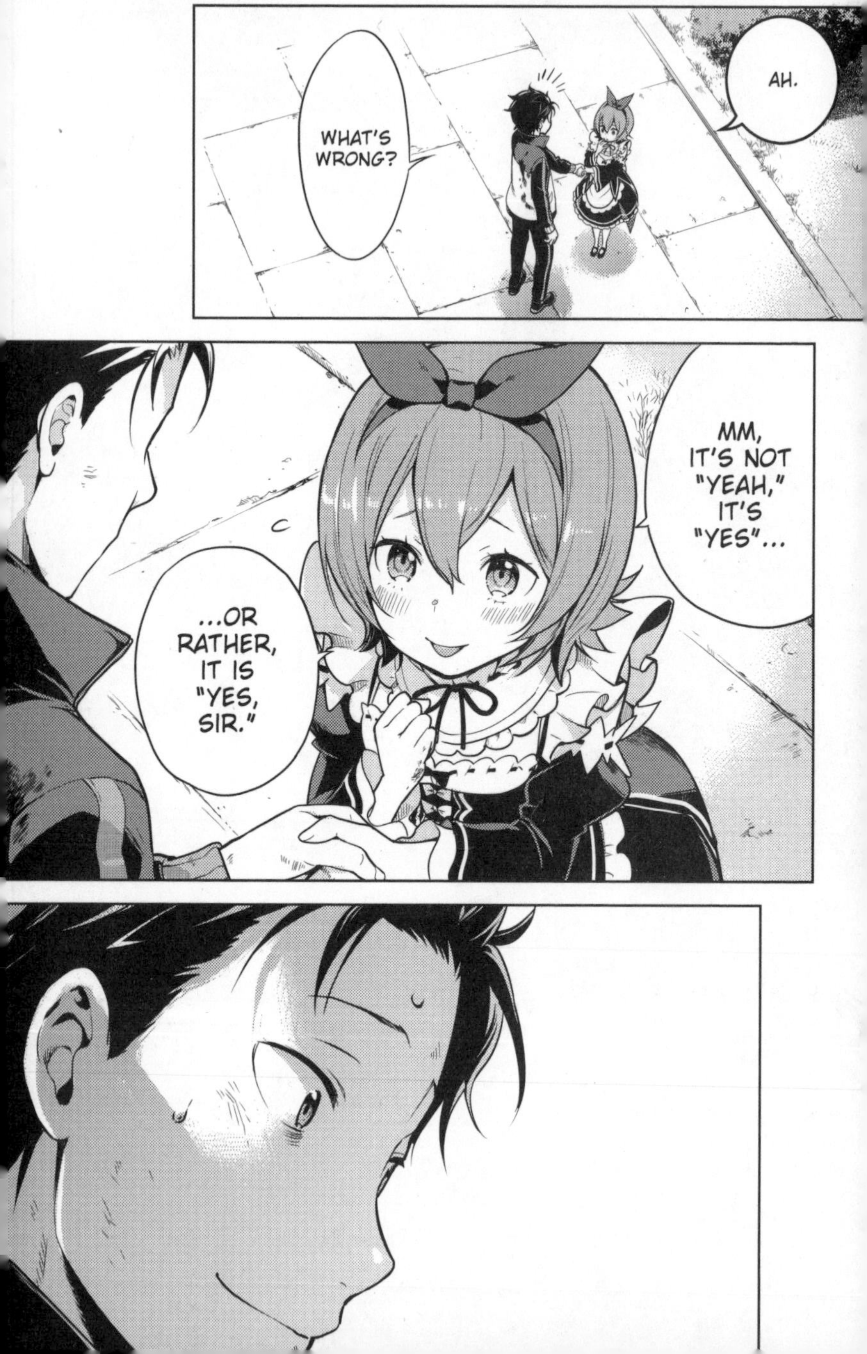
AH.
WHAT'S WRONG?
MM, IT'S NOT "YEAH," IT'S "YES"...
...OR RATHER, IT IS "YES, SIR."

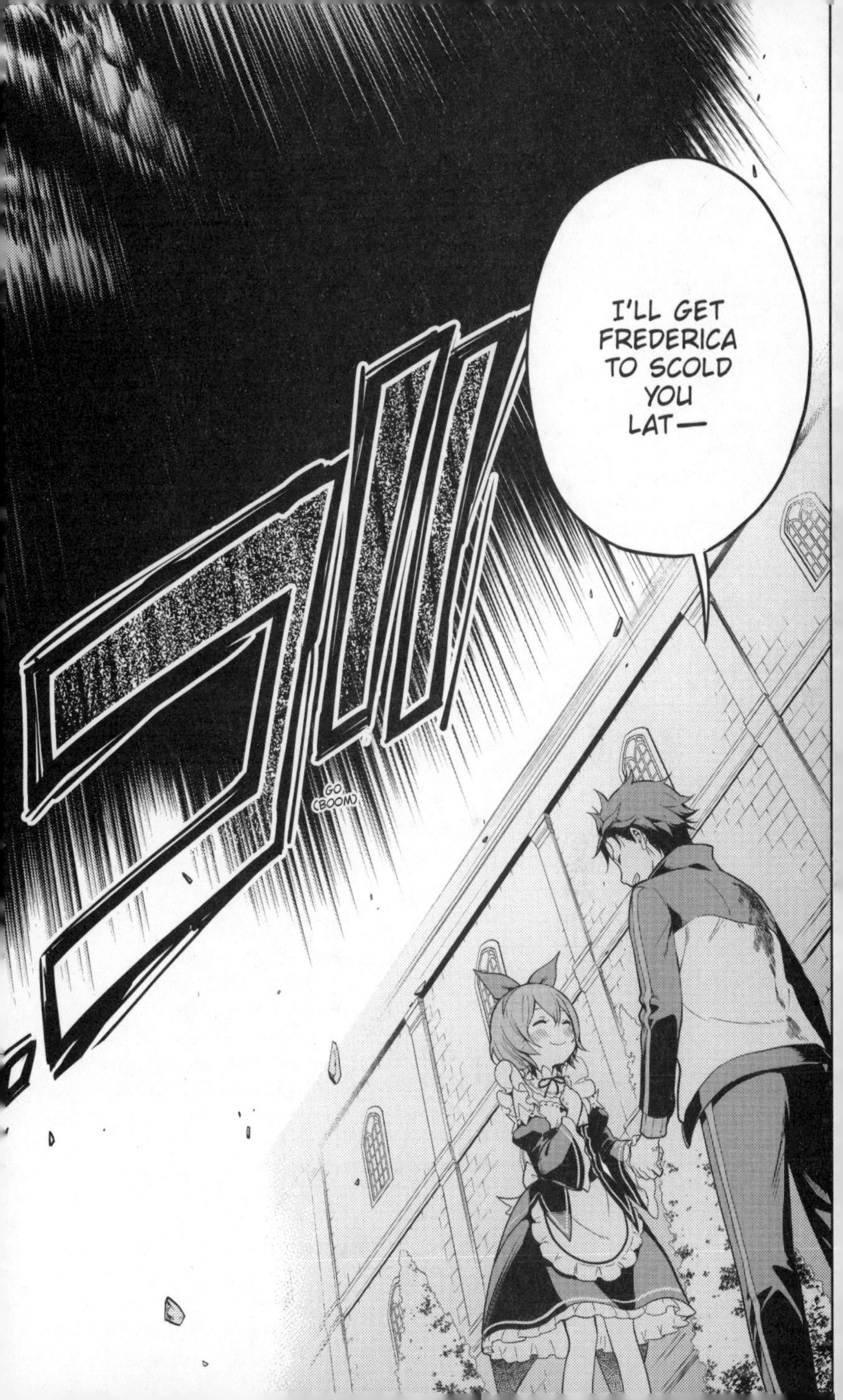
I'LL GET FREDERICA TO SCOLD YOU LAT—
GO (BOOM)

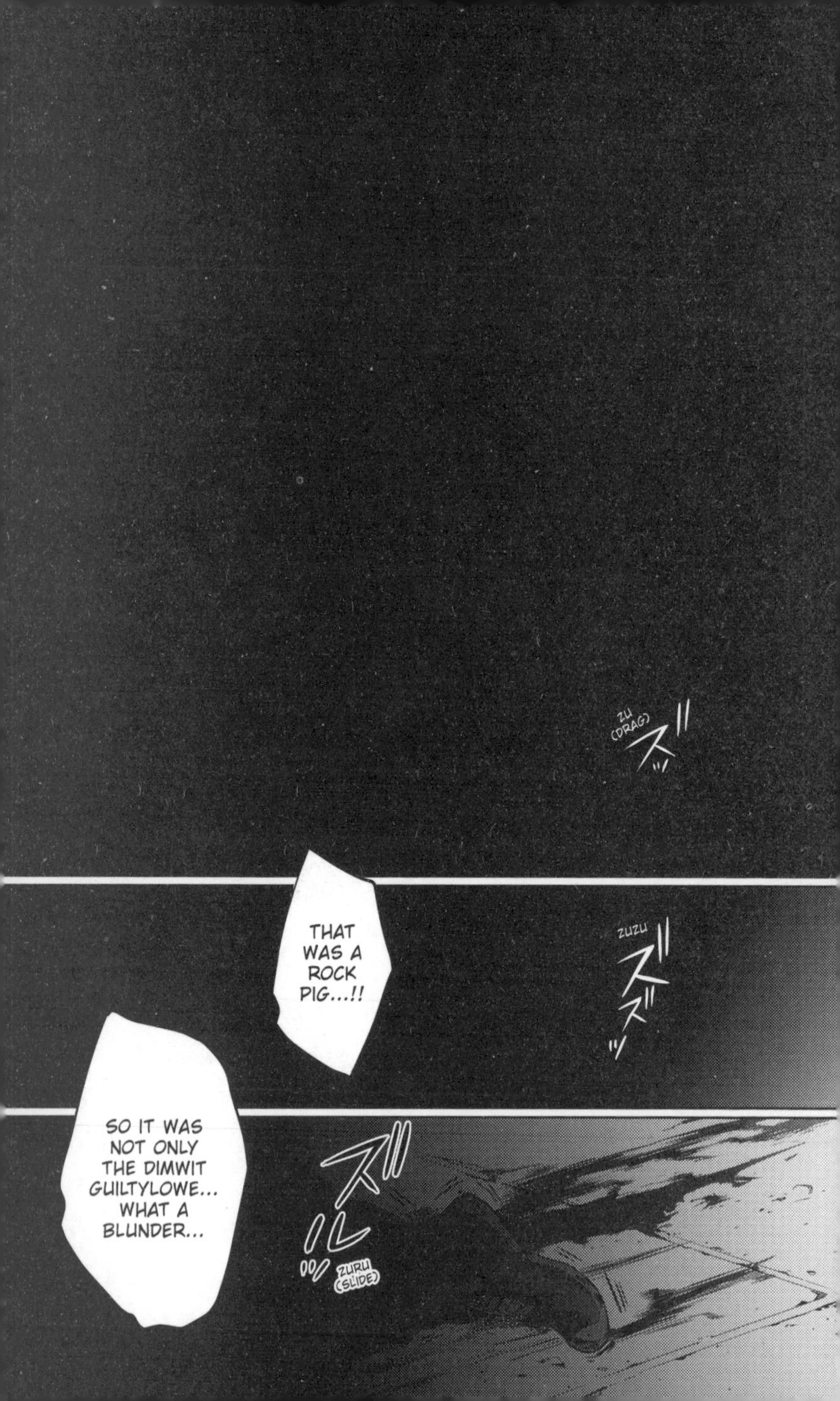
ZU (DRAG)
ZUZU
THAT WAS A ROCK PIG...!!
ZURU (SLIDE)
SO IT WAS NOT ONLY THE DIMWIT GUILTYLOWE... WHAT A BLUNDER...

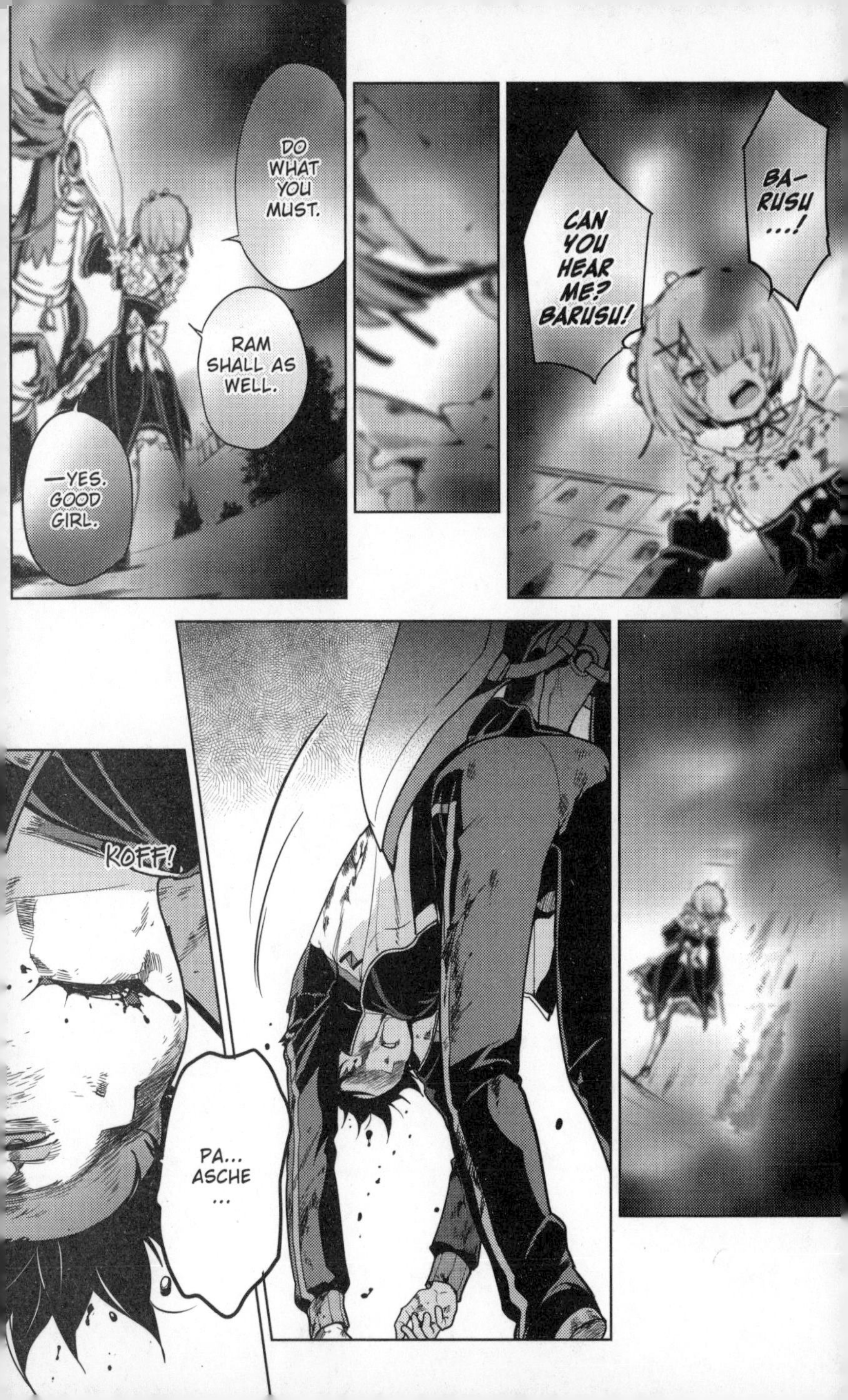
BA-RUSU...!
CAN YOU HEAR ME? BARUSU!
DO WHAT YOU MUST.
RAM SHALL AS WELL.
—YES. GOOD GIRL.
KOFF!
PA... ASCHE...

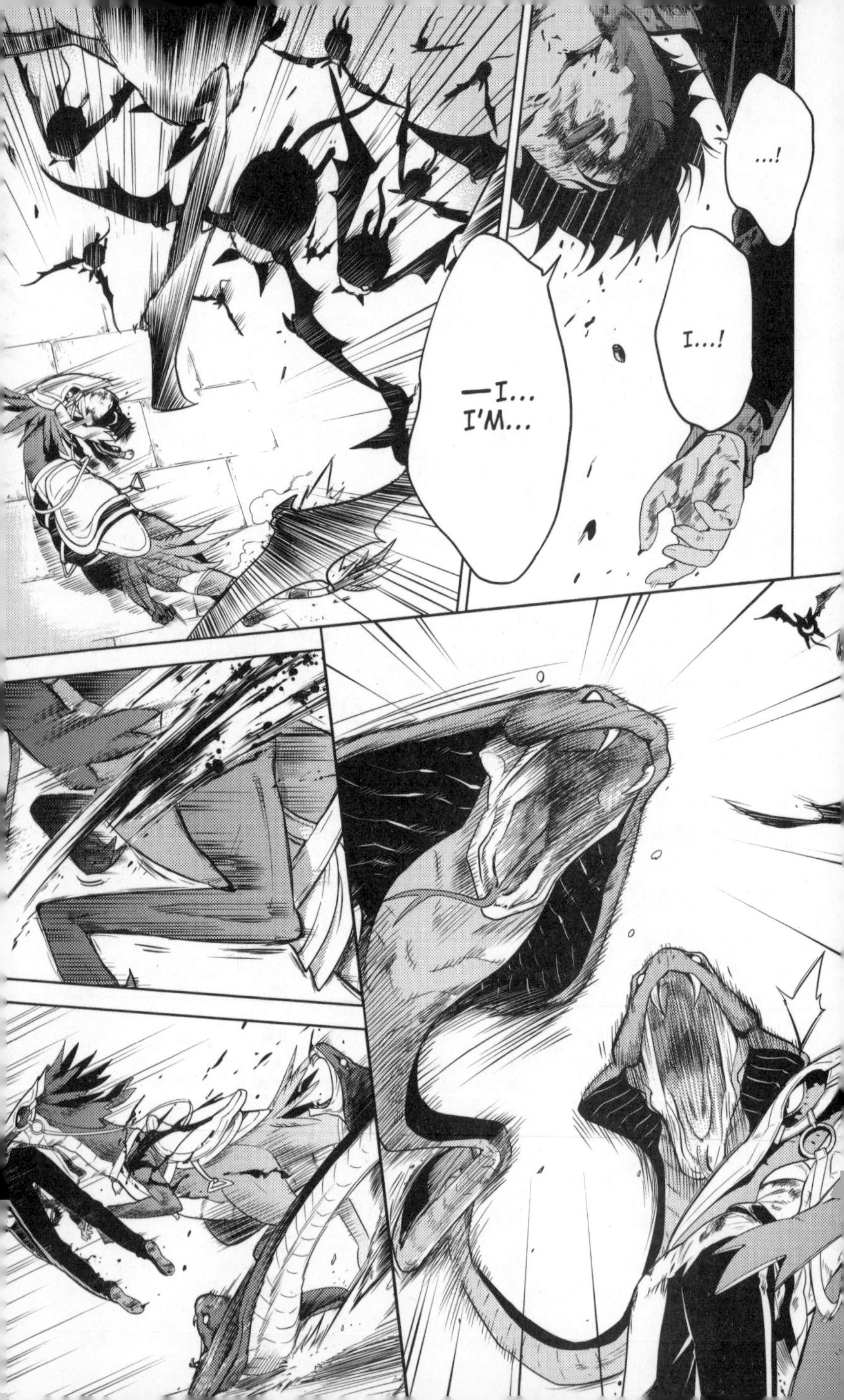
...!
I...!
—I...
I'M...

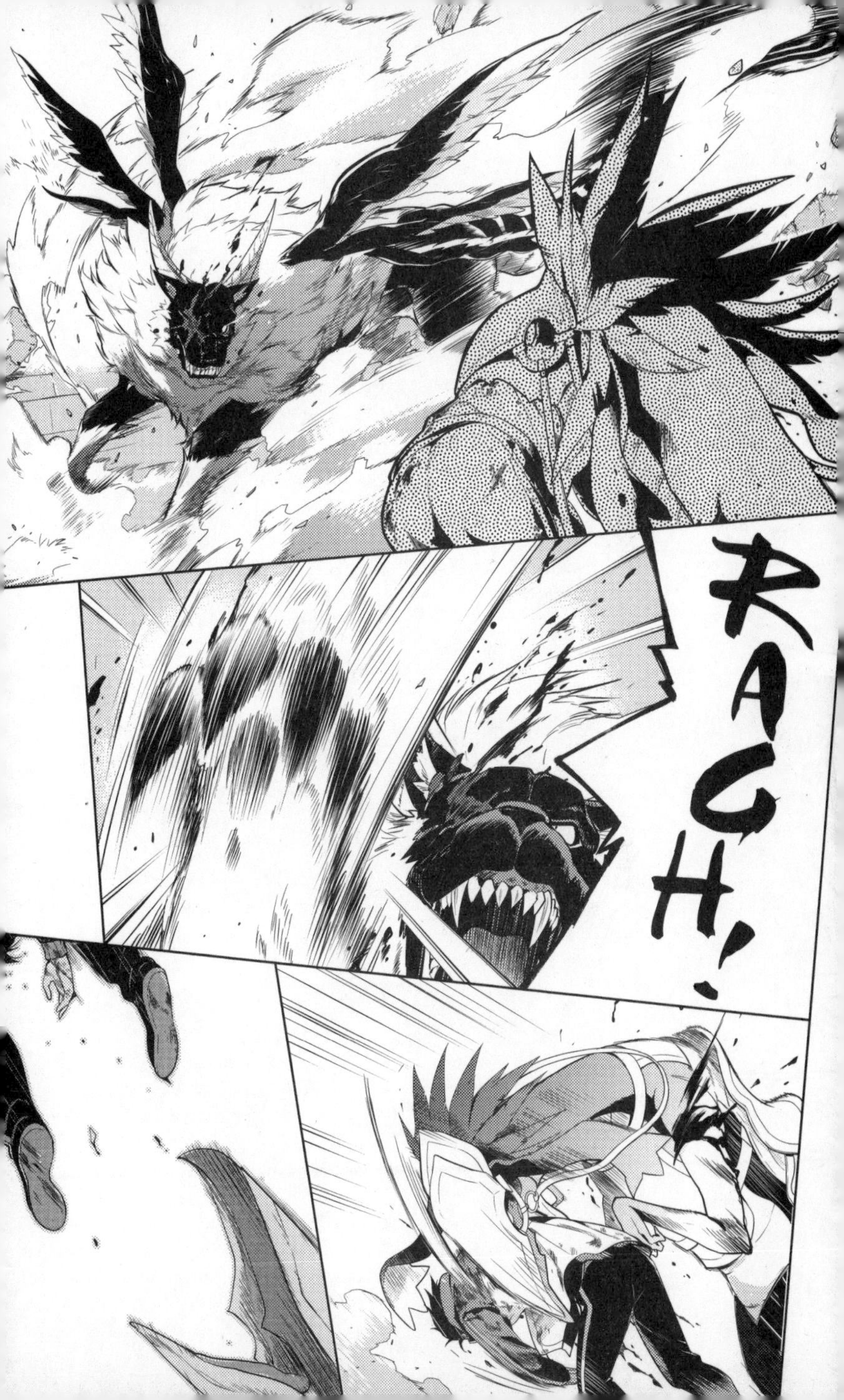
RACH!

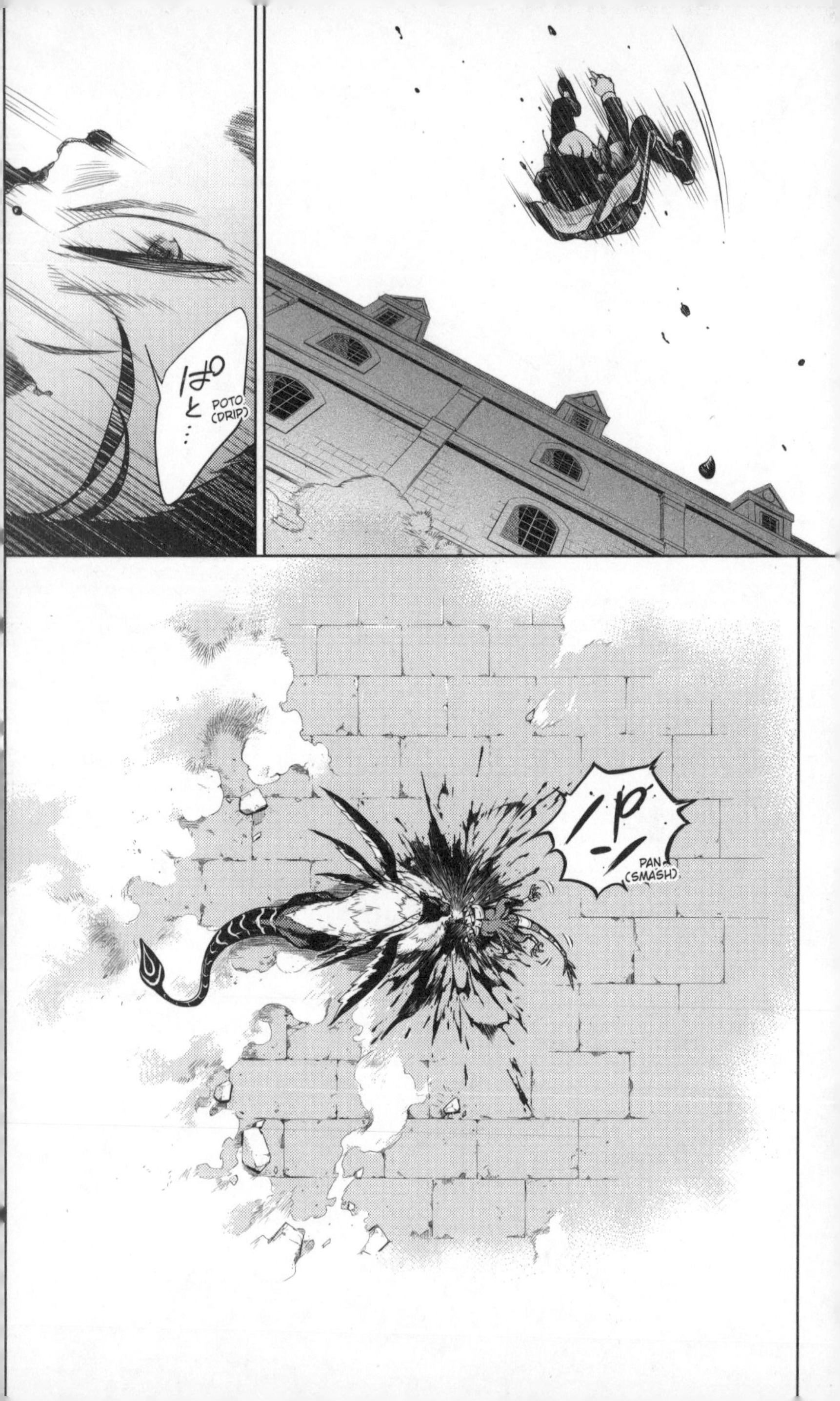
ぽと…
POTO (DRIP)
PAN (SMASH)

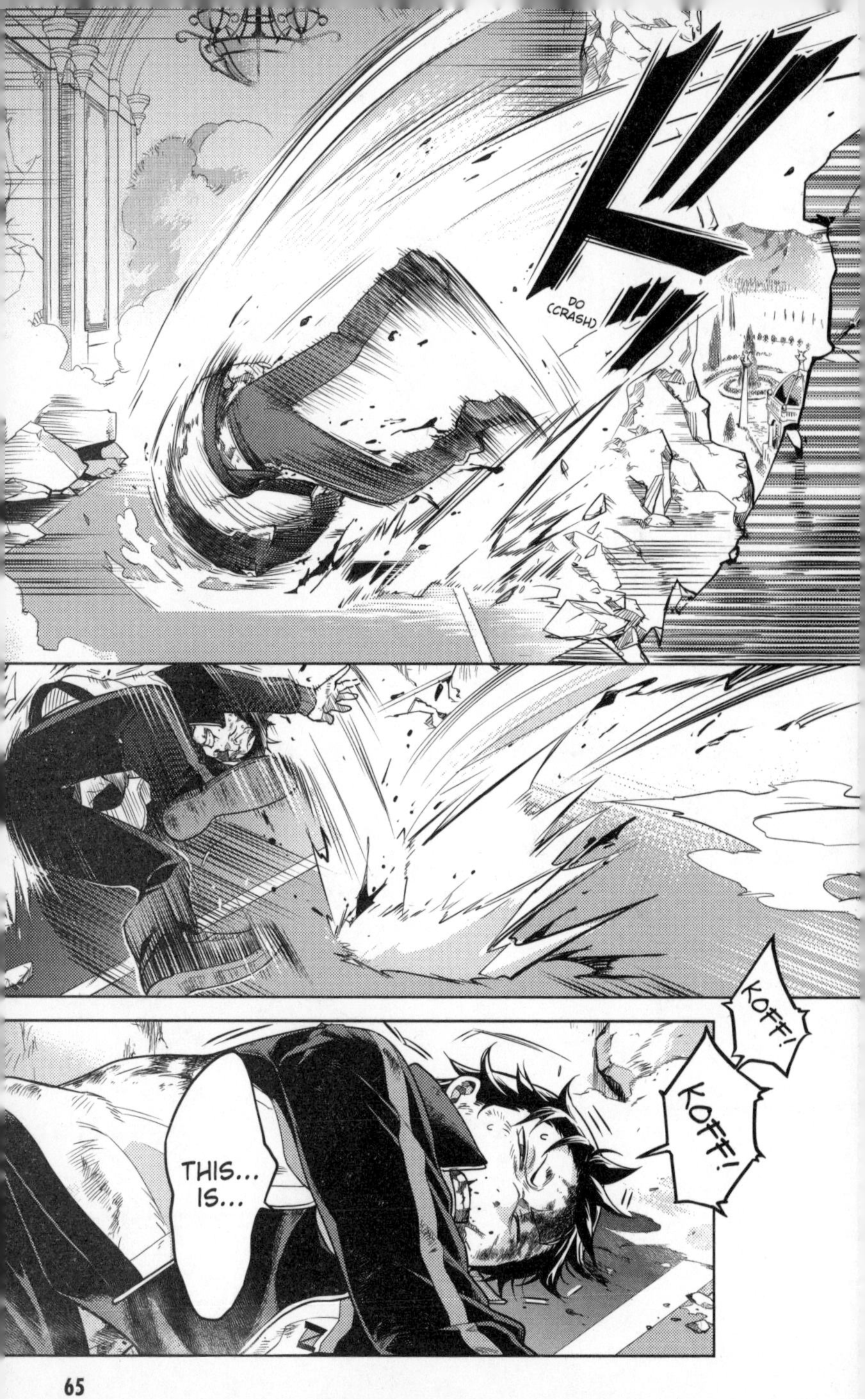
DO (CRASH)
KOFF!
KOFF!
THIS... IS...

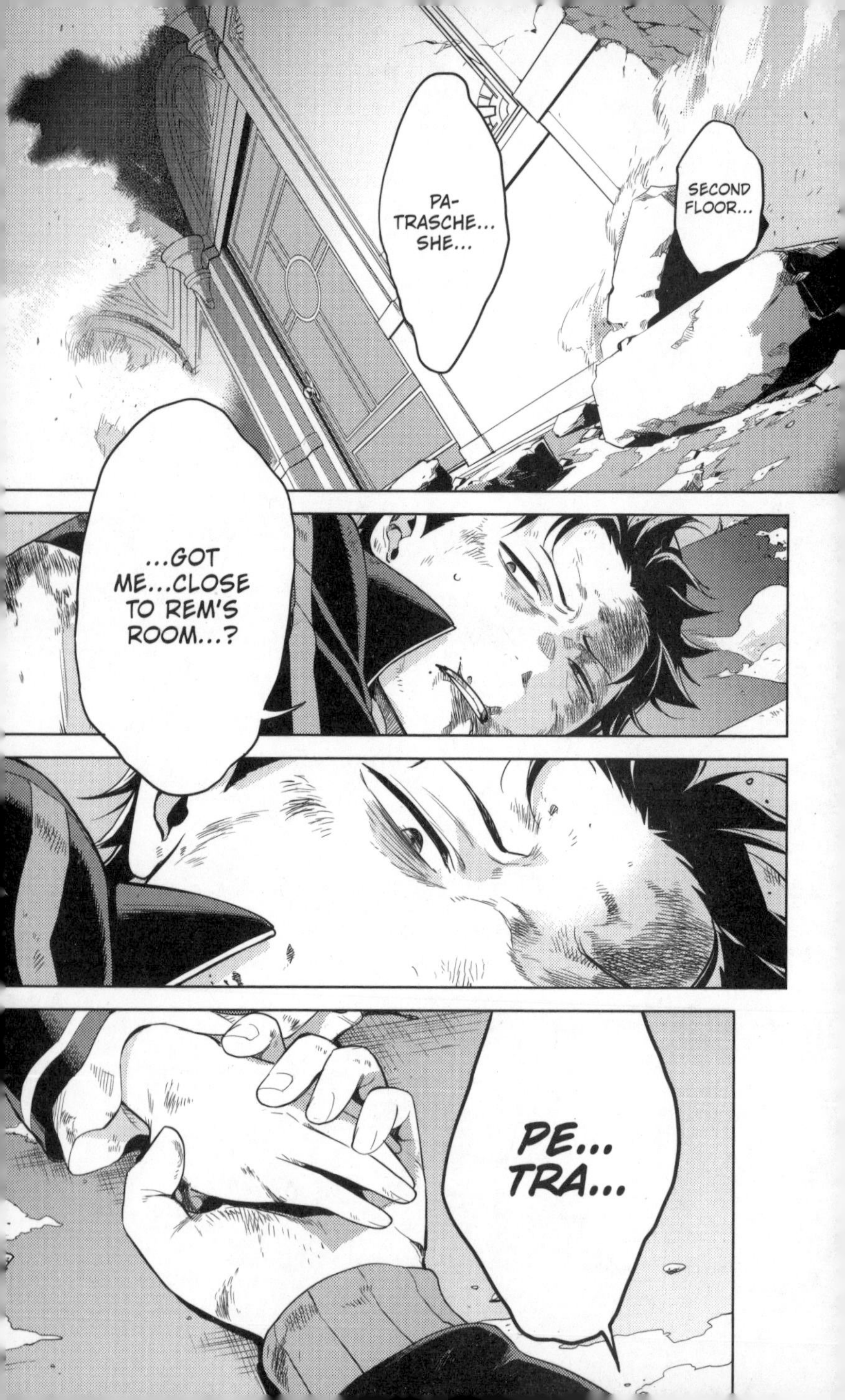
SECOND FLOOR...
PA-TRASCHE... SHE...
...GOT ME...CLOSE TO REM'S ROOM...?
PE... TRA...

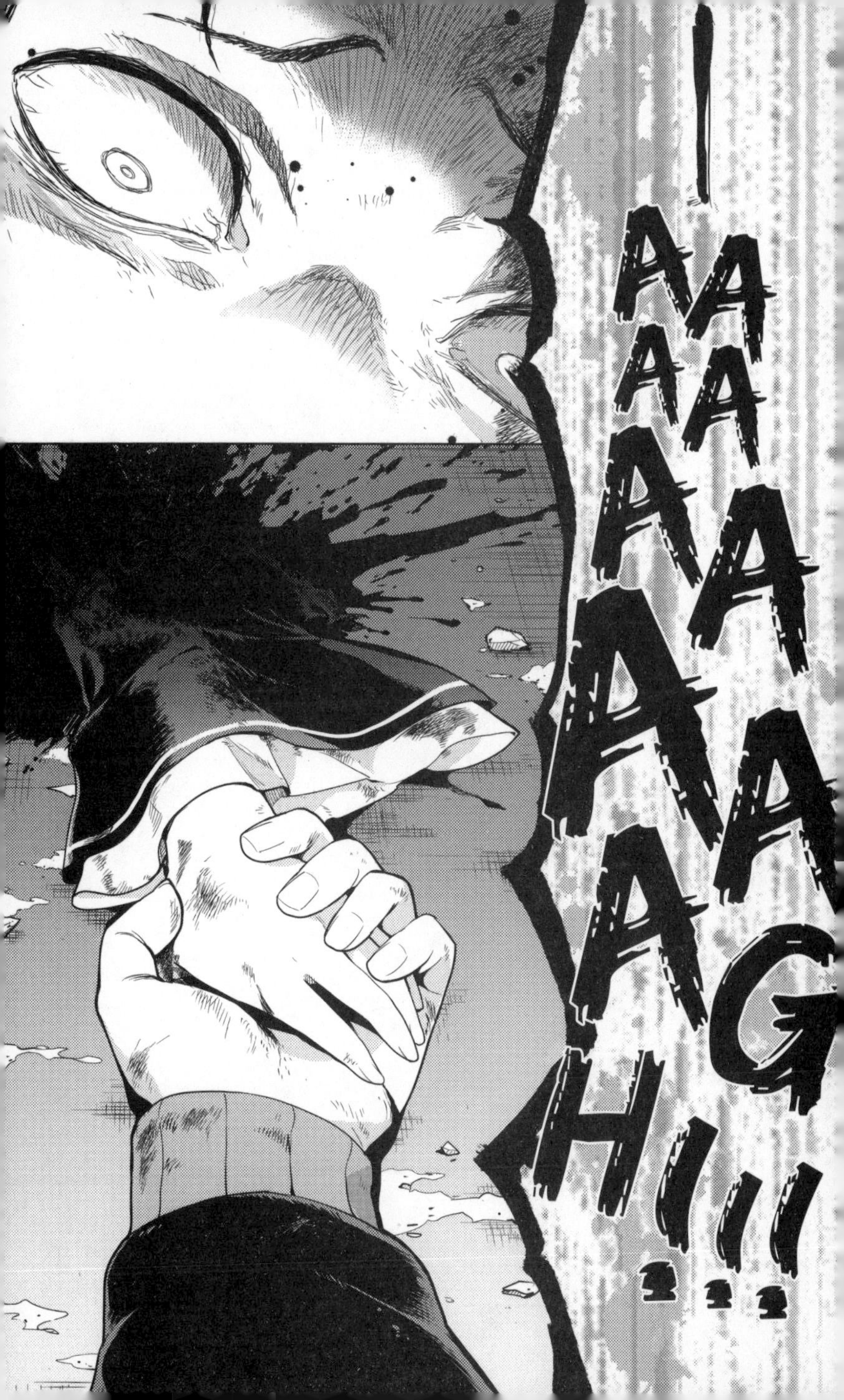
AAAAAAAAAAAGH!!!

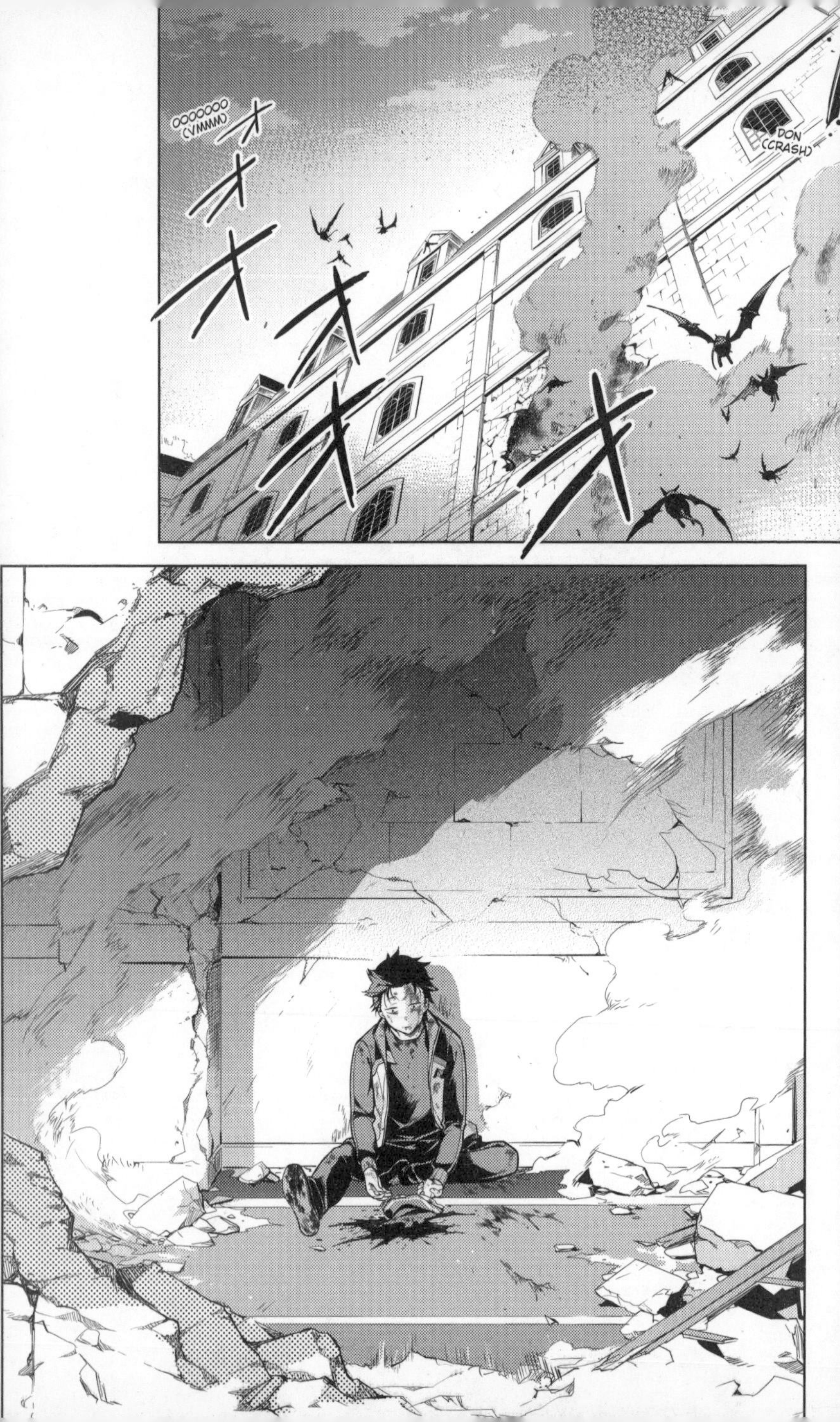
DON (CRASH)
OOOOOOO (VMMM)

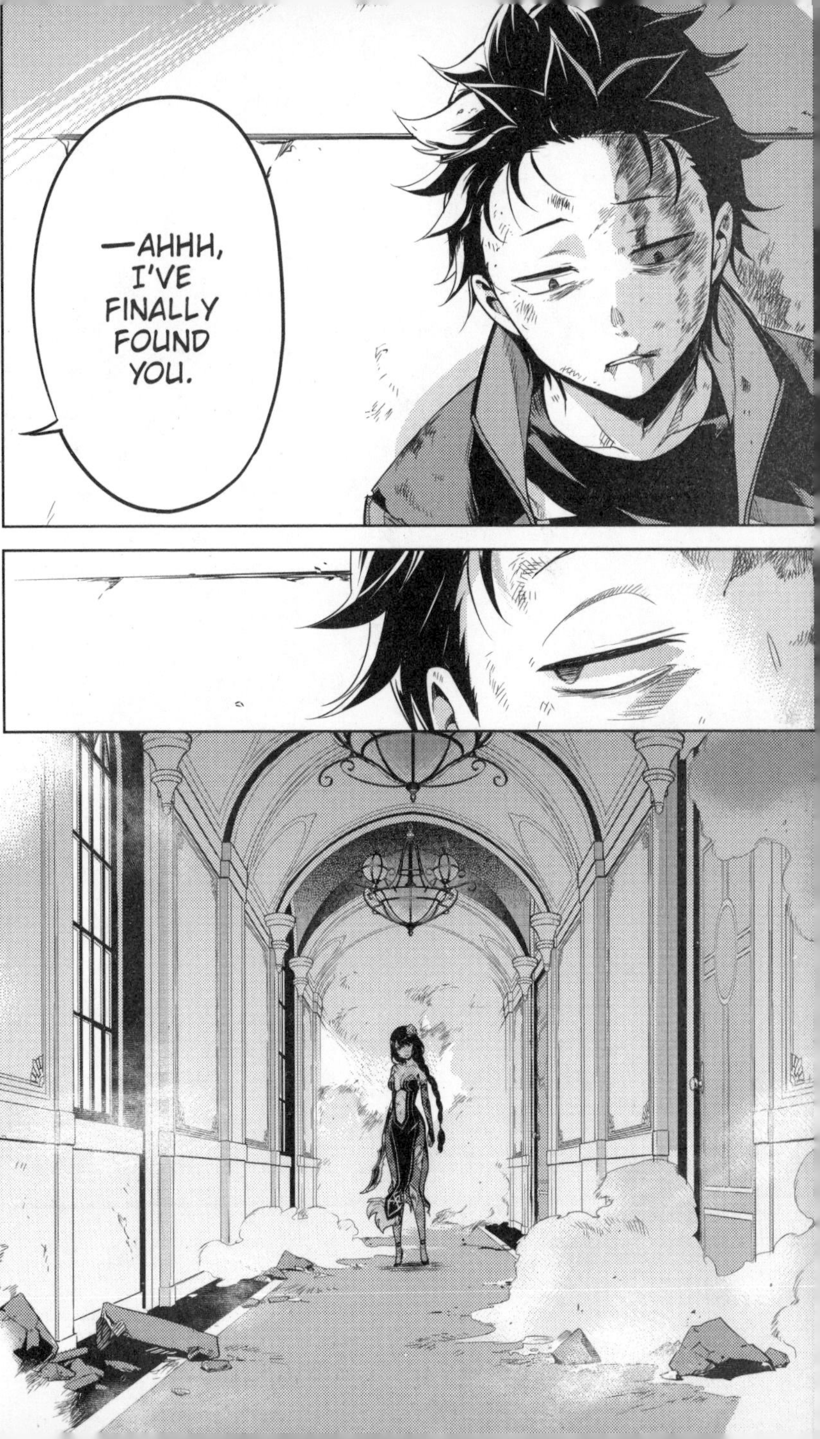
—AHHH, I'VE FINALLY FOUND YOU.

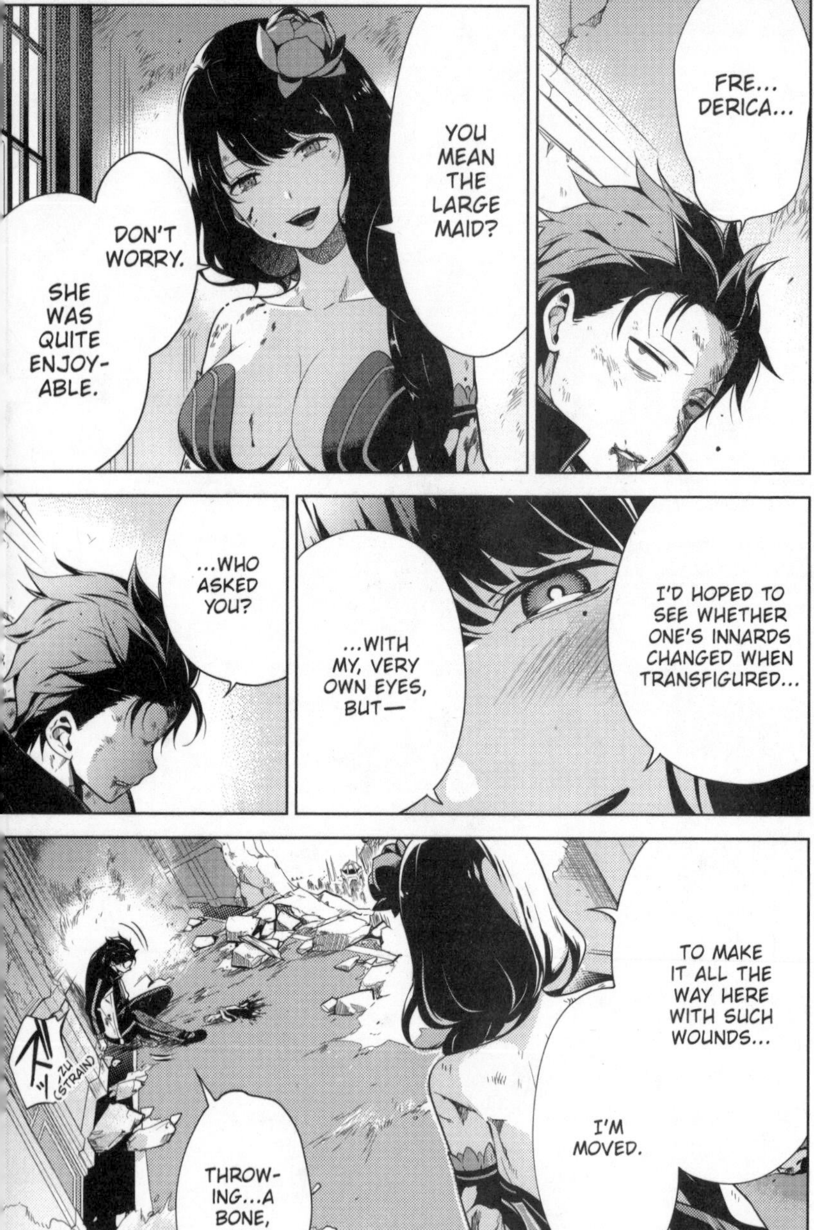
FRE... DERICA...
YOU MEAN THE LARGE MAID?
DON'T WORRY.
SHE WAS QUITE ENJOY-ABLE.
I'D HOPED TO SEE WHETHER ONE'S INNARDS CHANGED WHEN TRANSFIGURED...
...WITH MY, VERY OWN EYES, BUT—
...WHO ASKED YOU?
TO MAKE IT ALL THE WAY HERE WITH SUCH WOUNDS...
I'M MOVED.
ZU (STRAIN)
THROW-ING...A BONE, HUH?

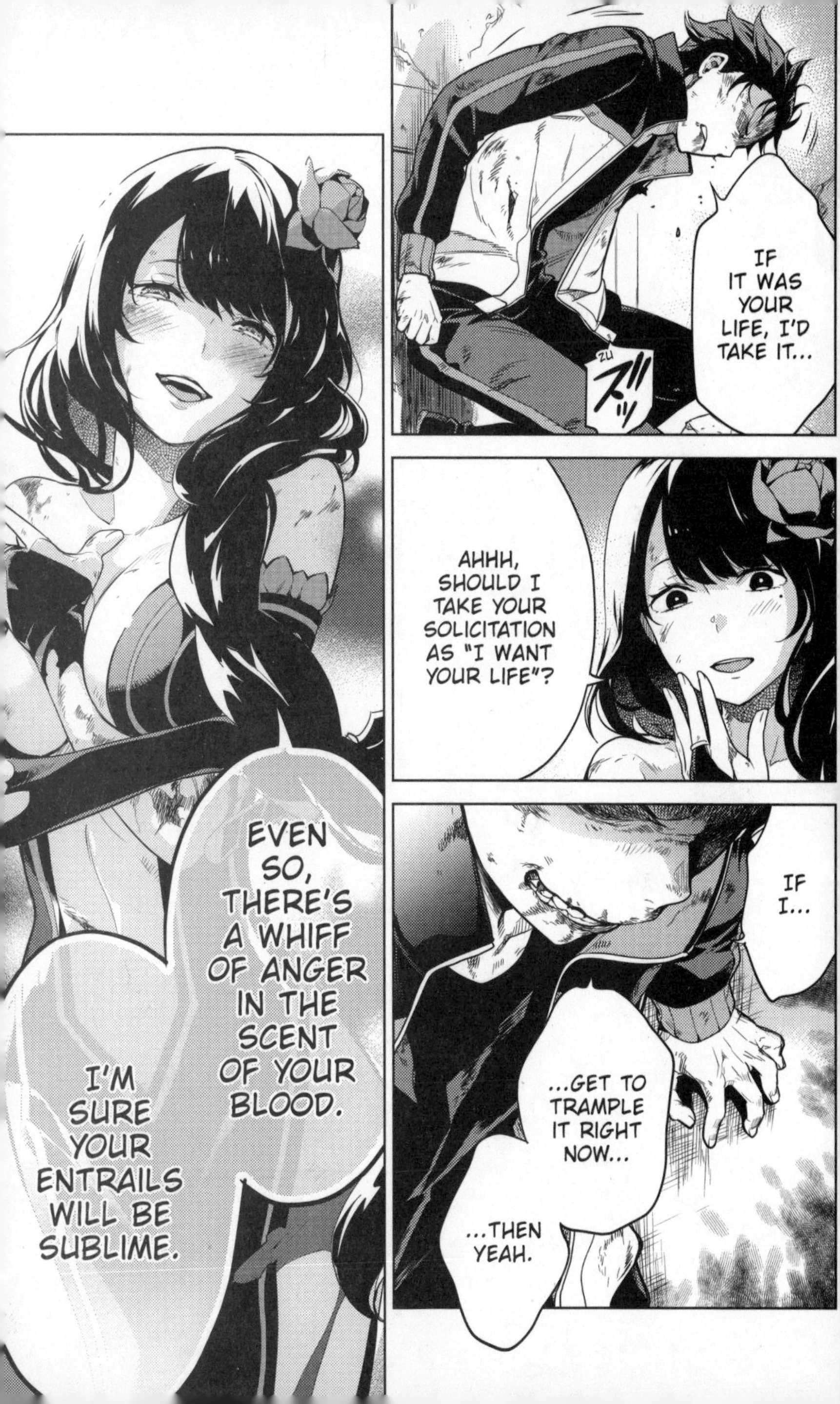
IF IT WAS YOUR LIFE, I'D TAKE IT...
ZU
ズッ
AHHH, SHOULD I TAKE YOUR SOLICITATION AS "I WANT YOUR LIFE"?
IF I...
...GET TO TRAMPLE IT RIGHT NOW...
...THEN YEAH.
EVEN SO, THERE'S A WHIFF OF ANGER IN THE SCENT OF YOUR BLOOD.
I'M SURE YOUR ENTRAILS WILL BE SUBLIME.

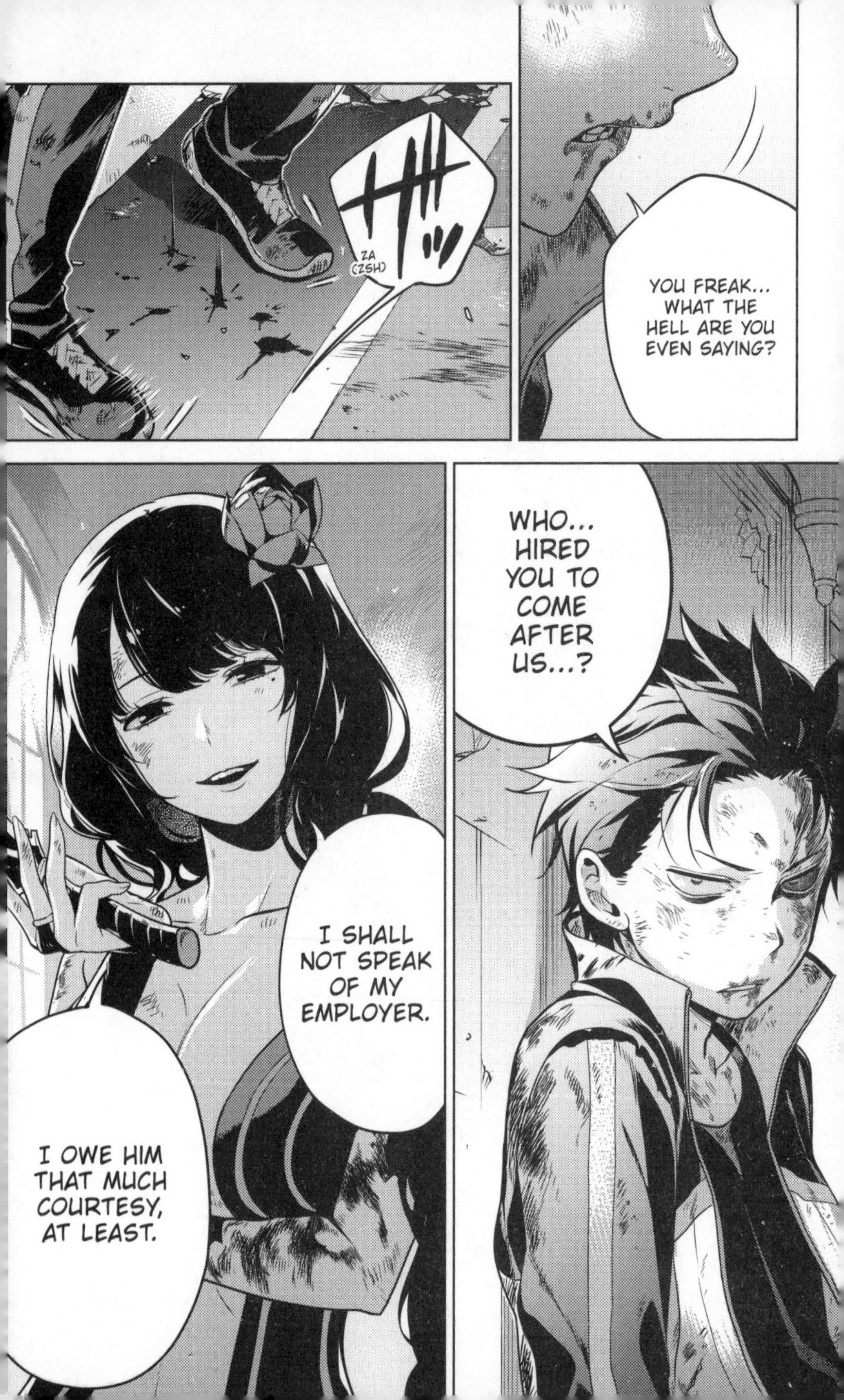
YOU FREAK... WHAT THE HELL ARE YOU EVEN SAYING?
ZA (ZSH)
WHO... HIRED YOU TO COME AFTER US...?
I SHALL NOT SPEAK OF MY EMPLOYER.
I OWE HIM THAT MUCH COURTESY, AT LEAST.

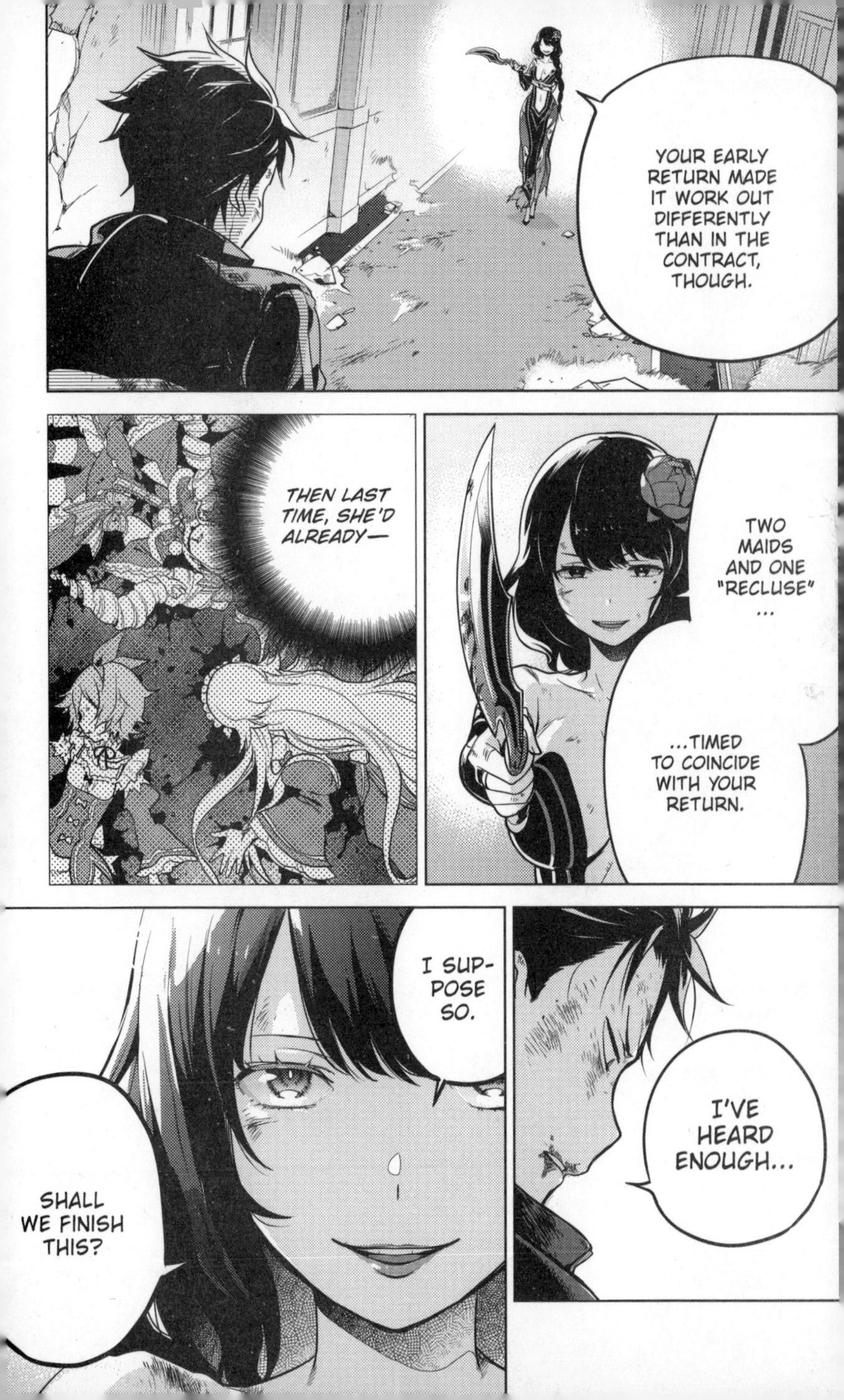
YOUR EARLY RETURN MADE IT WORK OUT DIFFERENTLY THAN IN THE CONTRACT, THOUGH.
TWO MAIDS AND ONE "RECLUSE" ...
...TIMED TO COINCIDE WITH YOUR RETURN.
THEN LAST TIME, SHE'D ALREADY—
I'VE HEARD ENOUGH...
I SUP-POSE SO.
SHALL WE FINISH THIS?

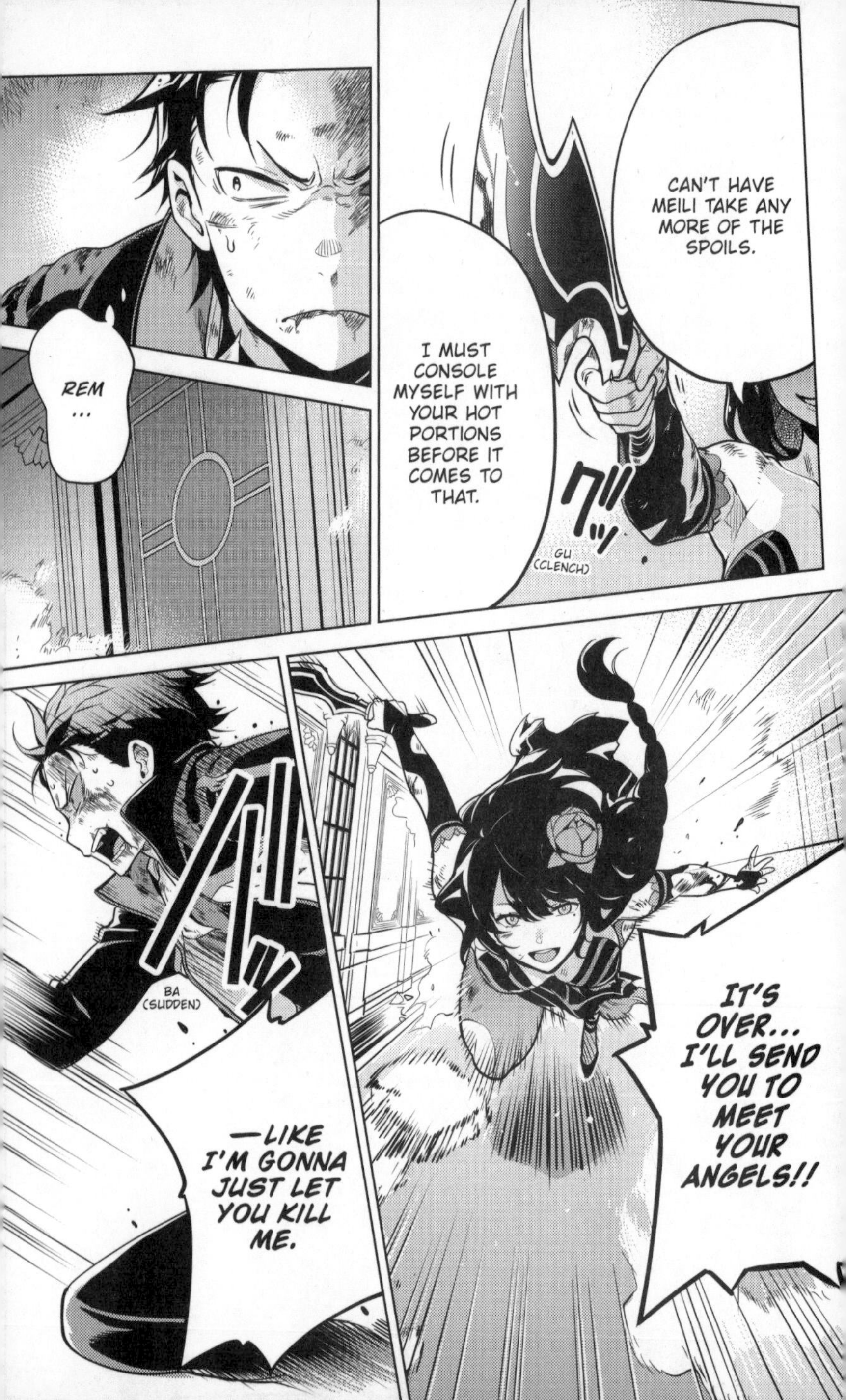
CAN'T HAVE MEILI TAKE ANY MORE OF THE SPOILS.
I MUST CONSOLE MYSELF WITH YOUR HOT PORTIONS BEFORE IT COMES TO THAT.
GU (CLENCH)
REM ...
IT'S OVER... I'LL SEND YOU TO MEET YOUR ANGELS!!
BA (SUDDEN)
—LIKE I'M GONNA JUST LET YOU KILL ME.

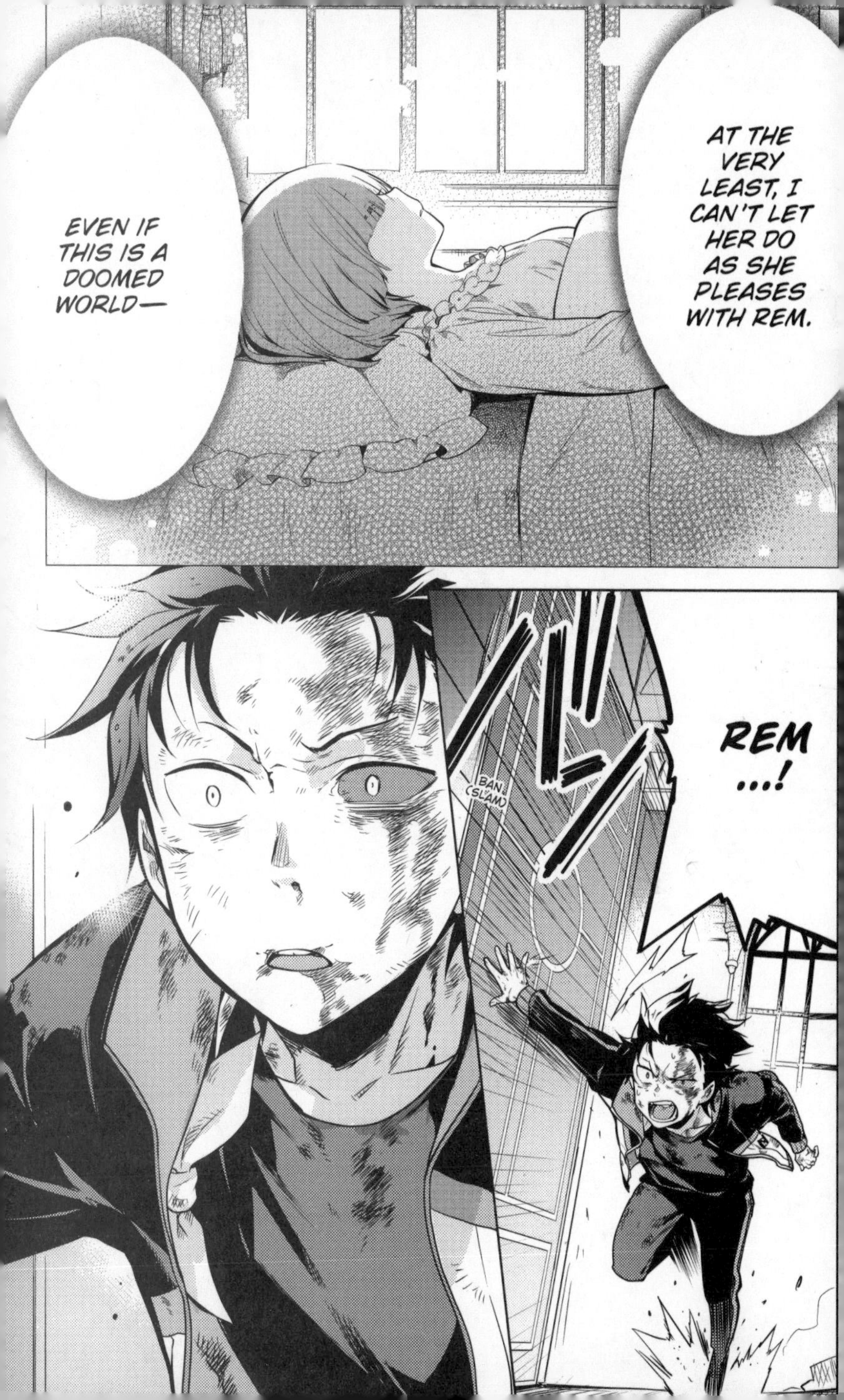
AT THE VERY LEAST, I CAN'T LET HER DO AS SHE PLEASES WITH REM.
EVEN IF THIS IS A DOOMED WORLD—
REM ...!
BAN (SLAM)

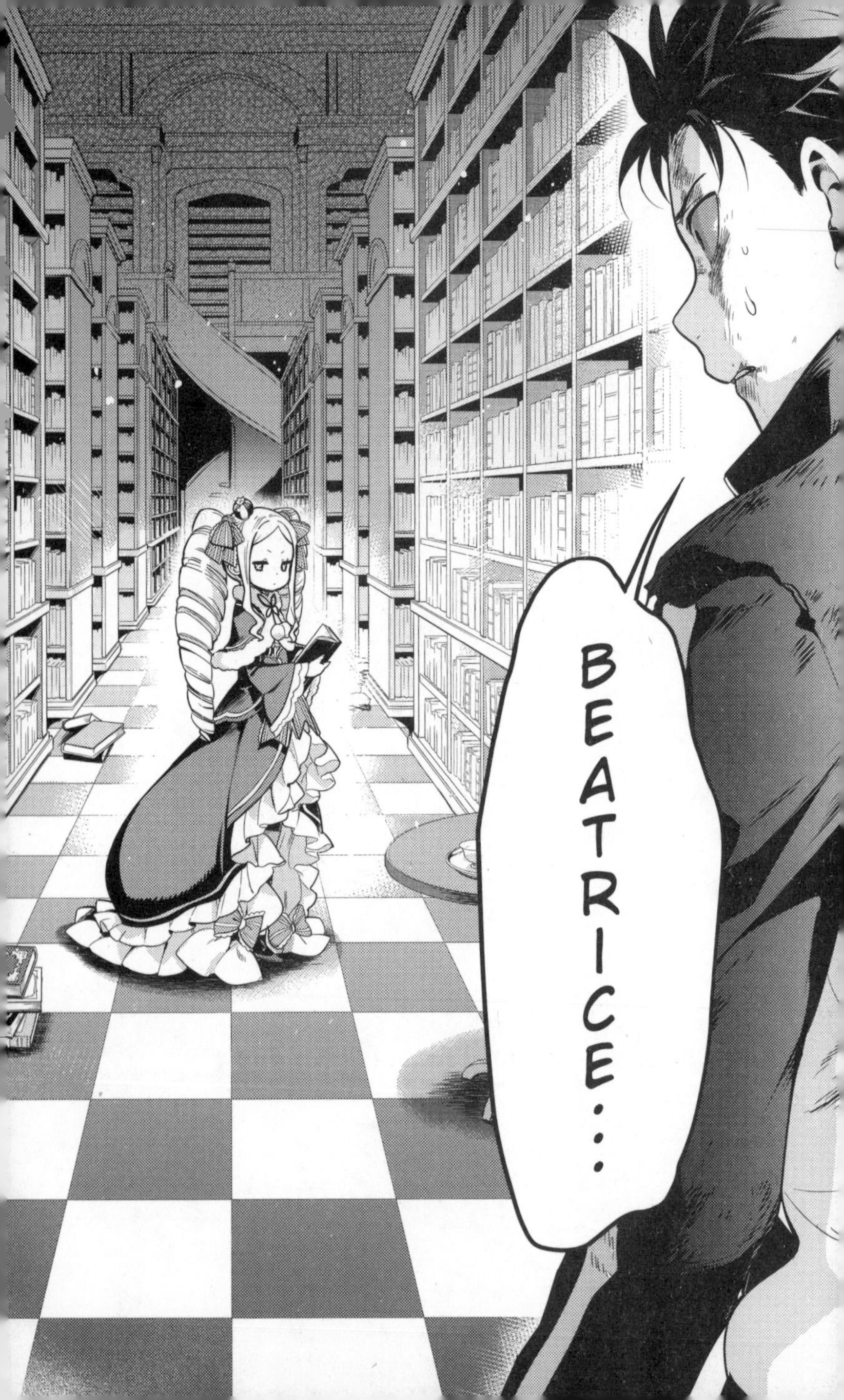
BEATRICE...

The only ability Subaru Natsuki gets when he's
summoned to another world is time travel via his own death.
But to save her, he'll die as many times as it takes.

Re:ZERO

-Starting Life in Another World-

Chapter 4: The Sanctuary and the Witch of Greed

Re:ZERO -Starting Life in Another World-

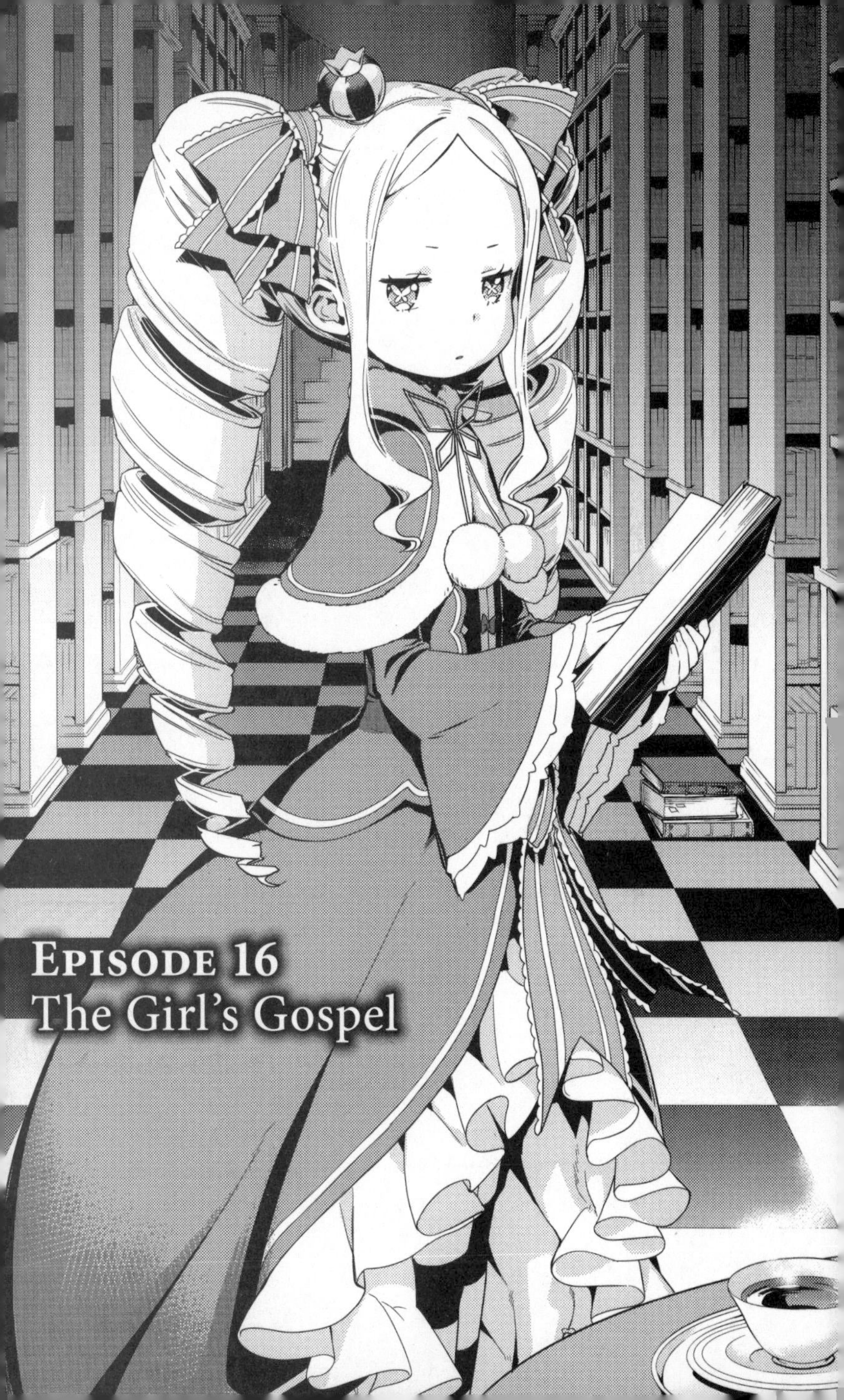
EPISODE 16
The Girl's Gospel

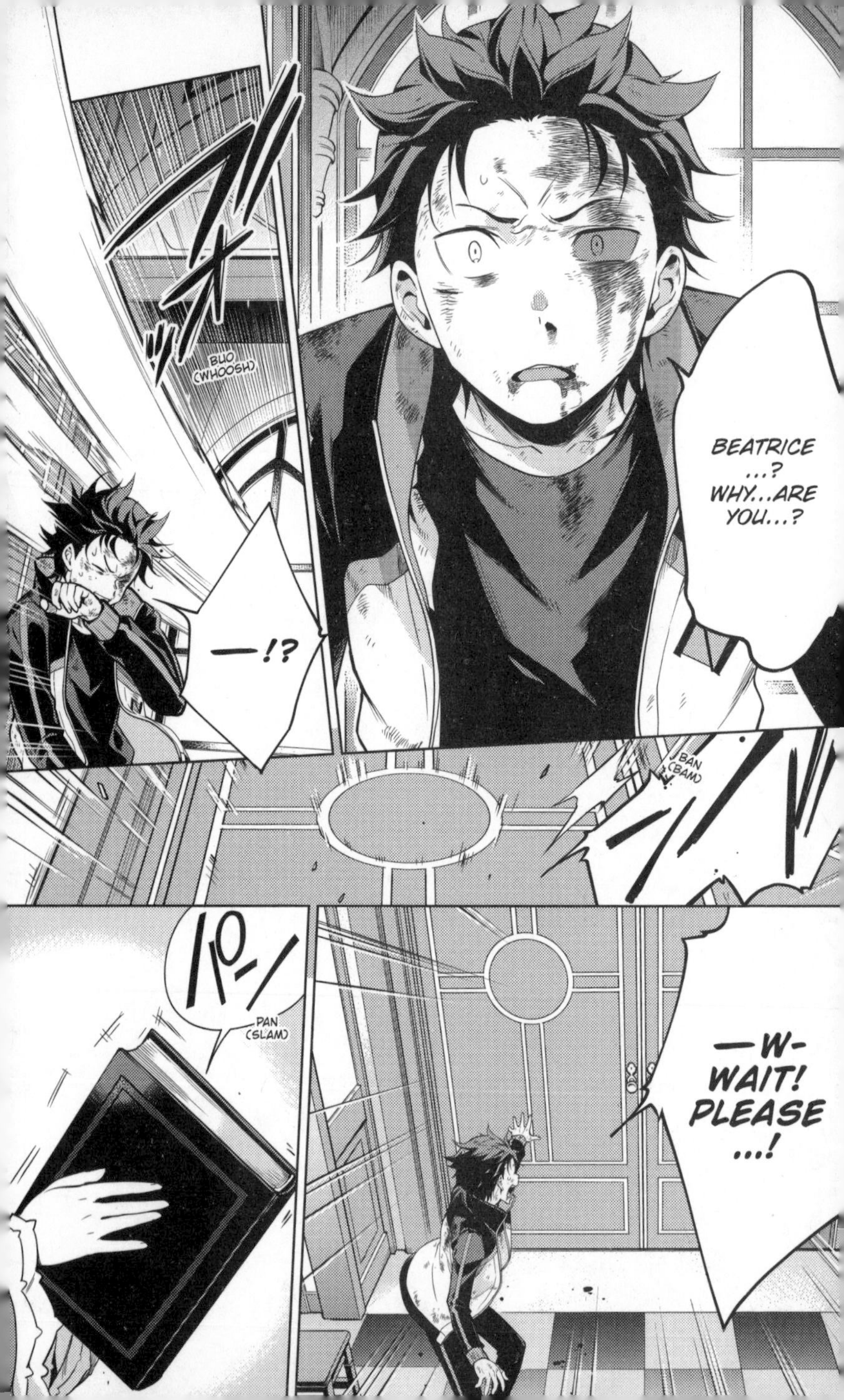
BEATRICE ...? WHY...ARE YOU...?
BUO (WHOOSH)
—!?
BAN (BAM)
—W-WAIT! PLEASE ...!
PAN (SLAM)

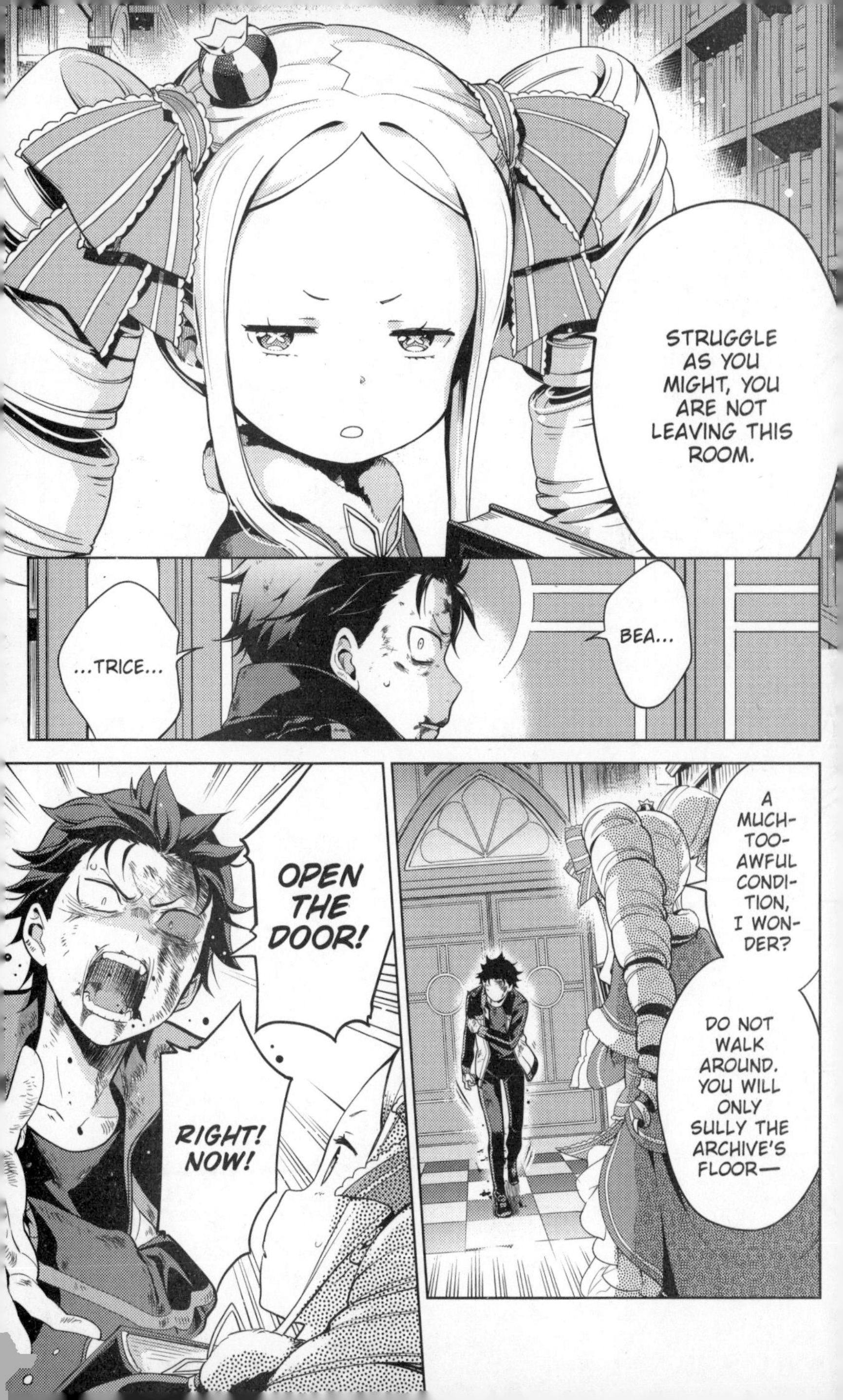
STRUGGLE AS YOU MIGHT, YOU ARE NOT LEAVING THIS ROOM.
BEA...
...TRICE...
A MUCH-TOO-AWFUL CONDITION, I WONDER?
DO NOT WALK AROUND. YOU WILL ONLY SULLY THE ARCHIVE'S FLOOR—
OPEN THE DOOR!
RIGHT! NOW!

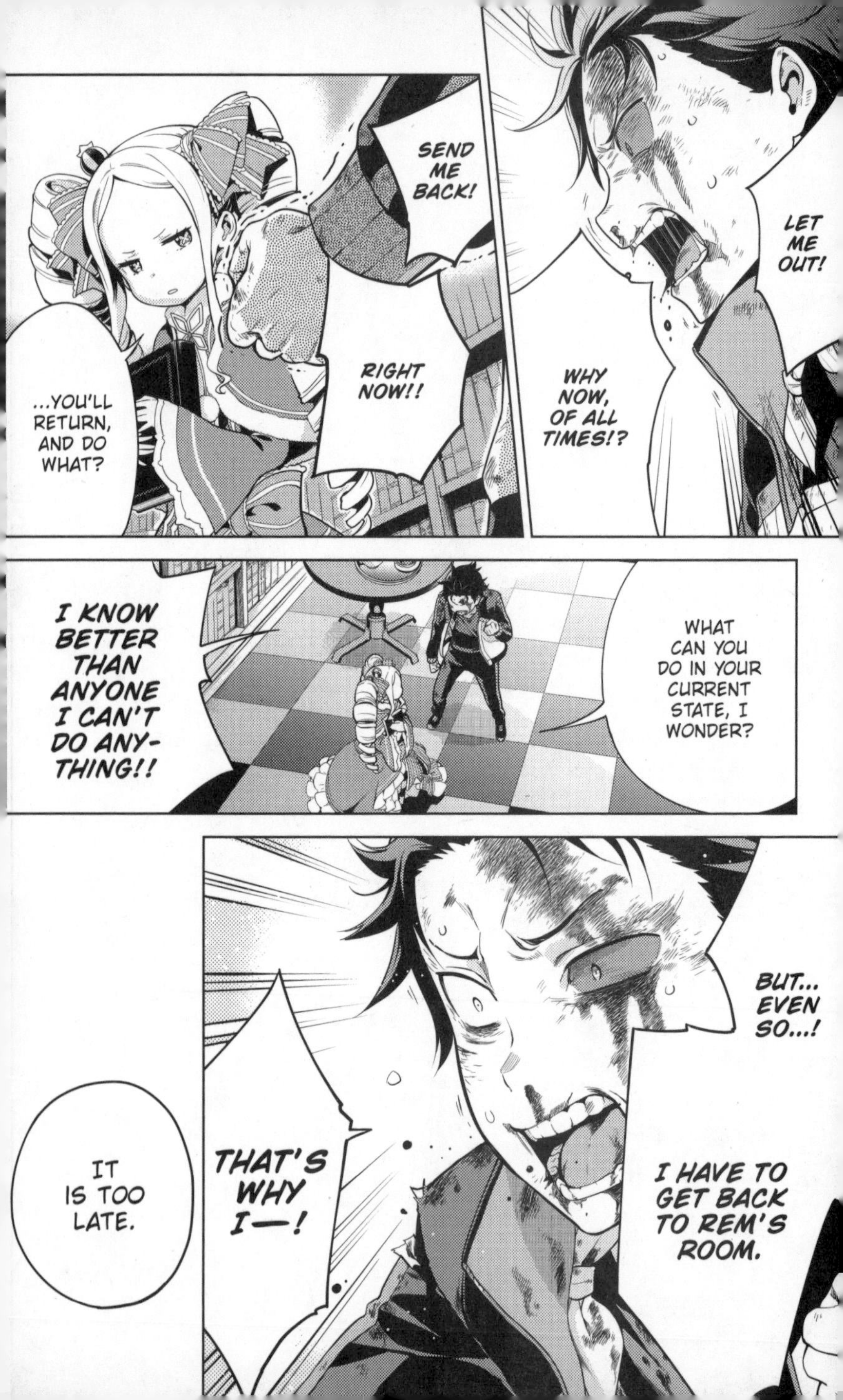
LET ME OUT!
WHY NOW, OF ALL TIMES!?
SEND ME BACK!
RIGHT NOW!!
...YOU'LL RETURN, AND DO WHAT?
WHAT CAN YOU DO IN YOUR CURRENT STATE, I WONDER?
I KNOW BETTER THAN ANYONE I CAN'T DO ANY-THING!!
BUT... EVEN SO...!
I HAVE TO GET BACK TO REM'S ROOM.
THAT'S WHY I—!
IT IS TOO LATE.

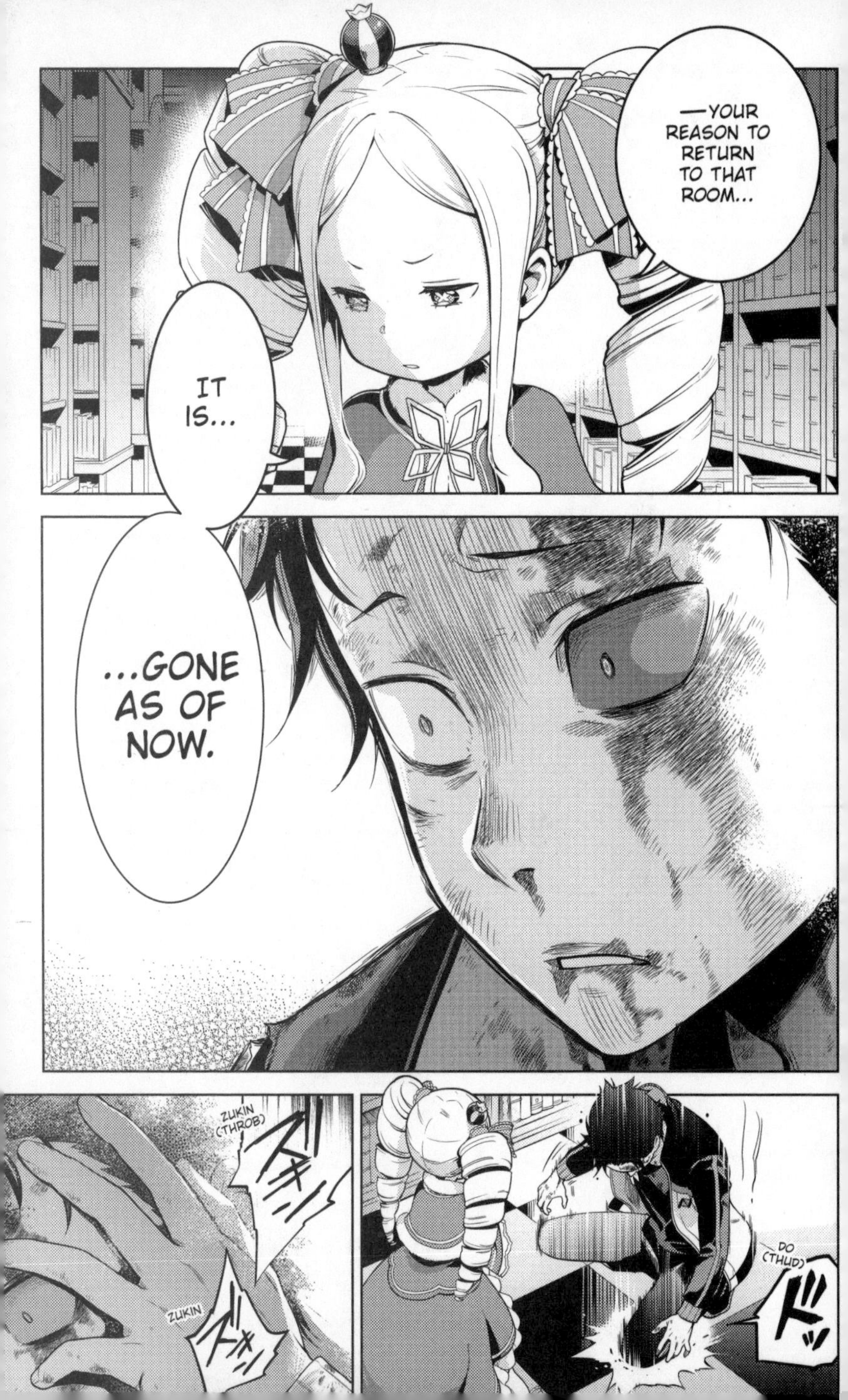
—YOUR REASON TO RETURN TO THAT ROOM...
IT IS...
...GONE AS OF NOW.
DO (THUD)
ZUKIN (THROB)
ZUKIN

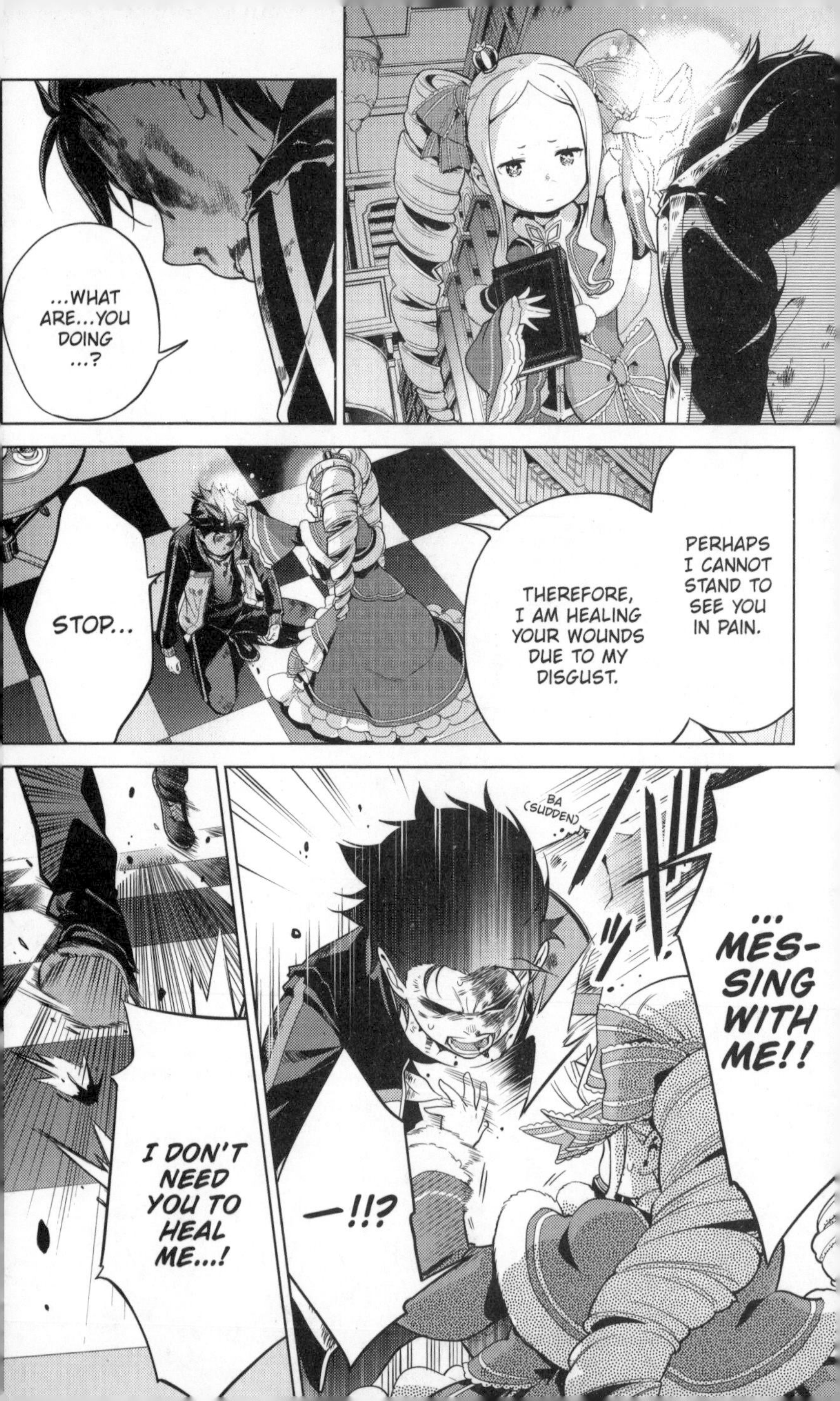
...WHAT ARE...YOU DOING ...?
PERHAPS I CANNOT STAND TO SEE YOU IN PAIN.
THEREFORE, I AM HEALING YOUR WOUNDS DUE TO MY DISGUST.
STOP...
... MES-SING WITH ME!!
BA (SUDDEN)
—!!?
I DON'T NEED YOU TO HEAL ME...!

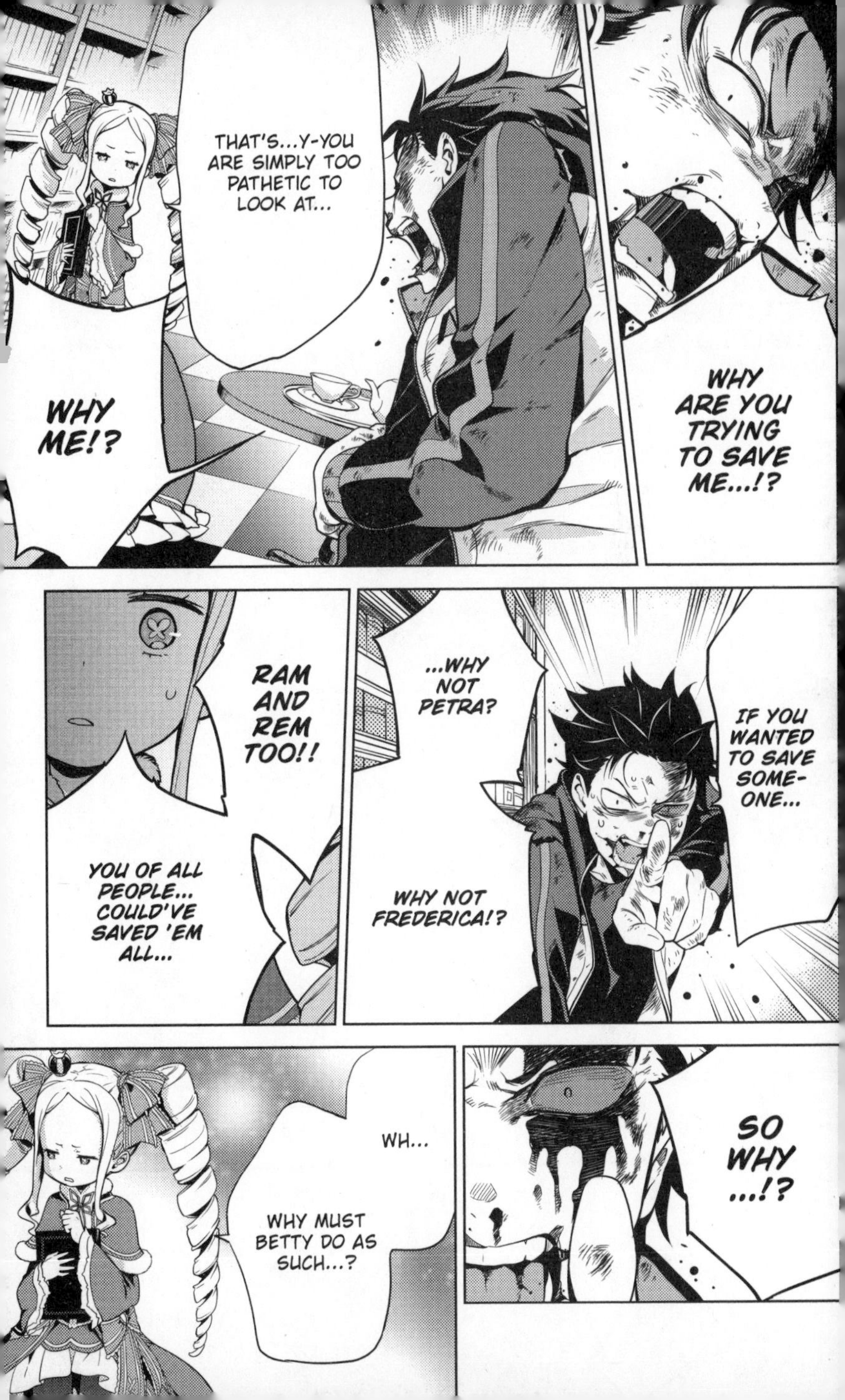
WHY ARE YOU TRYING TO SAVE ME...!?
THAT'S...Y-YOU ARE SIMPLY TOO PATHETIC TO LOOK AT...
WHY ME!?
IF YOU WANTED TO SAVE SOME-ONE...
...WHY NOT PETRA?
WHY NOT FREDERICA!?
RAM AND REM TOO!!
YOU OF ALL PEOPLE... COULD'VE SAVED 'EM ALL...
SO WHY...!?
WH...
WHY MUST BETTY DO AS SUCH...?

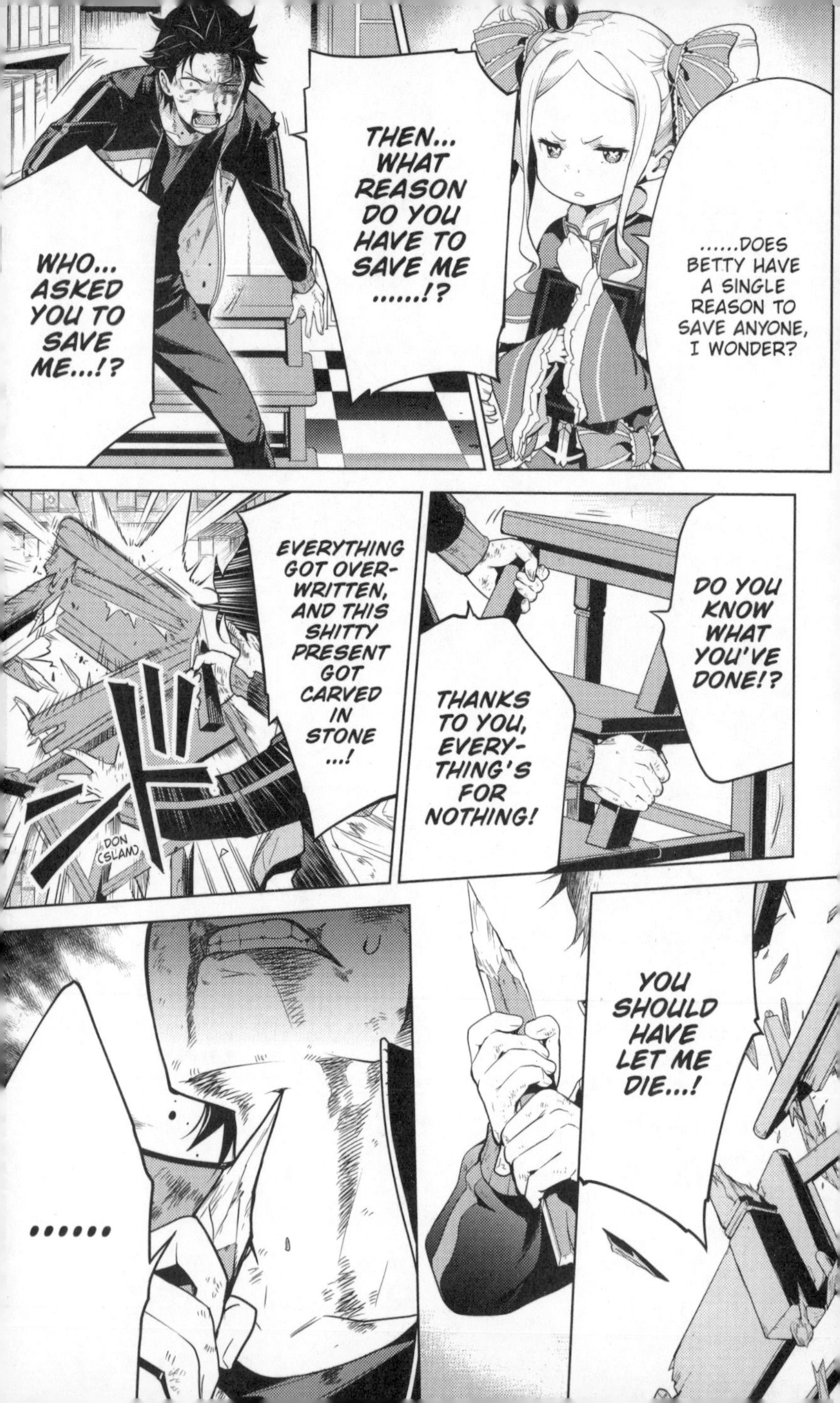
......DOES BETTY HAVE A SINGLE REASON TO SAVE ANYONE, I WONDER?
THEN... WHAT REASON DO YOU HAVE TO SAVE ME ......!?
WHO... ASKED YOU TO SAVE ME...!?
DO YOU KNOW WHAT YOU'VE DONE!?
THANKS TO YOU, EVERYTHING'S FOR NOTHING!
EVERYTHING GOT OVERWRITTEN, AND THIS SHITTY PRESENT GOT CARVED IN STONE ...!
DON (SLAM)
YOU SHOULD HAVE LET ME DIE...!
......

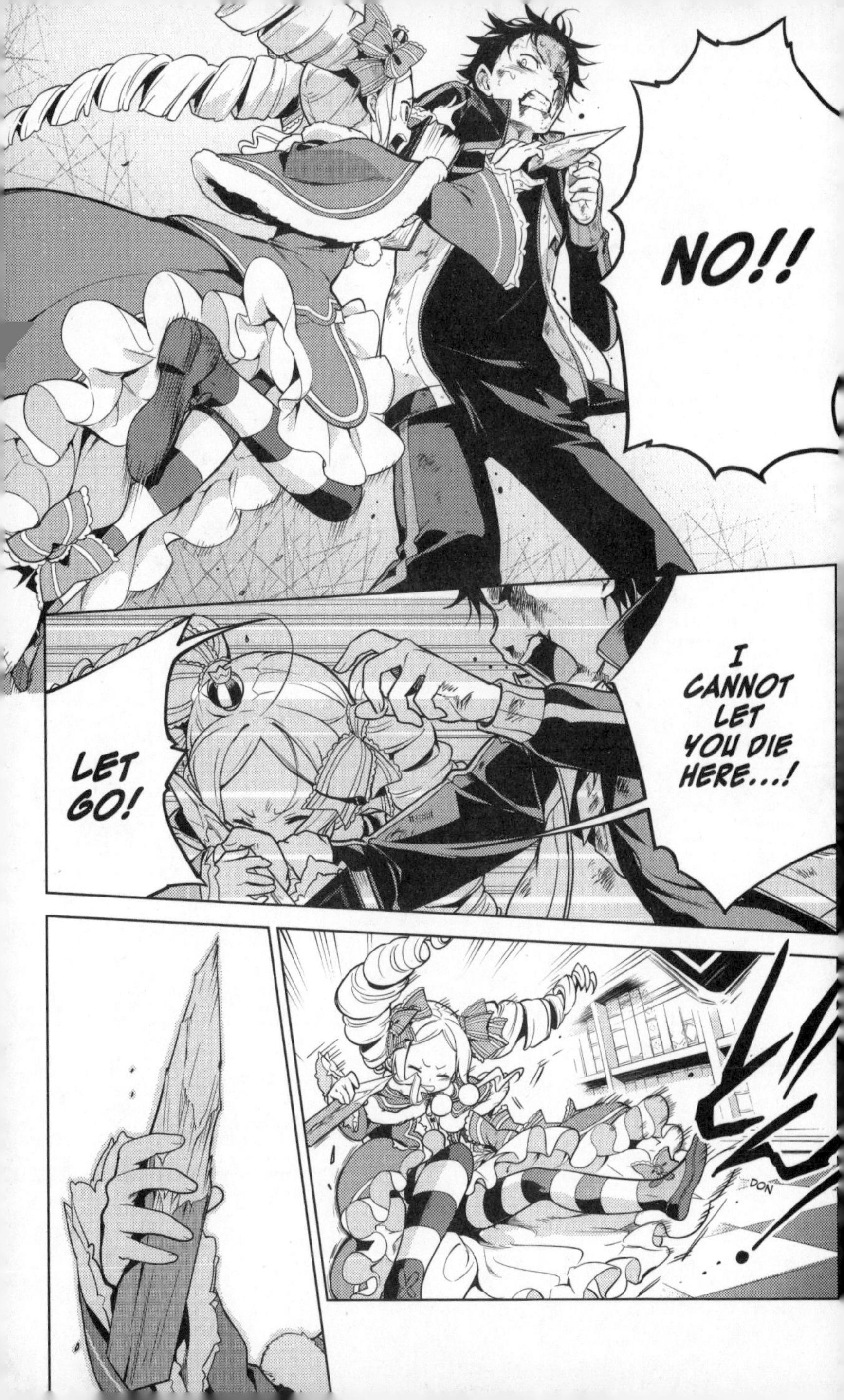
NO!!
I CANNOT LET YOU DIE HERE...!
LET GO!
DON

HAAH!

HAH!

GARAN
(PLINK)

WHY...

...DID YOU STOP ME...?

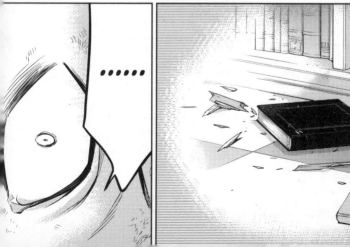

• • • • • •

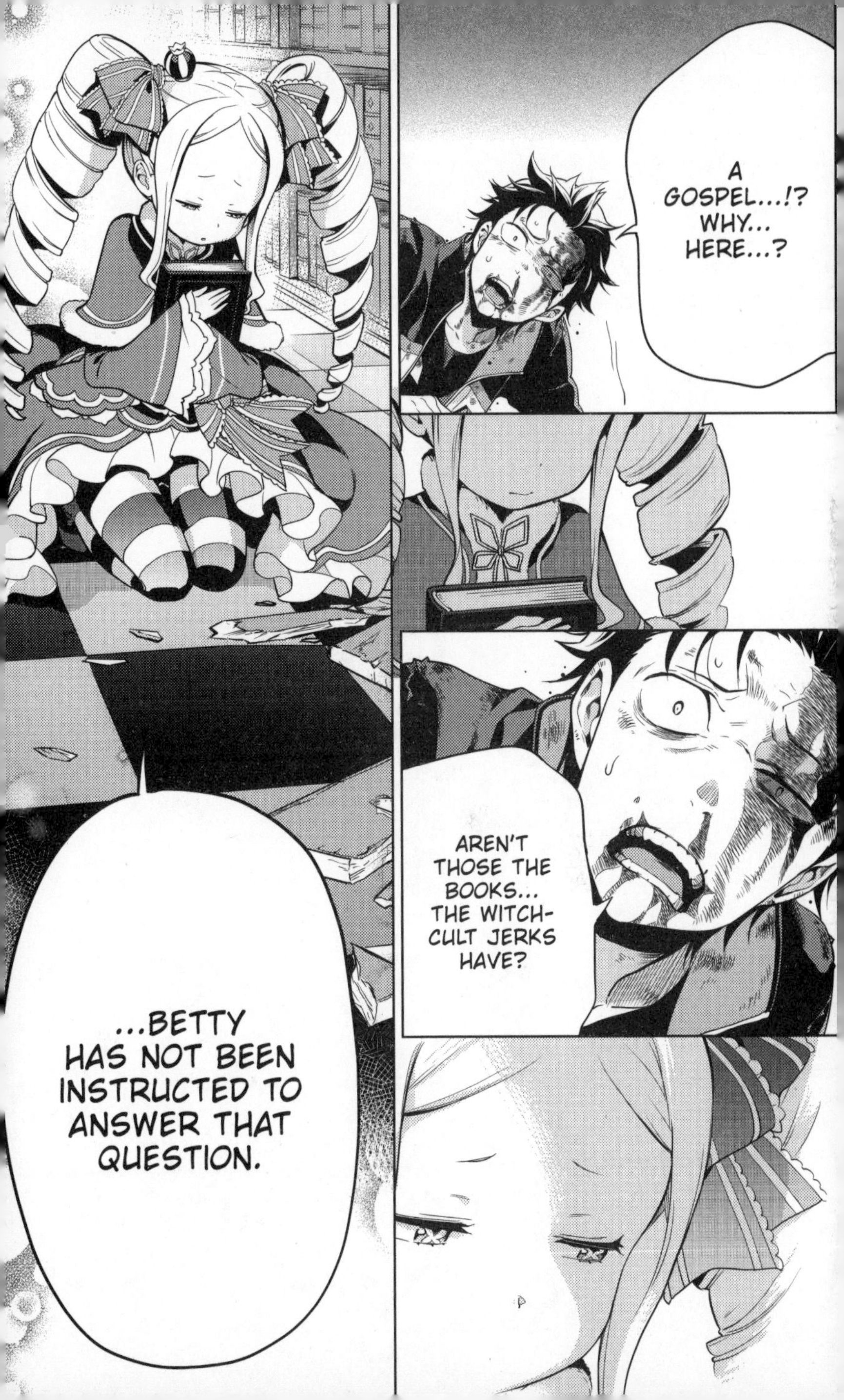
A GOSPEL...!? WHY... HERE...?
AREN'T THOSE THE BOOKS... THE WITCH-CULT JERKS HAVE?
...BETTY HAS NOT BEEN INSTRUCTED TO ANSWER THAT QUESTION.

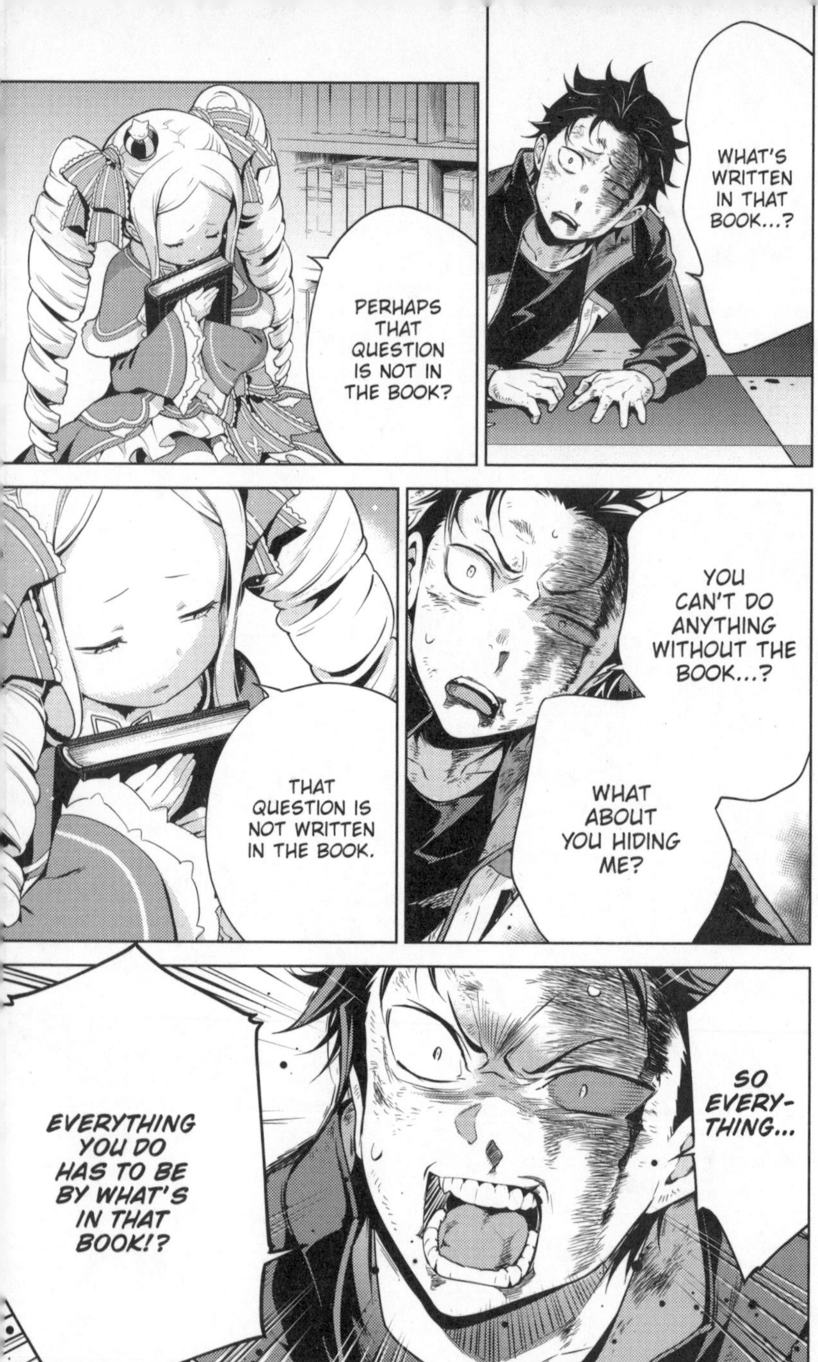
WHAT'S WRITTEN IN THAT BOOK...?
PERHAPS THAT QUESTION IS NOT IN THE BOOK?
YOU CAN'T DO ANYTHING WITHOUT THE BOOK...?
WHAT ABOUT YOU HIDING ME?
THAT QUESTION IS NOT WRITTEN IN THE BOOK.
SO EVERY-THING...
EVERYTHING YOU DO HAS TO BE BY WHAT'S IN THAT BOOK!?

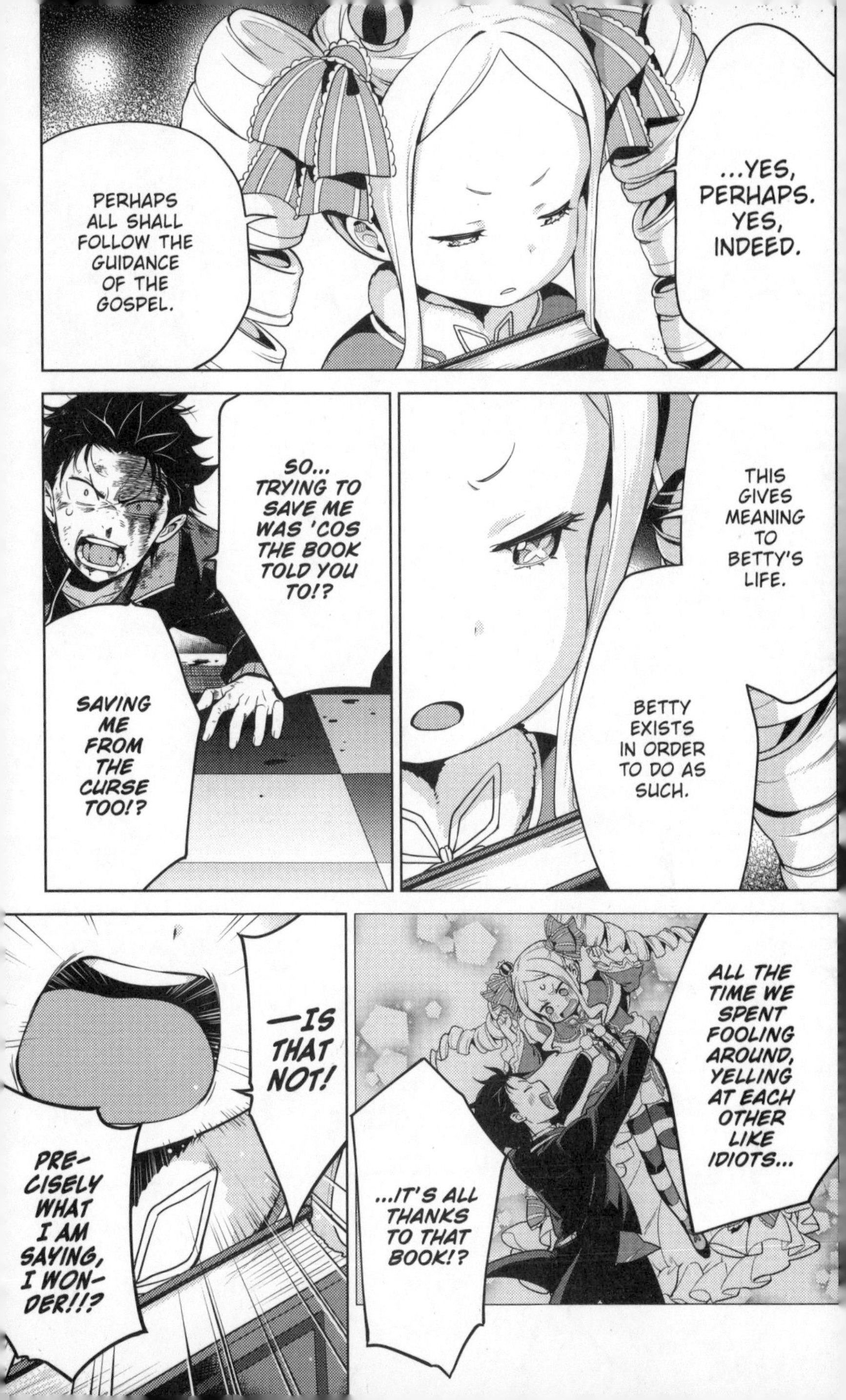
...YES, PERHAPS. YES, INDEED.
PERHAPS ALL SHALL FOLLOW THE GUIDANCE OF THE GOSPEL.
THIS GIVES MEANING TO BETTY'S LIFE.
BETTY EXISTS IN ORDER TO DO AS SUCH.
SO... TRYING TO SAVE ME WAS 'COS THE BOOK TOLD YOU TO!?
SAVING ME FROM THE CURSE TOO!?
ALL THE TIME WE SPENT FOOLING AROUND, YELLING AT EACH OTHER LIKE IDIOTS...
...IT'S ALL THANKS TO THAT BOOK!?
—IS THAT NOT!
PRECISELY WHAT I AM SAYING, I WONDER!!?

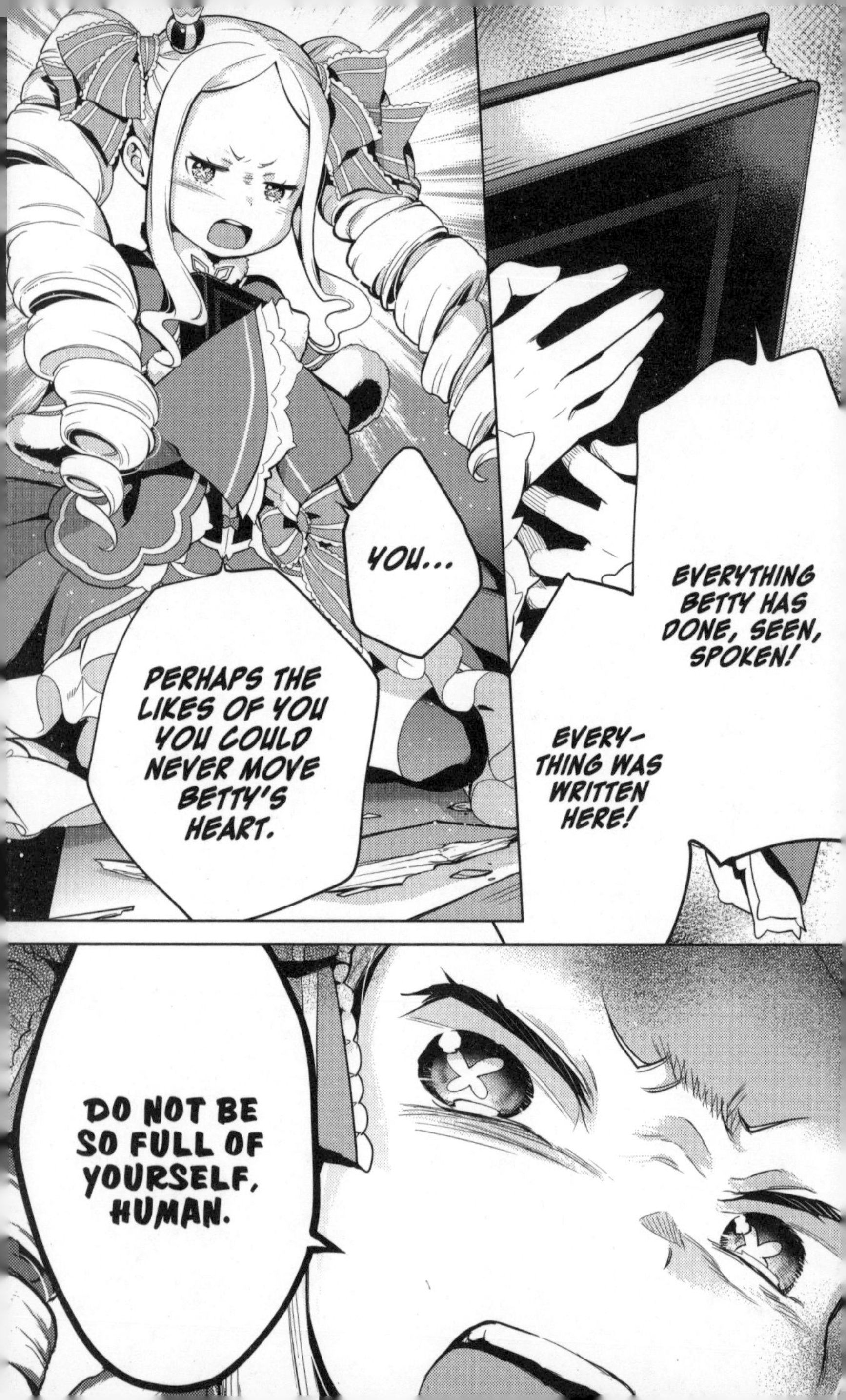
EVERYTHING BETTY HAS DONE, SEEN, SPOKEN!
EVERY-THING WAS WRITTEN HERE!
YOU...
PERHAPS THE LIKES OF YOU YOU COULD NEVER MOVE BETTY'S HEART.
DO NOT BE SO FULL OF YOURSELF, HUMAN.

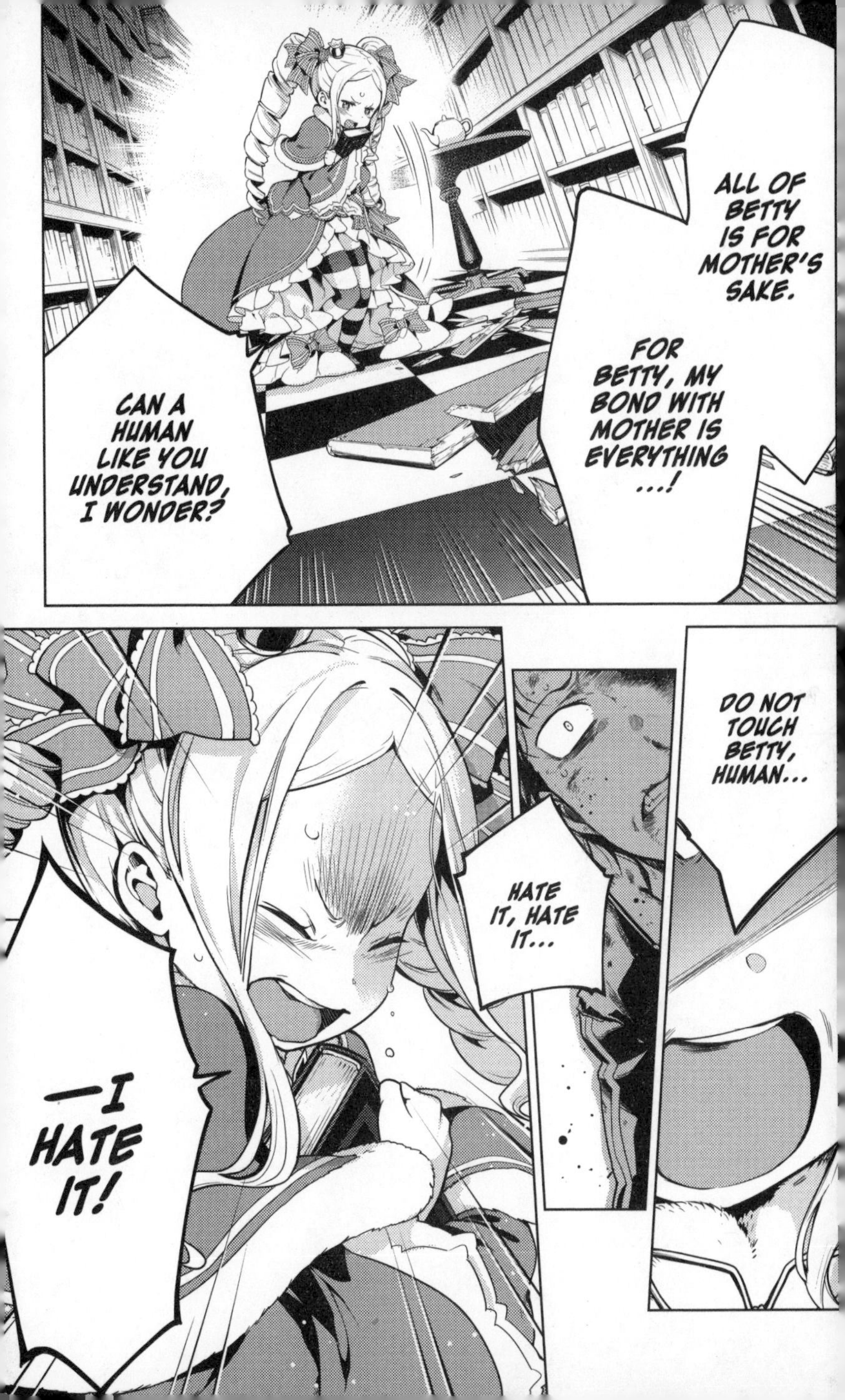
ALL OF BETTY IS FOR MOTHER'S SAKE.
FOR BETTY, MY BOND WITH MOTHER IS EVERYTHING...!
CAN A HUMAN LIKE YOU UNDERSTAND, I WONDER?
DO NOT TOUCH BETTY, HUMAN...
HATE IT, HATE IT...
—I HATE IT!

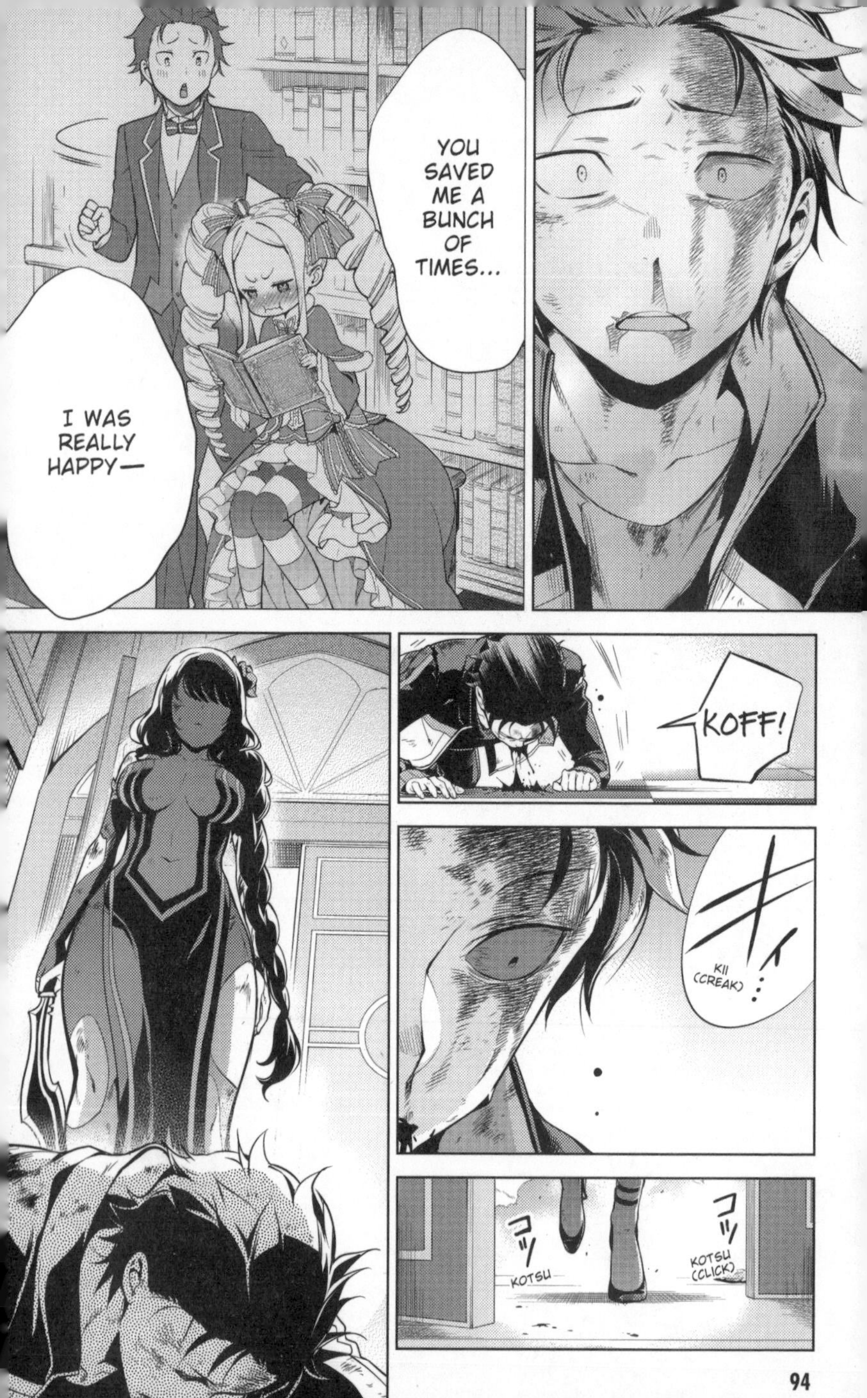
YOU SAVED ME A BUNCH OF TIMES...
I WAS REALLY HAPPY—
KOFF!
KII (CREAK)
KOTSU (CLICK)
KOTSU

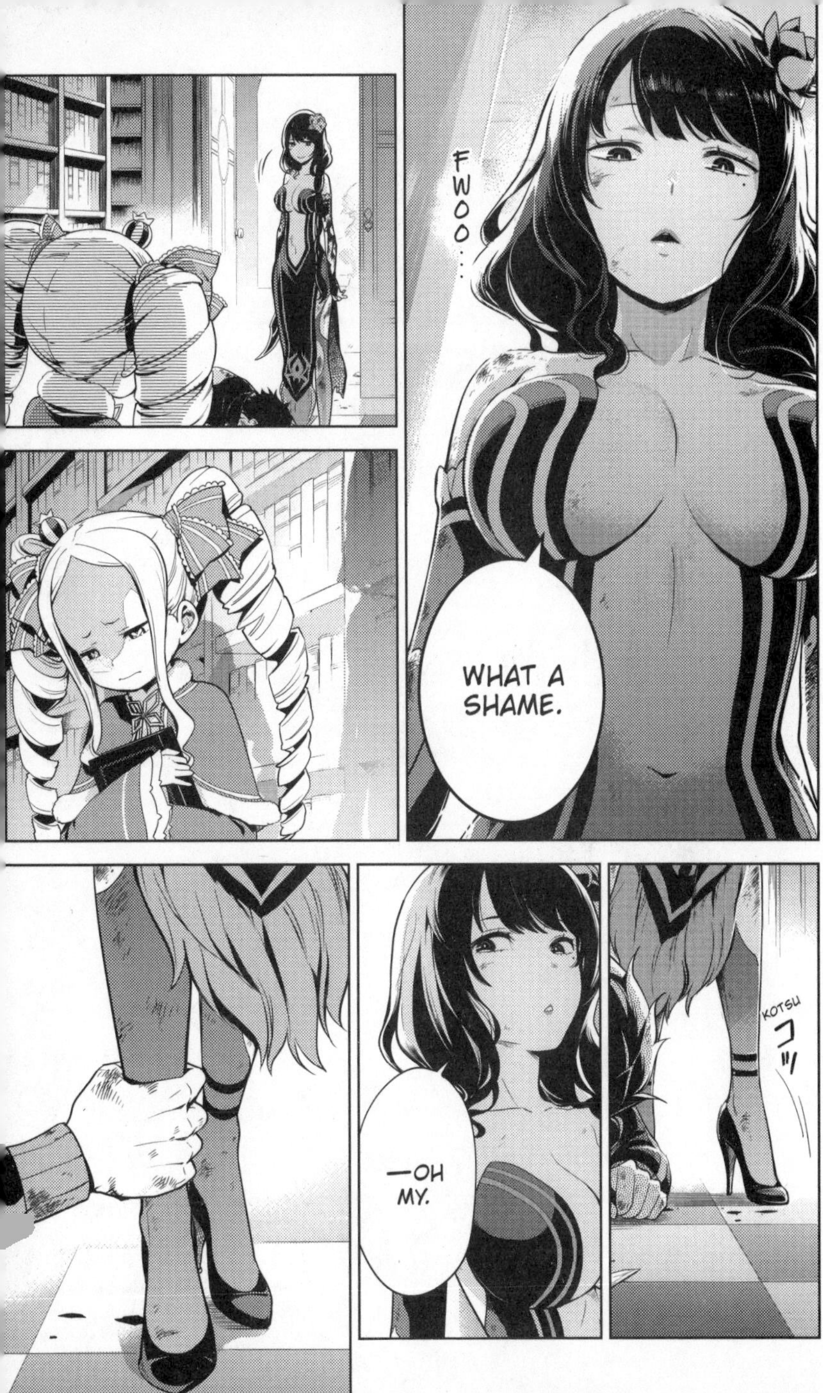
FWOO...
WHAT A SHAME.
KOTSU
コッ
—OH MY.

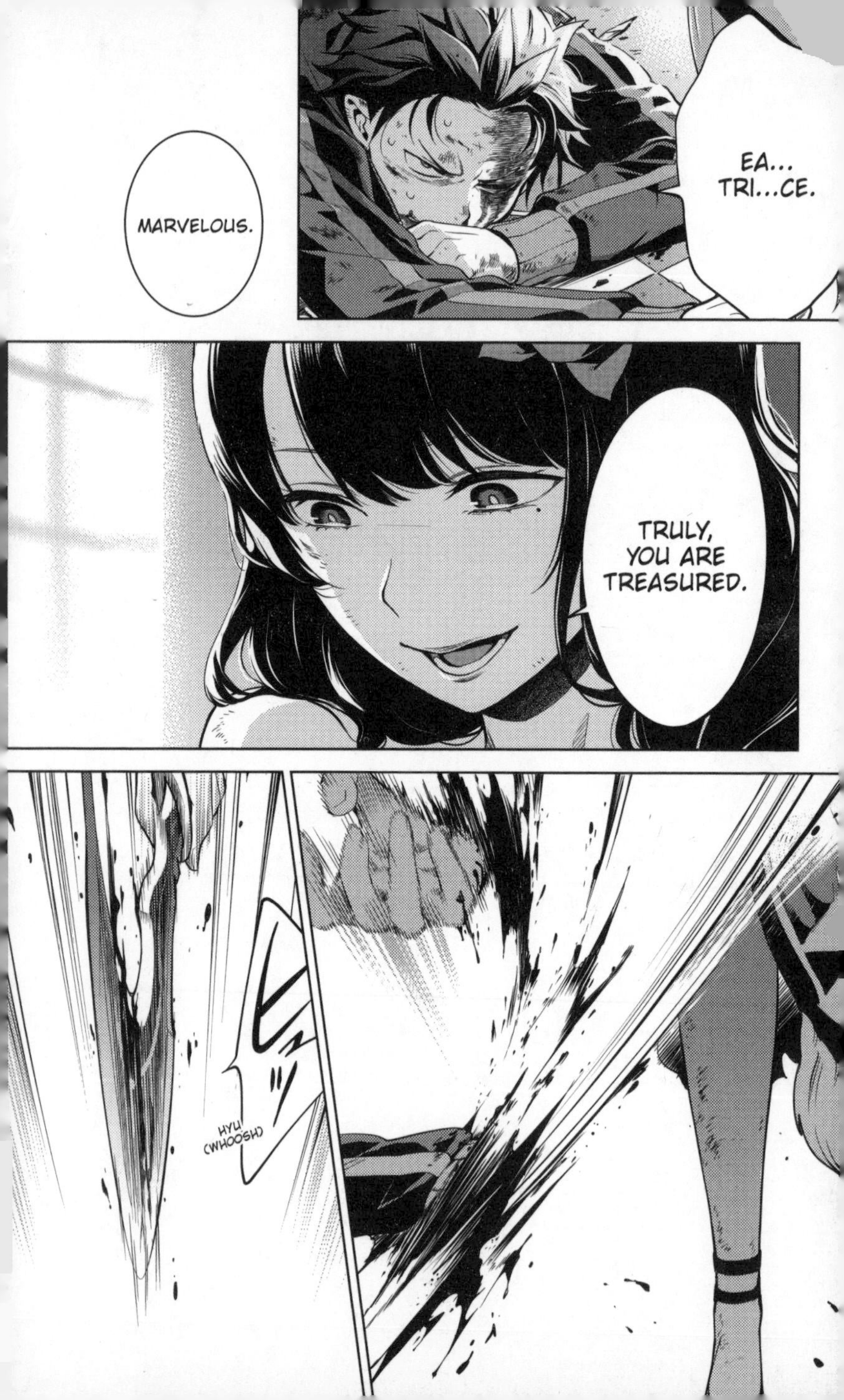
EA... TRI...CE.
MARVELOUS.
TRULY, YOU ARE TREASURED.
HYU (WHOOSH)

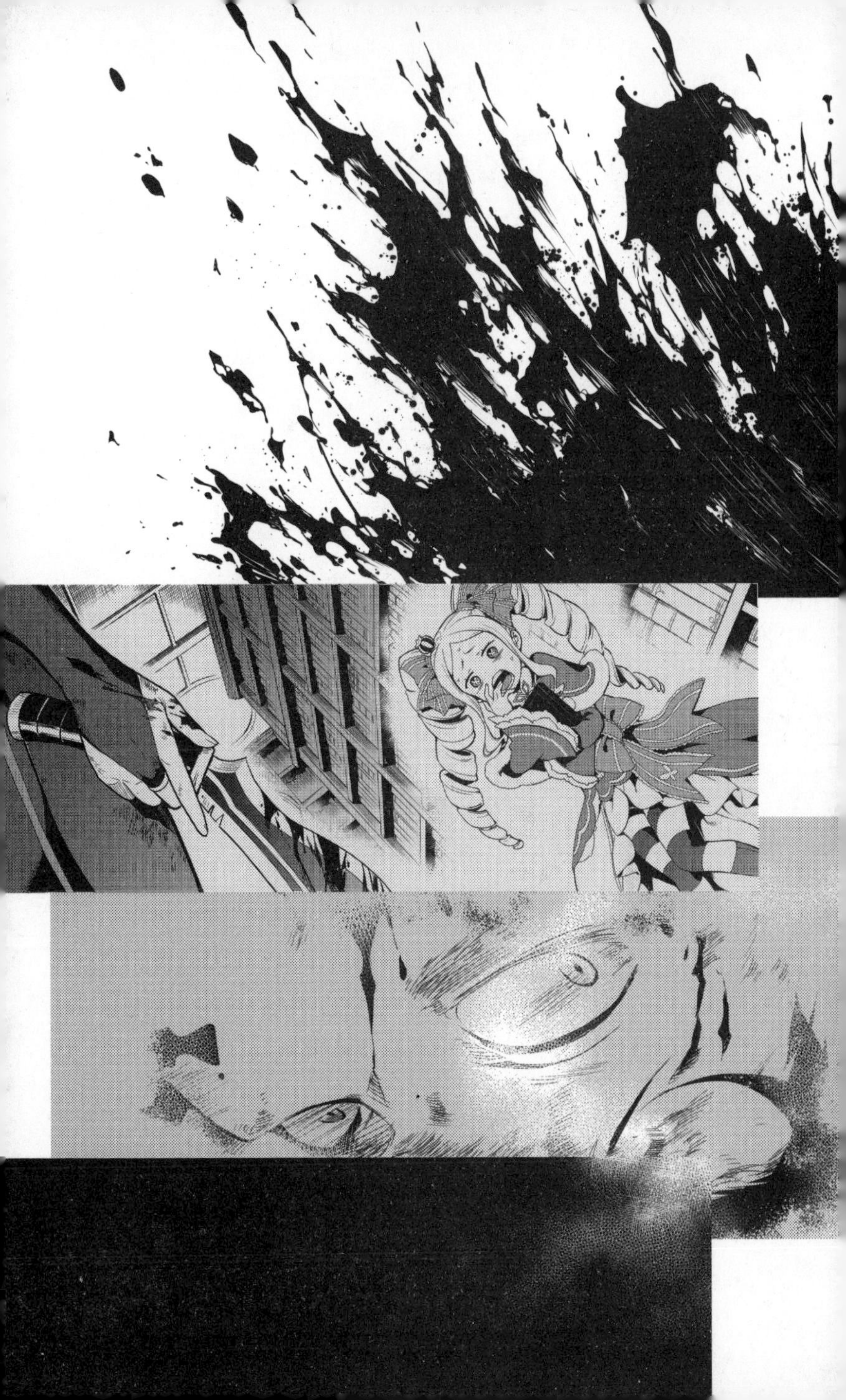

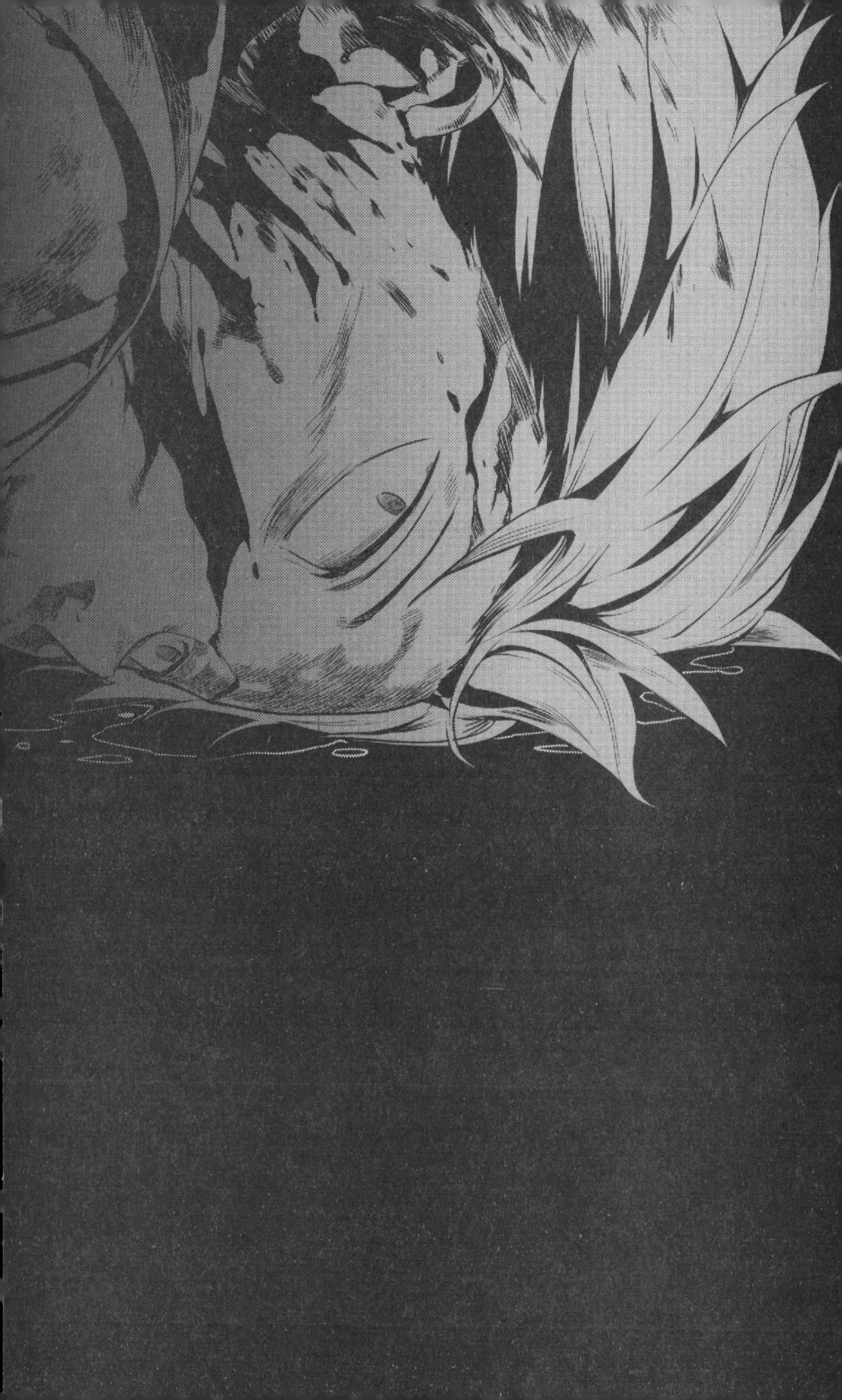

ゴオオオオ
GOOOO (RUUUMBLE)

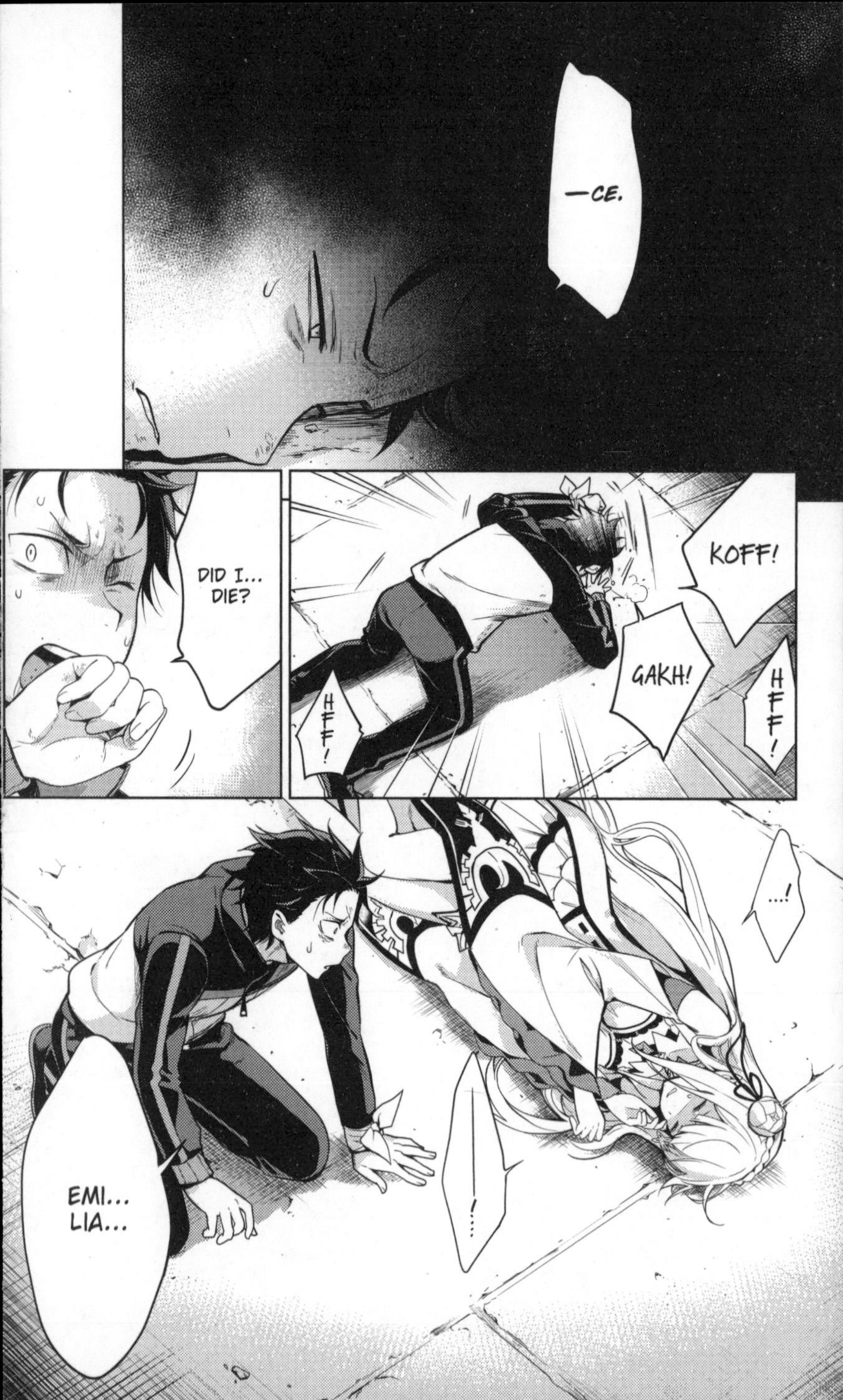
—CE.
KOFF!
GAKH!
HFF!
HFF!
DID I... DIE?
...!
...!
EMI... LIA...

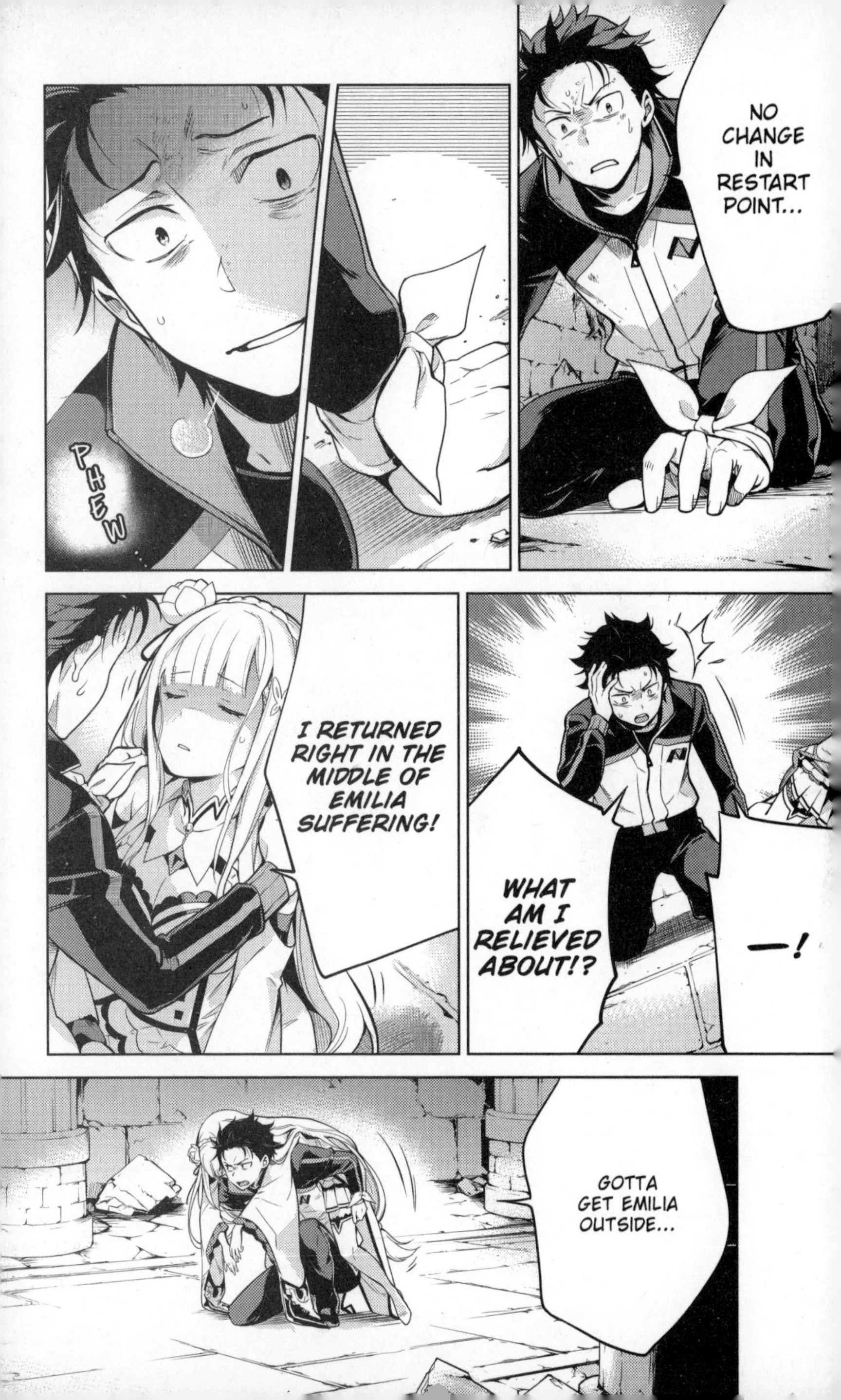
NO CHANGE IN RESTART POINT...
PHEW...
WHAT AM I RELIEVED ABOUT!?
—!
I RETURNED RIGHT IN THE MIDDLE OF EMILIA SUFFERING!
GOTTA GET EMILIA OUTSIDE...

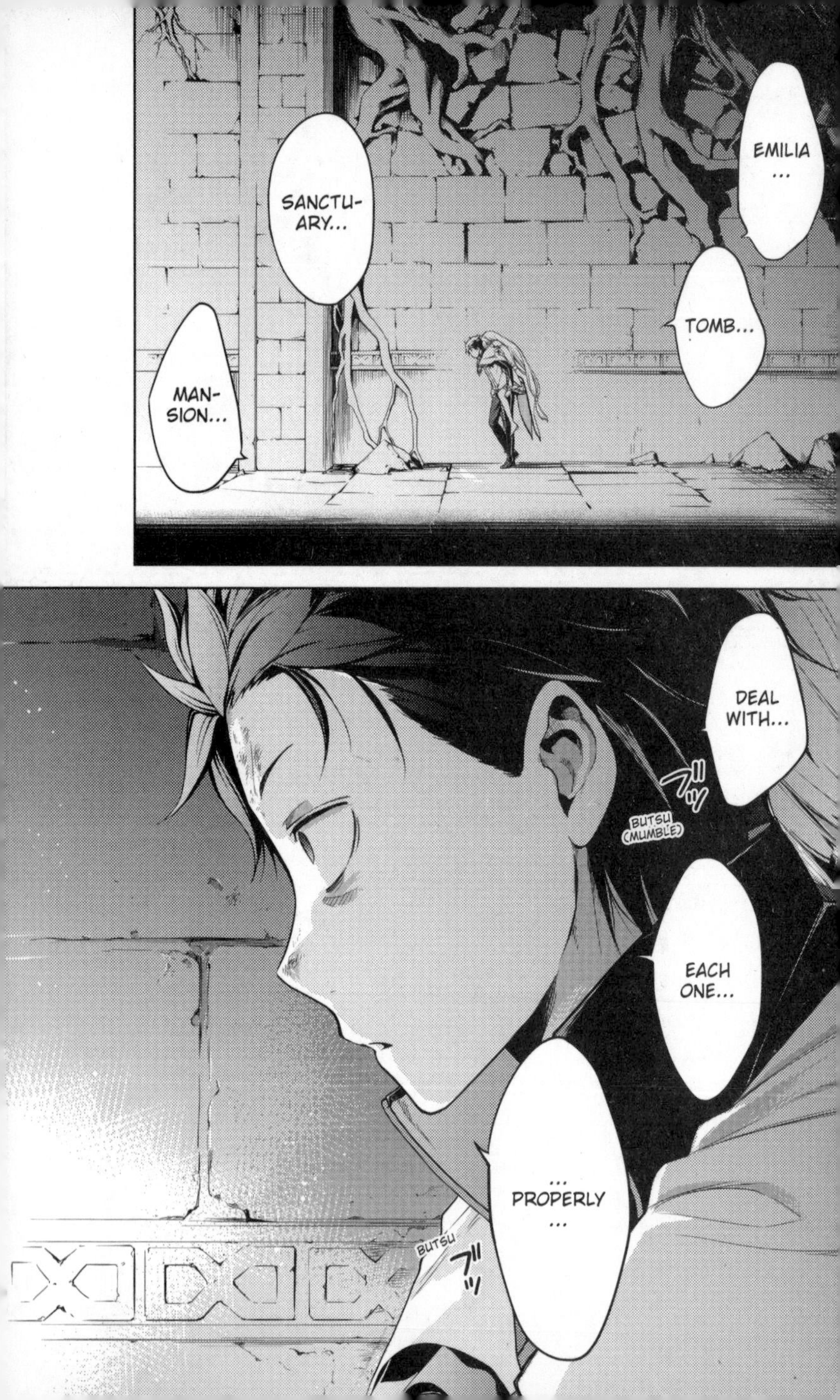
EMILIA...
TOMB...
SANCTUARY...
MANSION...
DEAL WITH...
BUTSU (MUMBLE)
EACH ONE...
...PROPERLY...
BUTSU

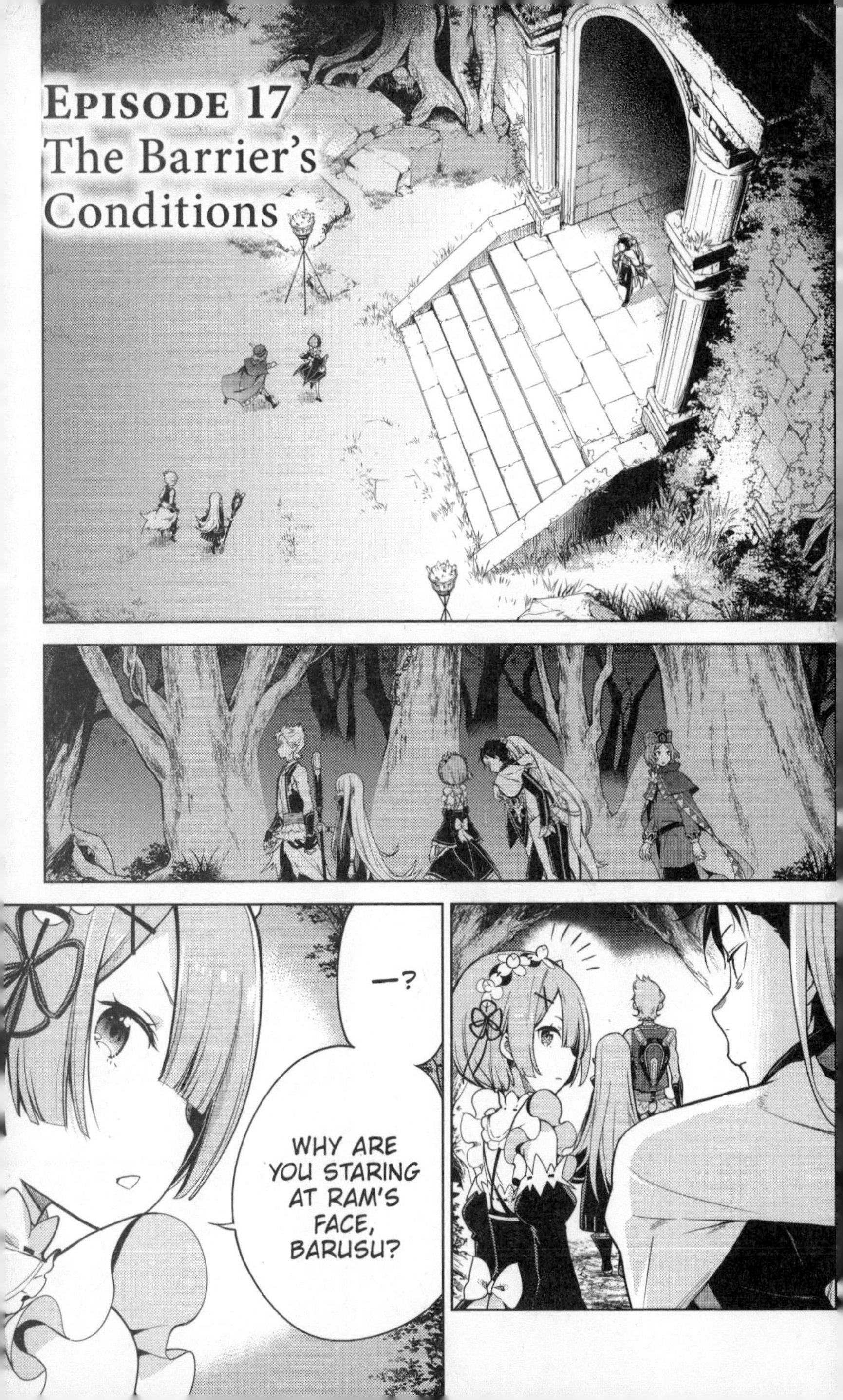
EPISODE 17
The Barrier's Conditions
—?
WHY ARE YOU STARING AT RAM'S FACE, BARUSU?

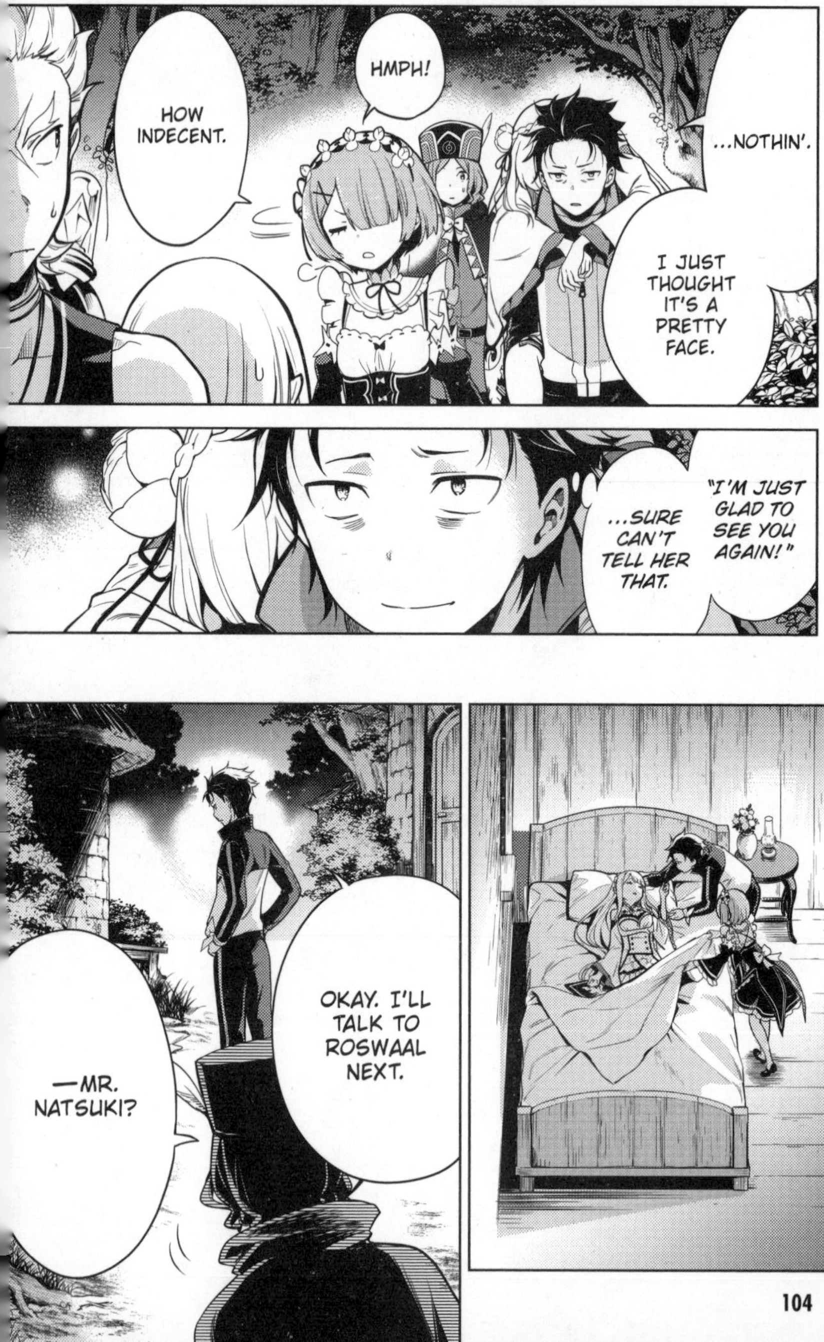
...NOTHIN'.
I JUST THOUGHT IT'S A PRETTY FACE.
HMPH!
HOW INDECENT.
"I'M JUST GLAD TO SEE YOU AGAIN!"
...SURE CAN'T TELL HER THAT.
OKAY. I'LL TALK TO ROSWAAL NEXT.
—MR. NATSUKI?

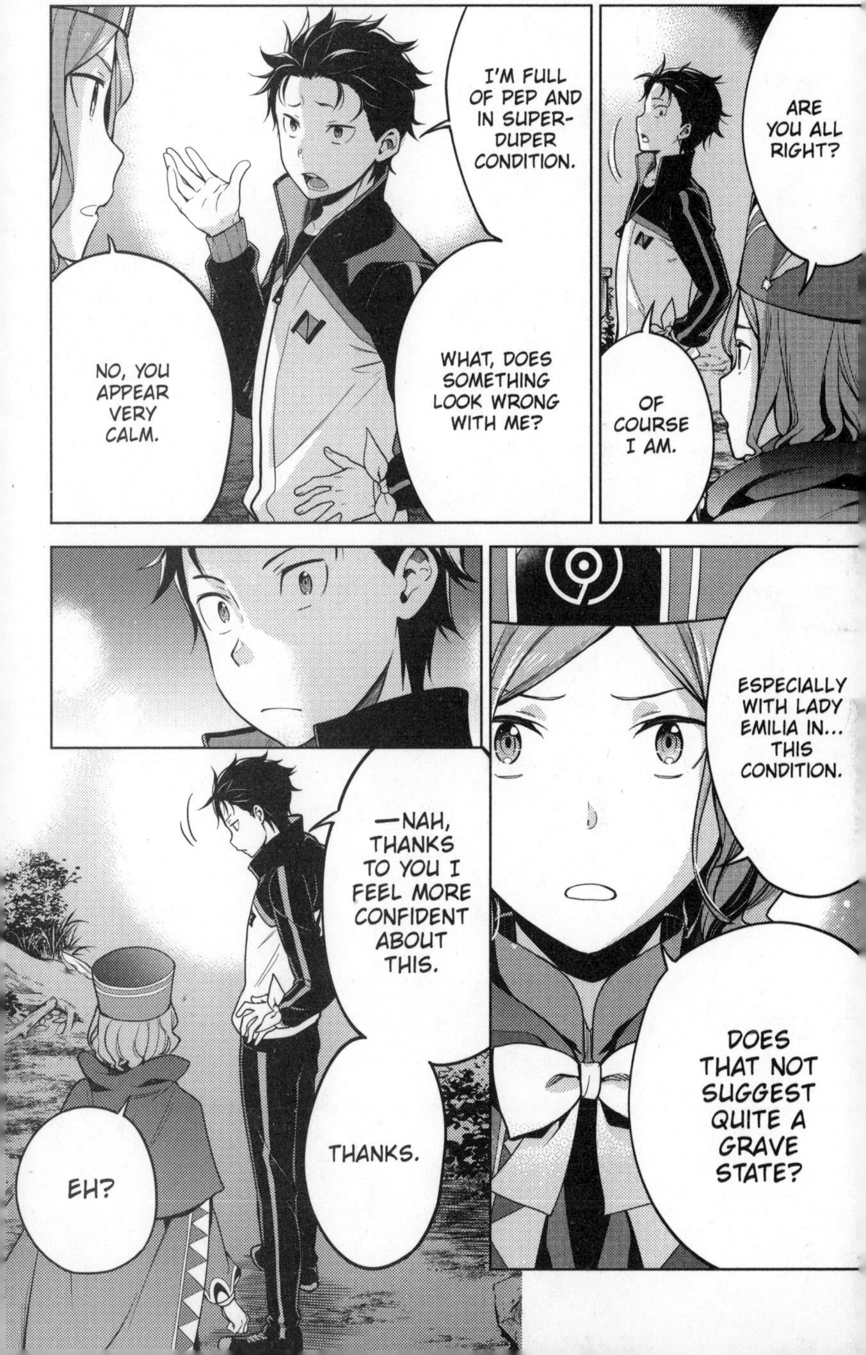
ARE YOU ALL RIGHT?
OF COURSE I AM.
I'M FULL OF PEP AND IN SUPER-DUPER CONDITION.
WHAT, DOES SOMETHING LOOK WRONG WITH ME?
NO, YOU APPEAR VERY CALM.
ESPECIALLY WITH LADY EMILIA IN... THIS CONDITION.
DOES THAT NOT SUGGEST QUITE A GRAVE STATE?
—NAH, THANKS TO YOU I FEEL MORE CONFIDENT ABOUT THIS.
THANKS.
EH?

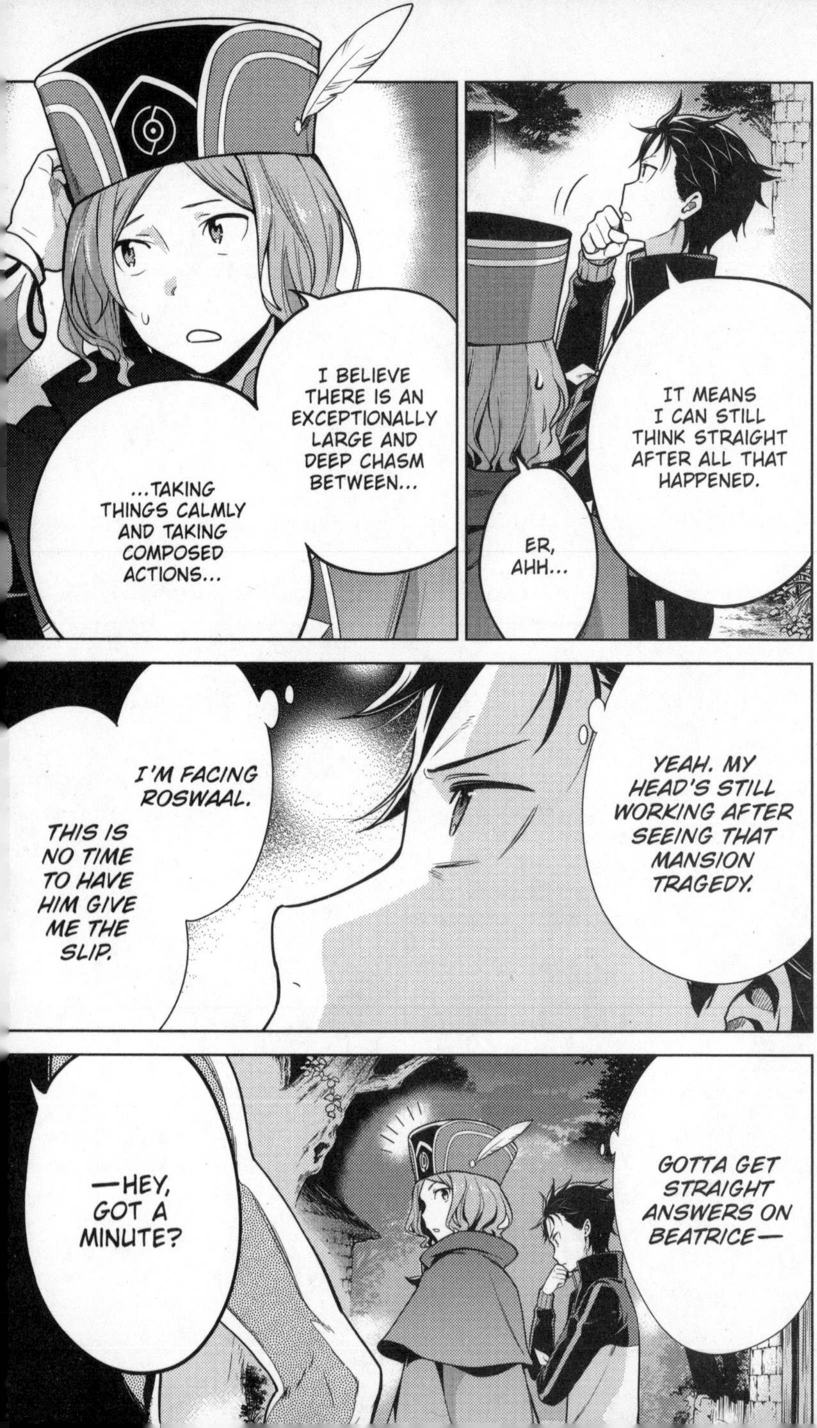
IT MEANS I CAN STILL THINK STRAIGHT AFTER ALL THAT HAPPENED.
ER, AHH...
I BELIEVE THERE IS AN EXCEPTIONALLY LARGE AND DEEP CHASM BETWEEN...
...TAKING THINGS CALMLY AND TAKING COMPOSED ACTIONS...
YEAH. MY HEAD'S STILL WORKING AFTER SEEING THAT MANSION TRAGEDY.
I'M FACING ROSWAAL.
THIS IS NO TIME TO HAVE HIM GIVE ME THE SLIP.
GOTTA GET STRAIGHT ANSWERS ON BEATRICE—
—HEY, GOT A MINUTE?

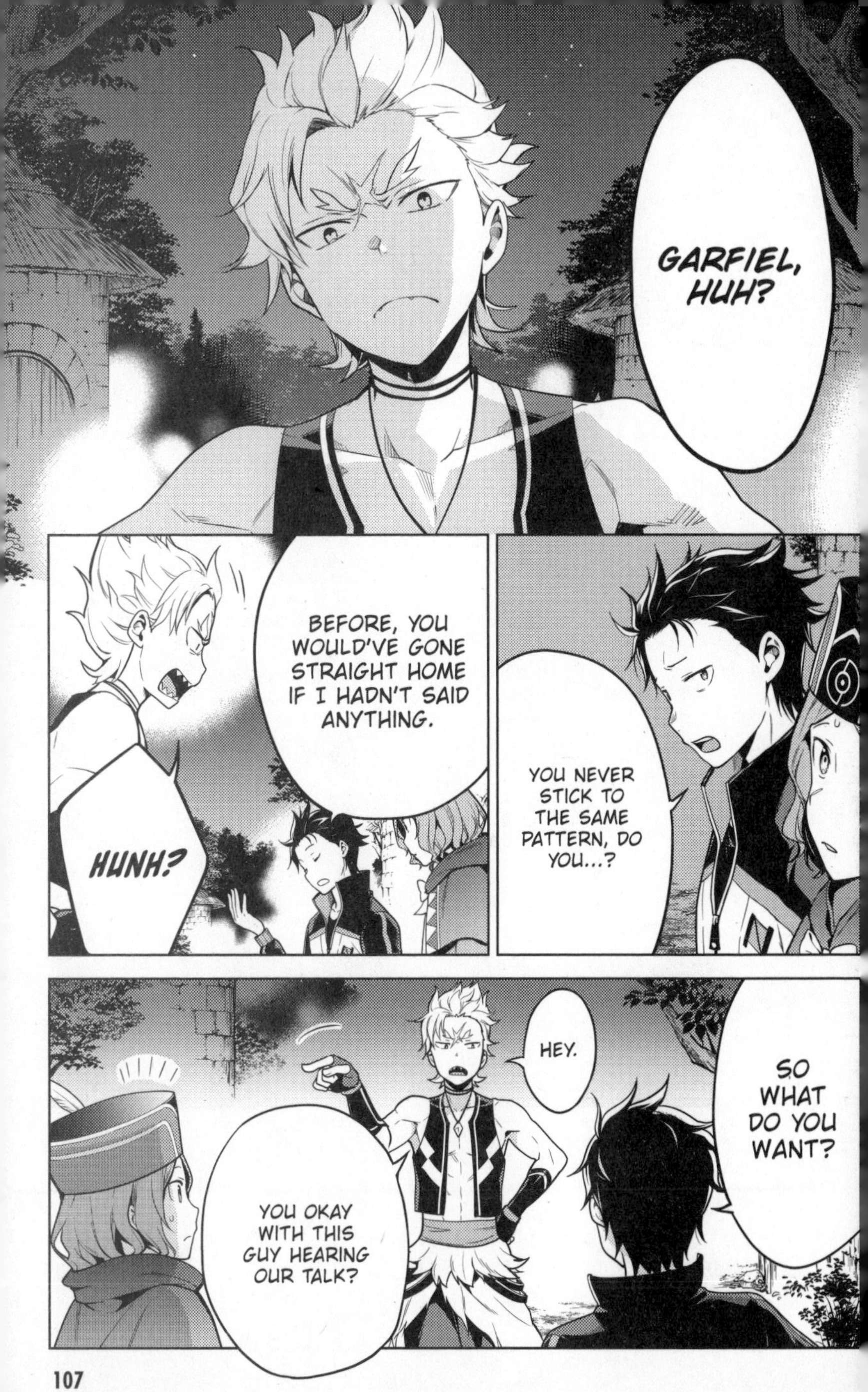
GARFIEL, HUH?
YOU NEVER STICK TO THE SAME PATTERN, DO YOU...?
BEFORE, YOU WOULD'VE GONE STRAIGHT HOME IF I HADN'T SAID ANYTHING.
HUNH?
SO WHAT DO YOU WANT?
HEY.
YOU OKAY WITH THIS GUY HEARING OUR TALK?

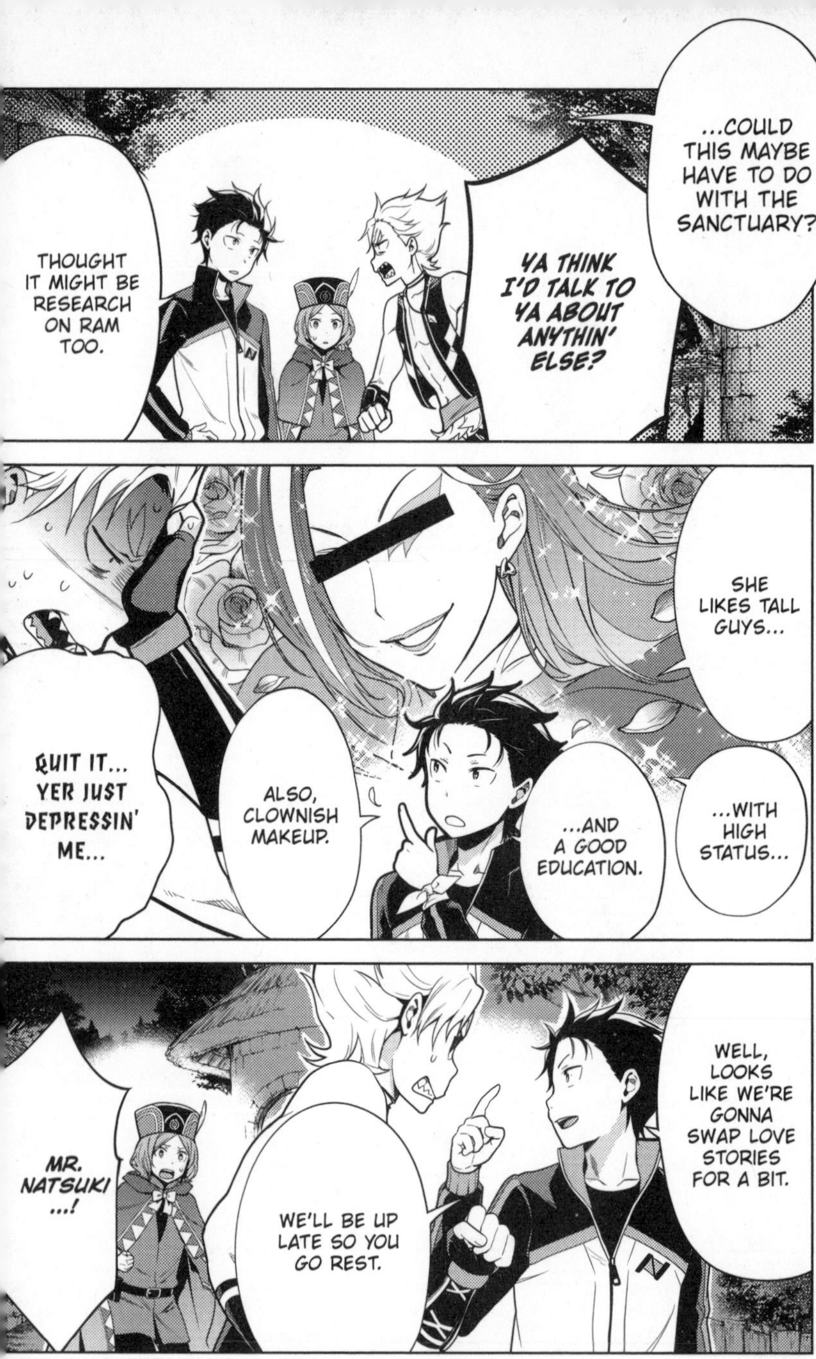
...COULD THIS MAYBE HAVE TO DO WITH THE SANCTUARY?
YA THINK I'D TALK TO YA ABOUT ANYTHIN' ELSE?
THOUGHT IT MIGHT BE RESEARCH ON RAM TOO.
SHE LIKES TALL GUYS...
...WITH HIGH STATUS...
...AND A GOOD EDUCATION.
ALSO, CLOWNISH MAKEUP.
QUIT IT... YER JUST DEPRESSIN' ME...
WELL, LOOKS LIKE WE'RE GONNA SWAP LOVE STORIES FOR A BIT.
WE'LL BE UP LATE SO YOU GO REST.
MR. NATSUKI ...!

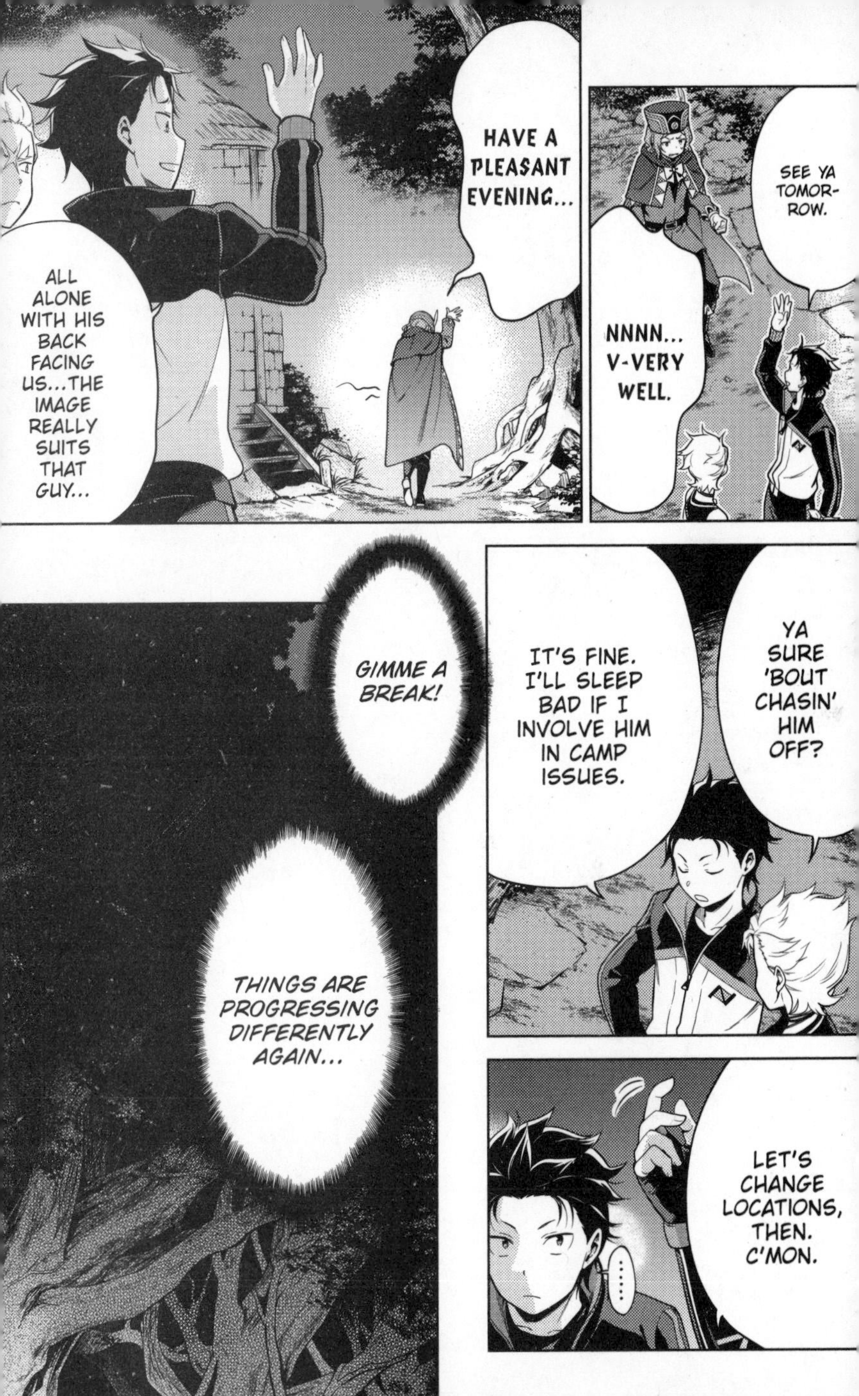
SEE YA TOMORROW.
NNNN... V-VERY WELL.
HAVE A PLEASANT EVENING...
ALL ALONE WITH HIS BACK FACING US...THE IMAGE REALLY SUITS THAT GUY...
YA SURE 'BOUT CHASIN' HIM OFF?
IT'S FINE. I'LL SLEEP BAD IF I INVOLVE HIM IN CAMP ISSUES.
LET'S CHANGE LOCATIONS, THEN. C'MON.
......
GIMME A BREAK!
THINGS ARE PROGRESSING DIFFERENTLY AGAIN...

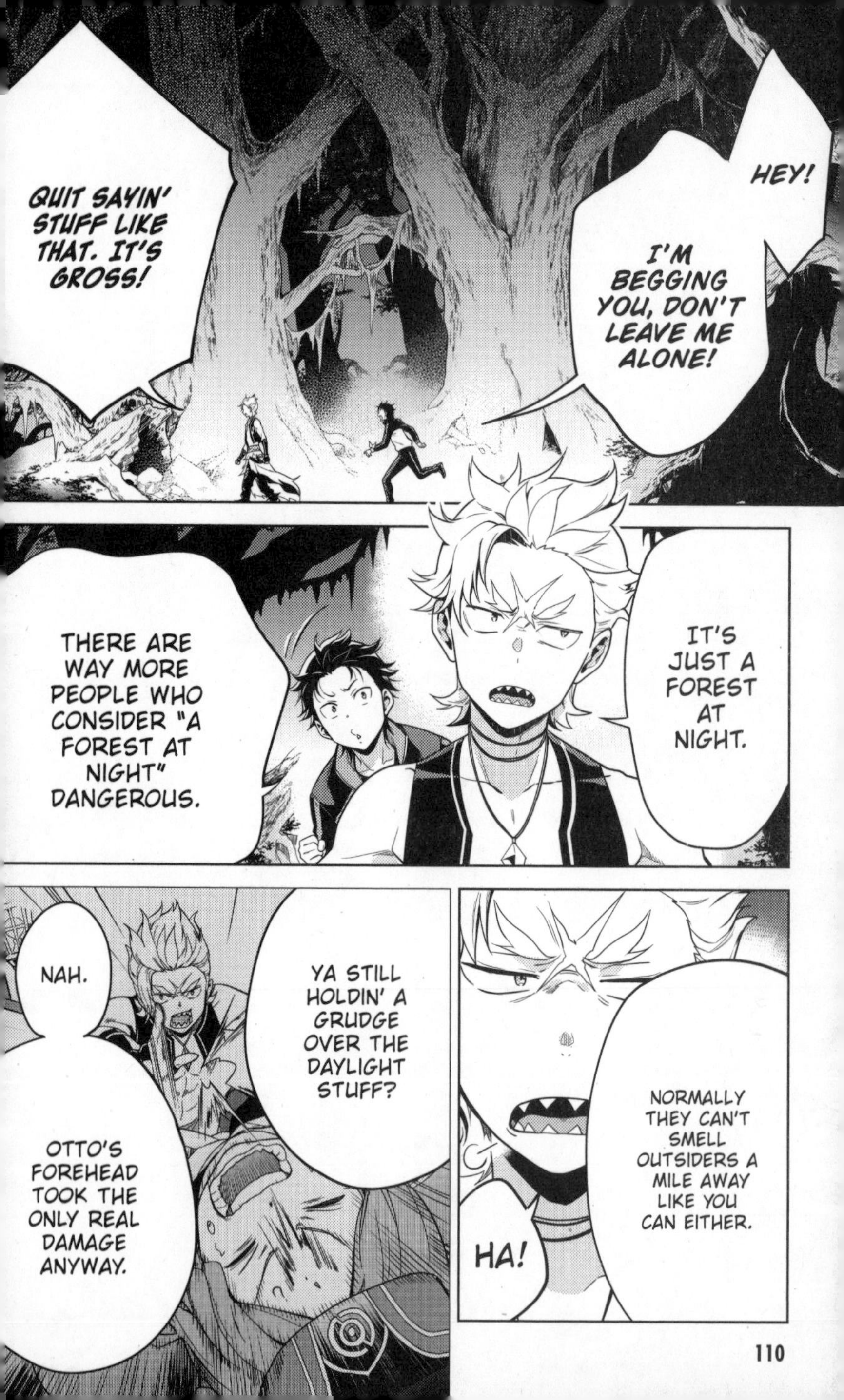
HEY!
I'M BEGGING YOU, DON'T LEAVE ME ALONE!
QUIT SAYIN' STUFF LIKE THAT. IT'S GROSS!
IT'S JUST A FOREST AT NIGHT.
THERE ARE WAY MORE PEOPLE WHO CONSIDER "A FOREST AT NIGHT" DANGEROUS.
NORMALLY THEY CAN'T SMELL OUTSIDERS A MILE AWAY LIKE YOU CAN EITHER.
HA!
YA STILL HOLDIN' A GRUDGE OVER THE DAYLIGHT STUFF?
NAH.
OTTO'S FOREHEAD TOOK THE ONLY REAL DAMAGE ANYWAY.

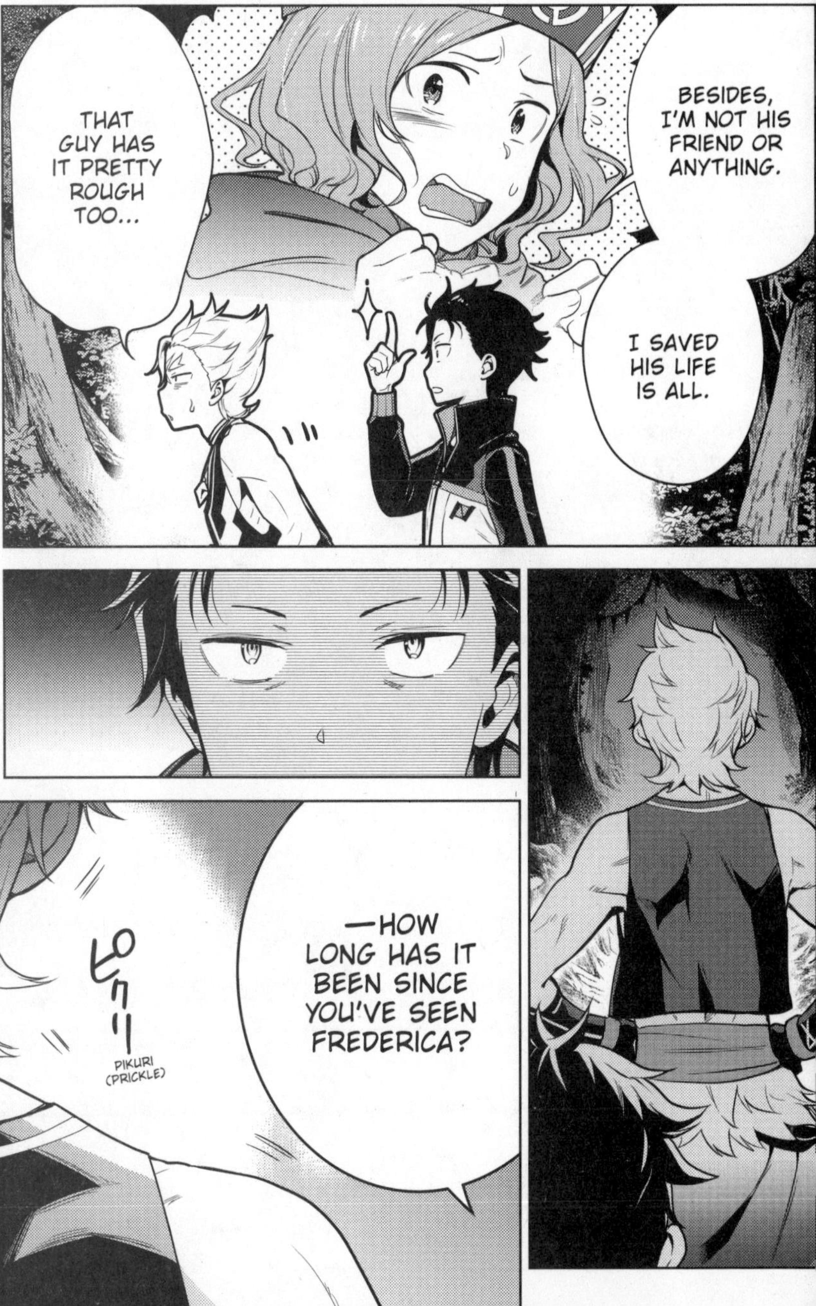
BESIDES, I'M NOT HIS FRIEND OR ANYTHING.
I SAVED HIS LIFE IS ALL.
THAT GUY HAS IT PRETTY ROUGH TOO...
—HOW LONG HAS IT BEEN SINCE YOU'VE SEEN FREDERICA?
ピクリ
PIKURI (PRICKLE)

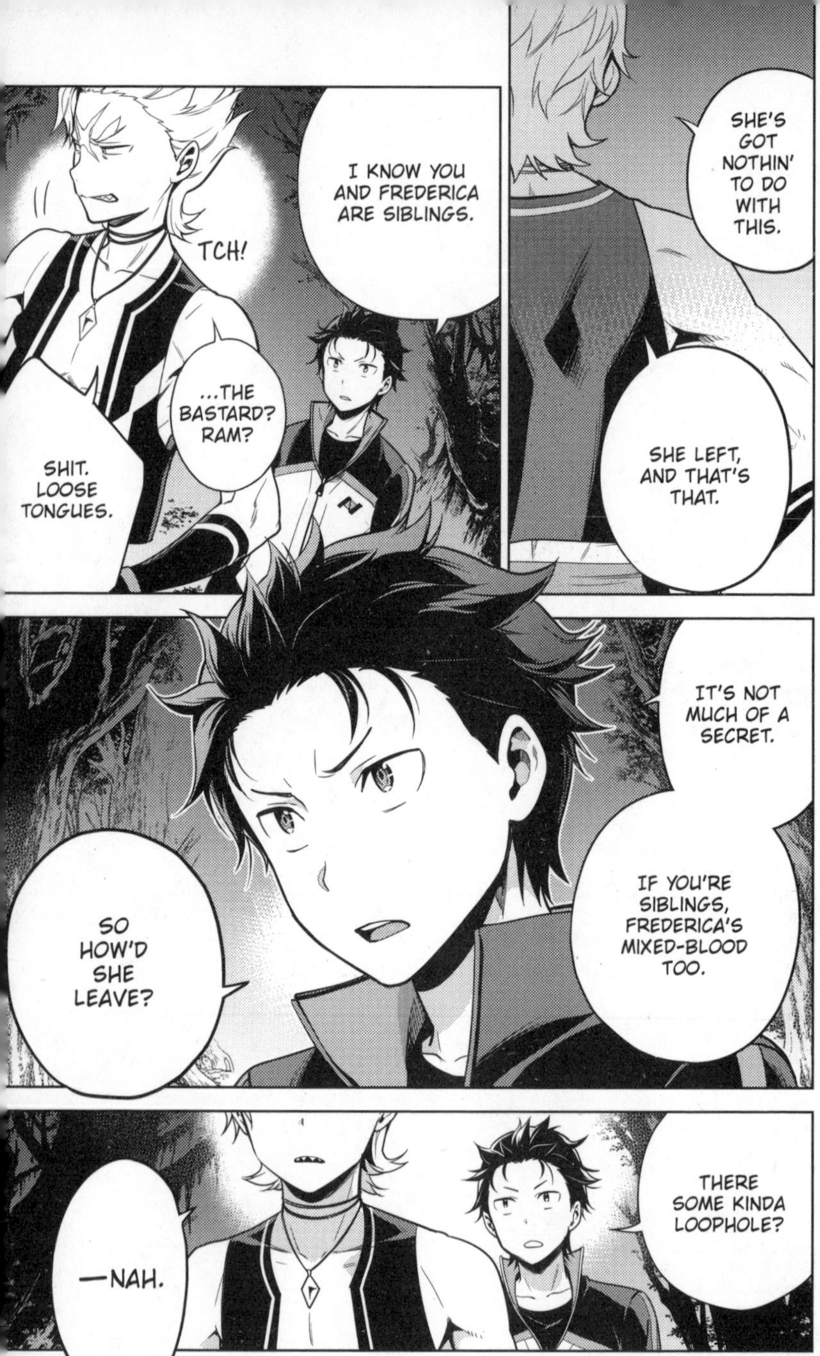
SHE'S GOT NOTHIN' TO DO WITH THIS.
SHE LEFT, AND THAT'S THAT.
I KNOW YOU AND FREDERICA ARE SIBLINGS.
TCH!
...THE BASTARD? RAM?
SHIT. LOOSE TONGUES.
IT'S NOT MUCH OF A SECRET.
IF YOU'RE SIBLINGS, FREDERICA'S MIXED-BLOOD TOO.
SO HOW'D SHE LEAVE?
THERE SOME KINDA LOOPHOLE?
—NAH.

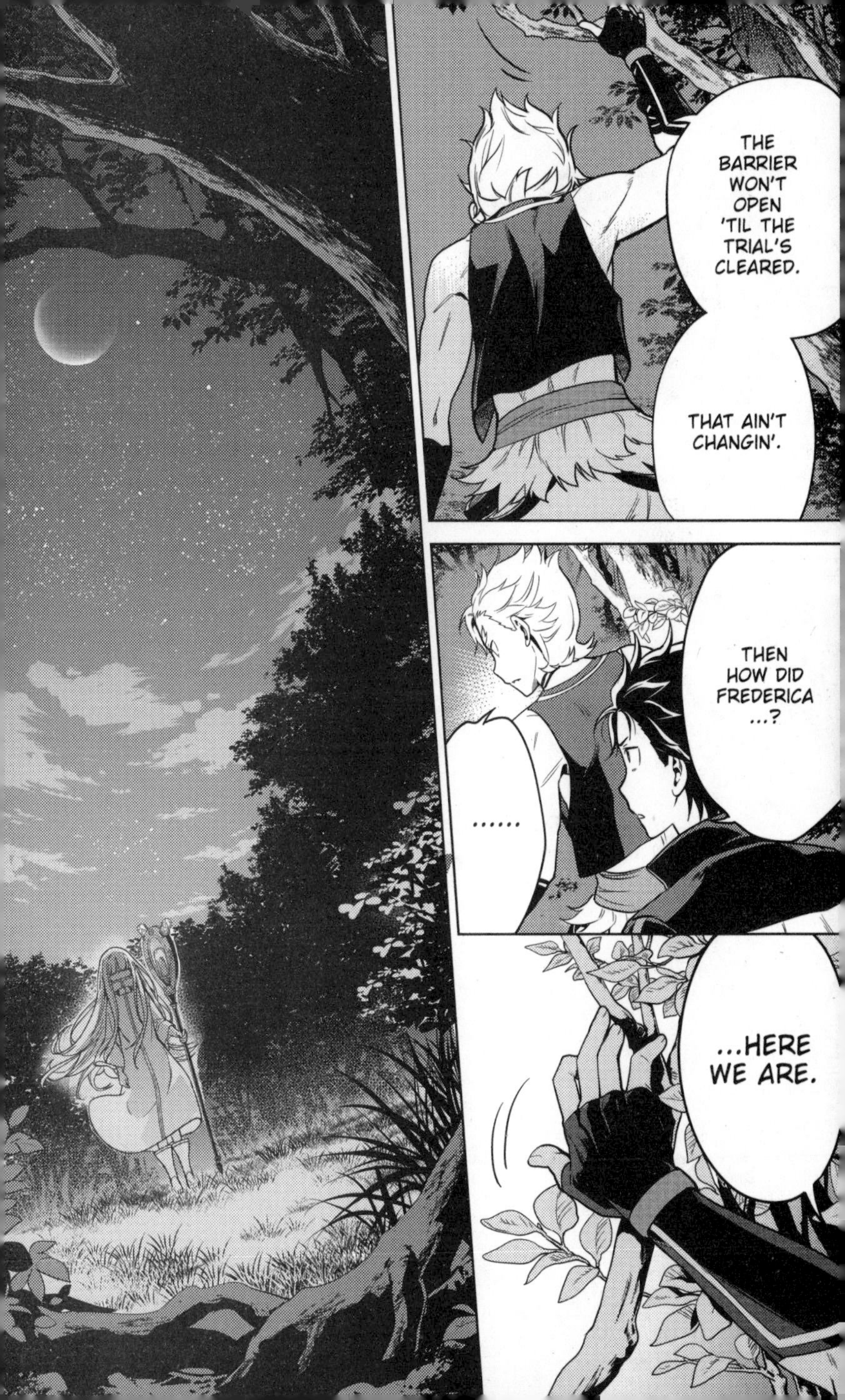
THE BARRIER WON'T OPEN 'TIL THE TRIAL'S CLEARED.
THAT AIN'T CHANGIN'.
THEN HOW DID FREDERICA ...?
......
...HERE WE ARE.

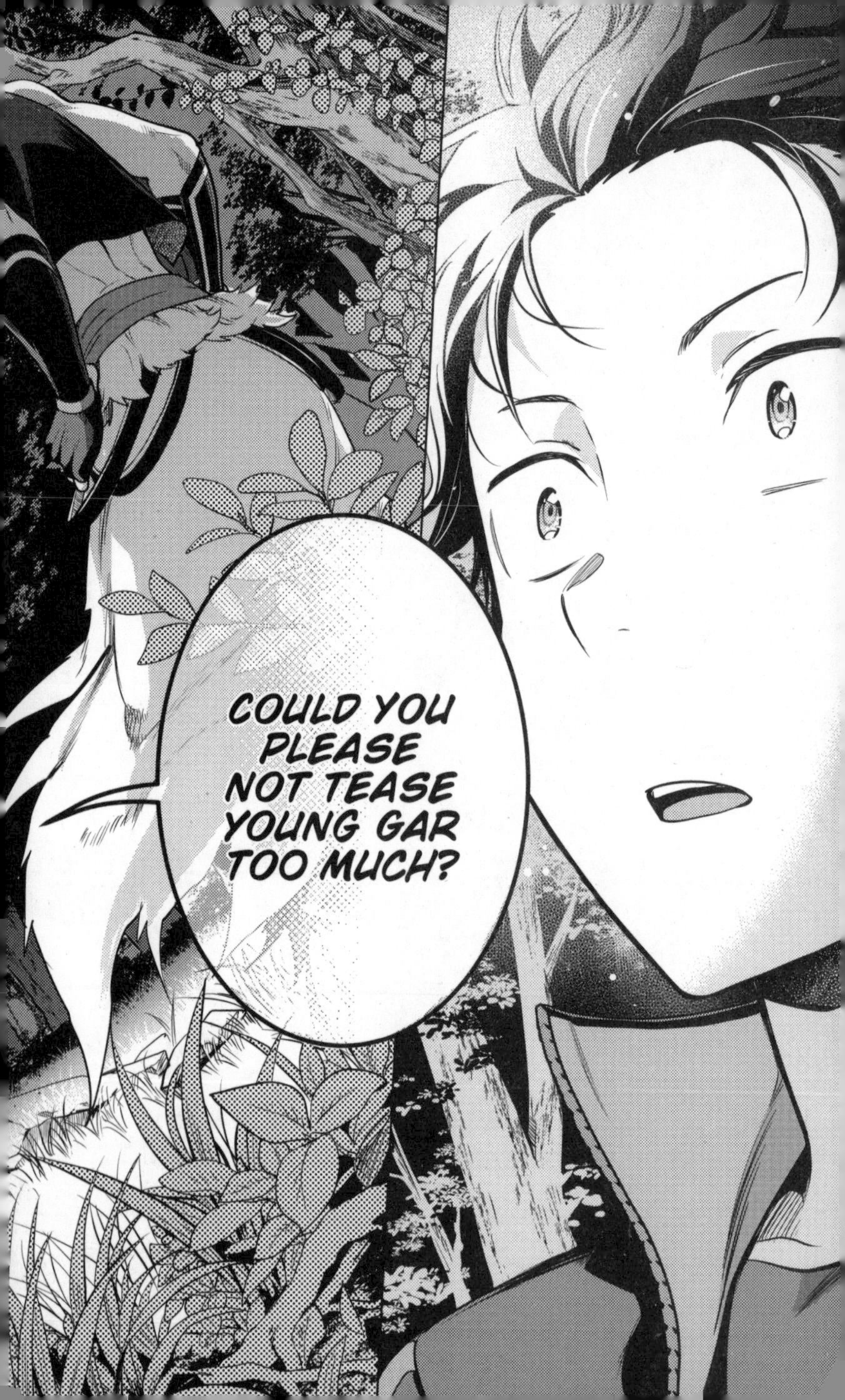
COULD YOU PLEASE NOT TEASE YOUNG GAR TOO MUCH?

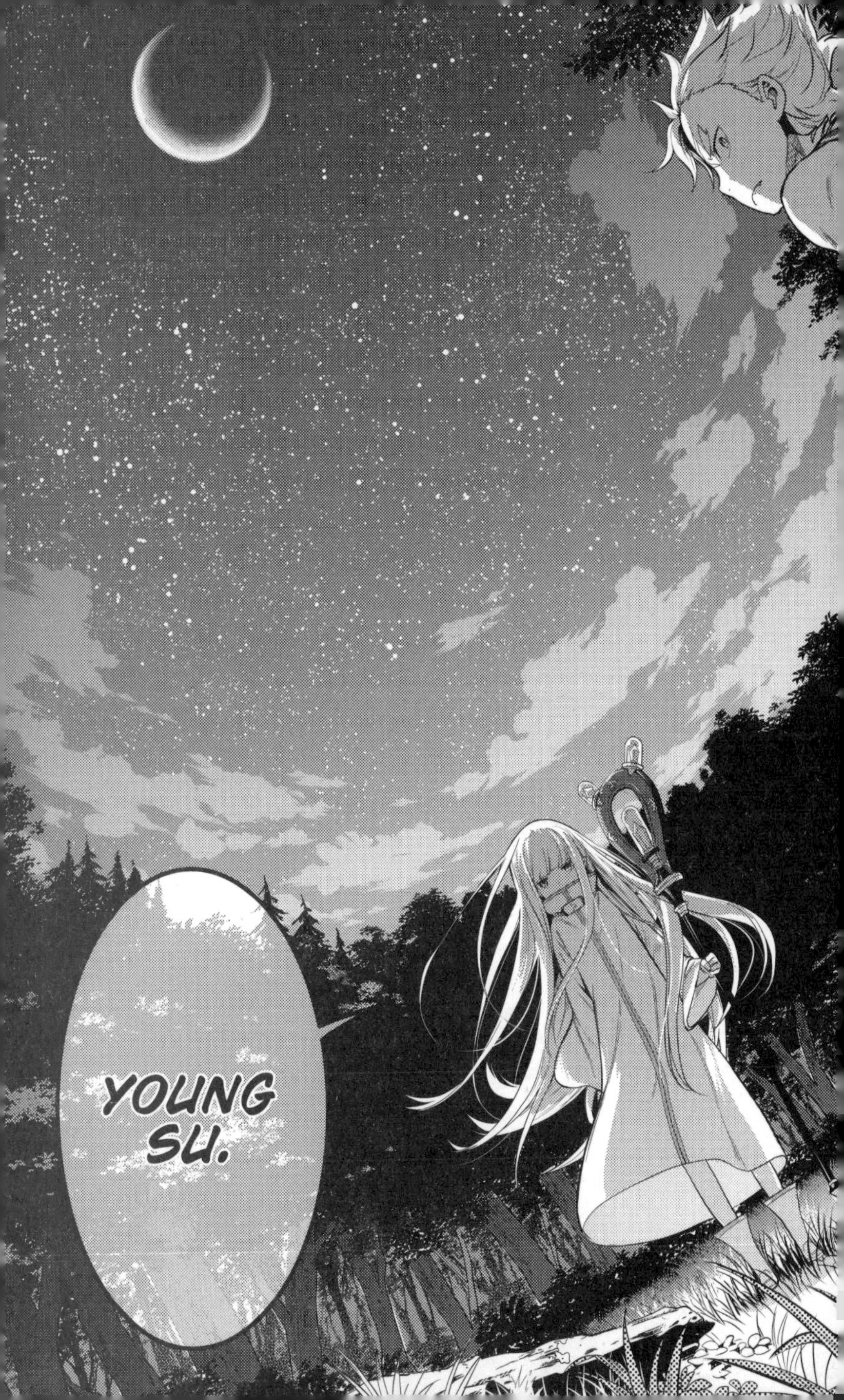
YOUNG SU.

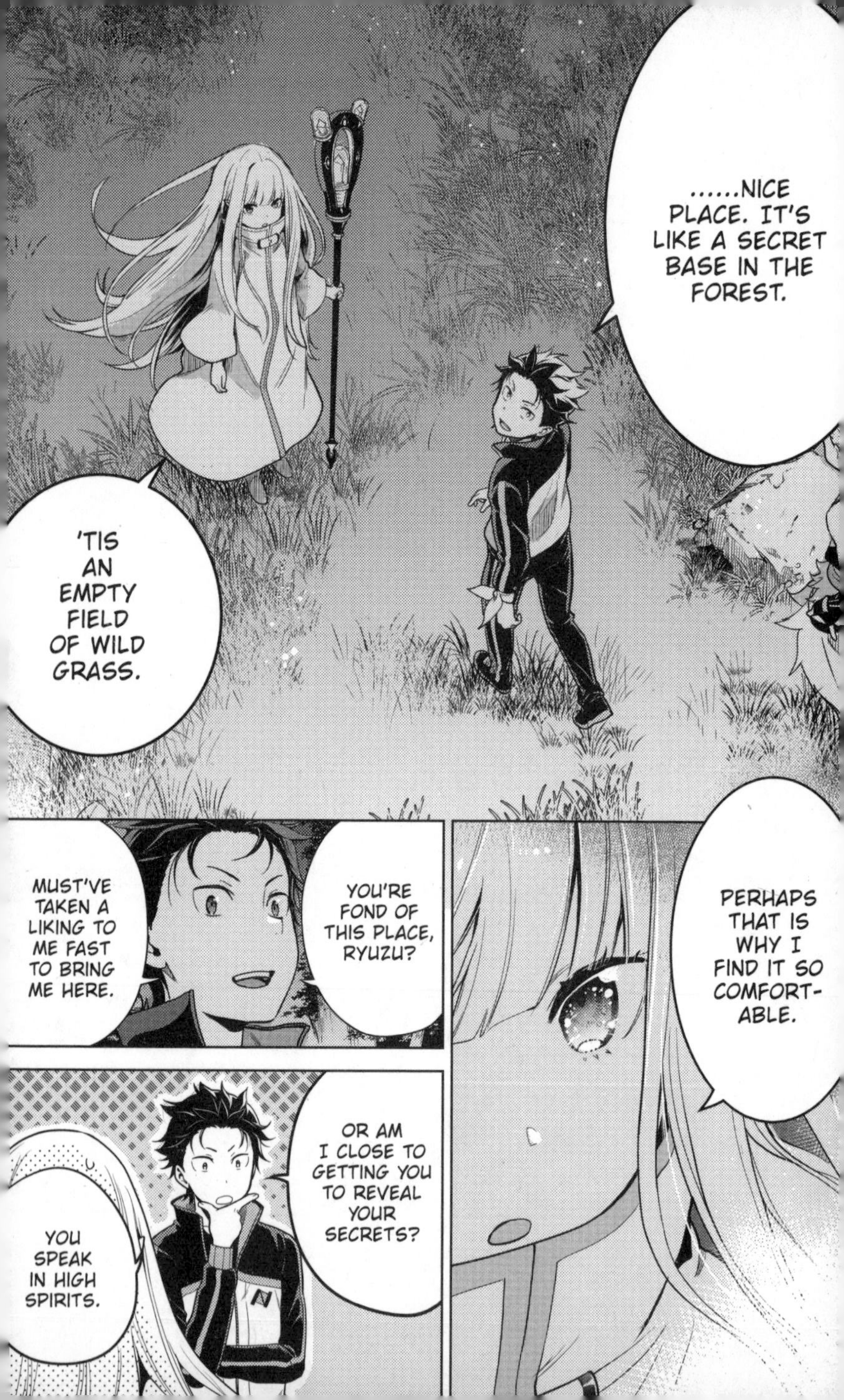
......NICE PLACE. IT'S LIKE A SECRET BASE IN THE FOREST.
'TIS AN EMPTY FIELD OF WILD GRASS.
PERHAPS THAT IS WHY I FIND IT SO COMFORT-ABLE.
YOU'RE FOND OF THIS PLACE, RYUZU?
MUST'VE TAKEN A LIKING TO ME FAST TO BRING ME HERE.
OR AM I CLOSE TO GETTING YOU TO REVEAL YOUR SECRETS?
YOU SPEAK IN HIGH SPIRITS.

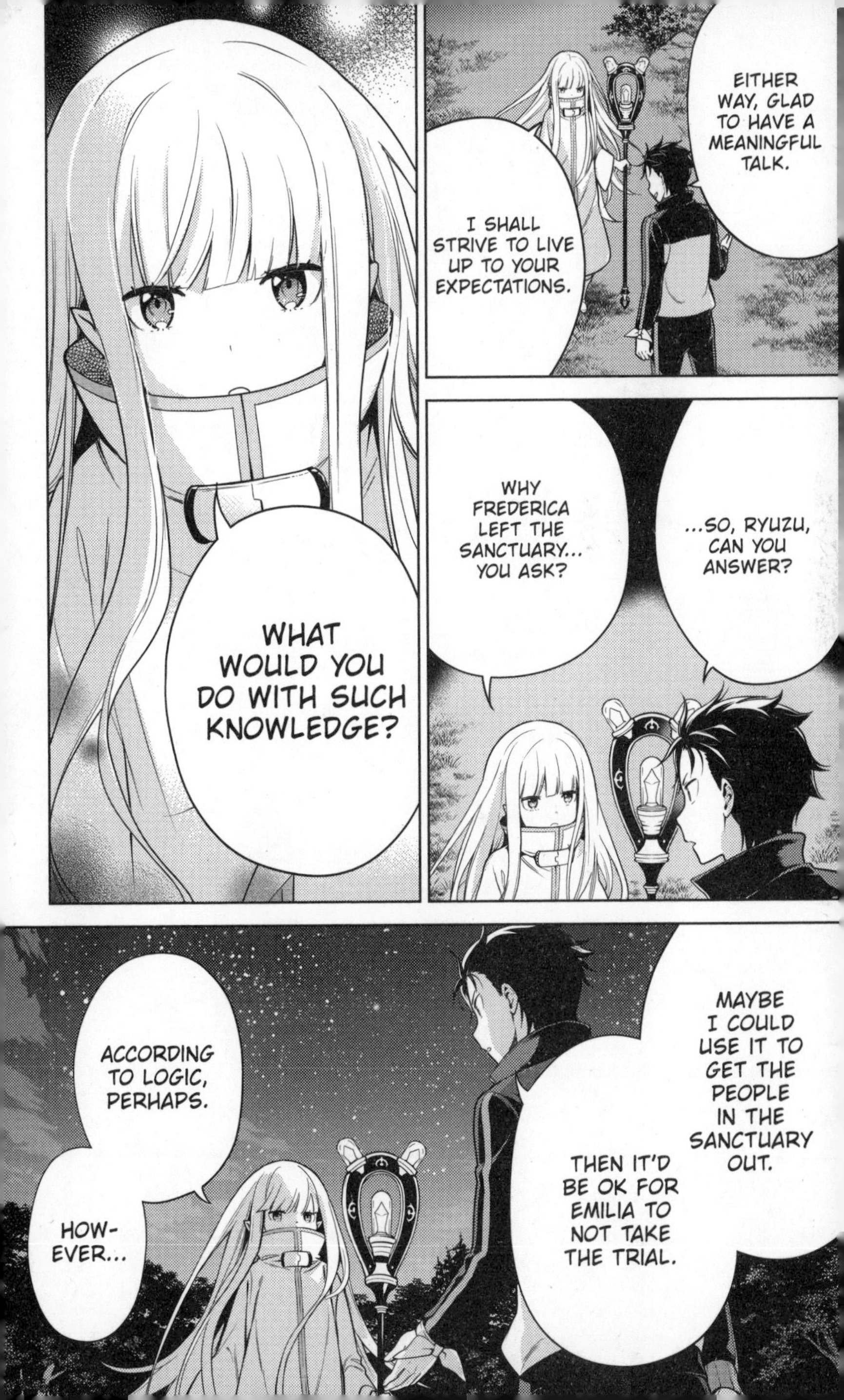
EITHER WAY, GLAD TO HAVE A MEANINGFUL TALK.
I SHALL STRIVE TO LIVE UP TO YOUR EXPECTATIONS.
...SO, RYUZU, CAN YOU ANSWER?
WHY FREDERICA LEFT THE SANCTUARY... YOU ASK?
WHAT WOULD YOU DO WITH SUCH KNOWLEDGE?
MAYBE I COULD USE IT TO GET THE PEOPLE IN THE SANCTUARY OUT.
THEN IT'D BE OK FOR EMILIA TO NOT TAKE THE TRIAL.
ACCORDING TO LOGIC, PERHAPS.
HOW-EVER...

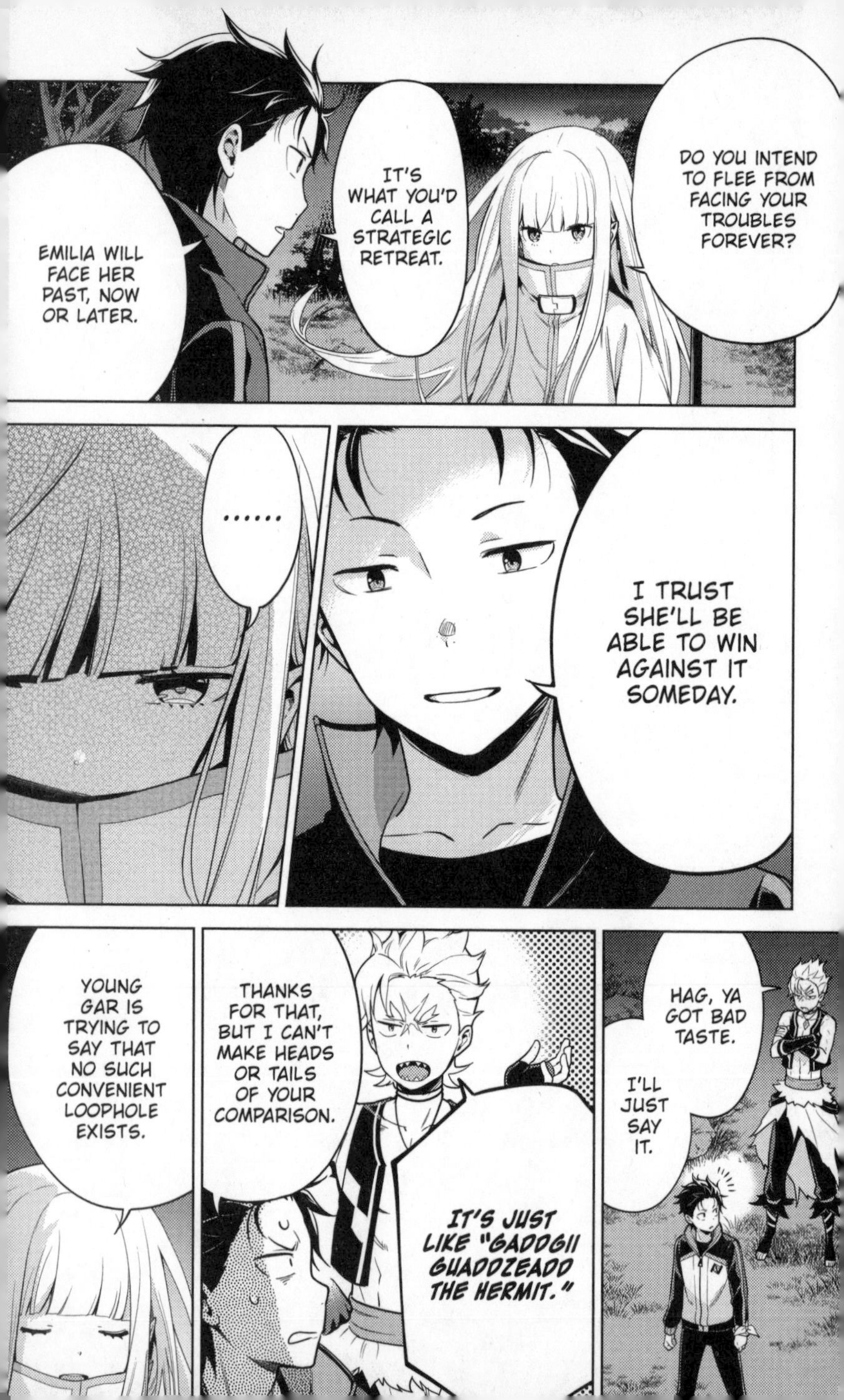
DO YOU INTEND TO FLEE FROM FACING YOUR TROUBLES FOREVER?
IT'S WHAT YOU'D CALL A STRATEGIC RETREAT.
EMILIA WILL FACE HER PAST, NOW OR LATER.
I TRUST SHE'LL BE ABLE TO WIN AGAINST IT SOMEDAY.
......
HAG, YA GOT BAD TASTE.
I'LL JUST SAY IT.
IT'S JUST LIKE "GADDGII GUADDZEADD THE HERMIT."
THANKS FOR THAT, BUT I CAN'T MAKE HEADS OR TAILS OF YOUR COMPARISON.
YOUNG GAR IS TRYING TO SAY THAT NO SUCH CONVENIENT LOOPHOLE EXISTS.

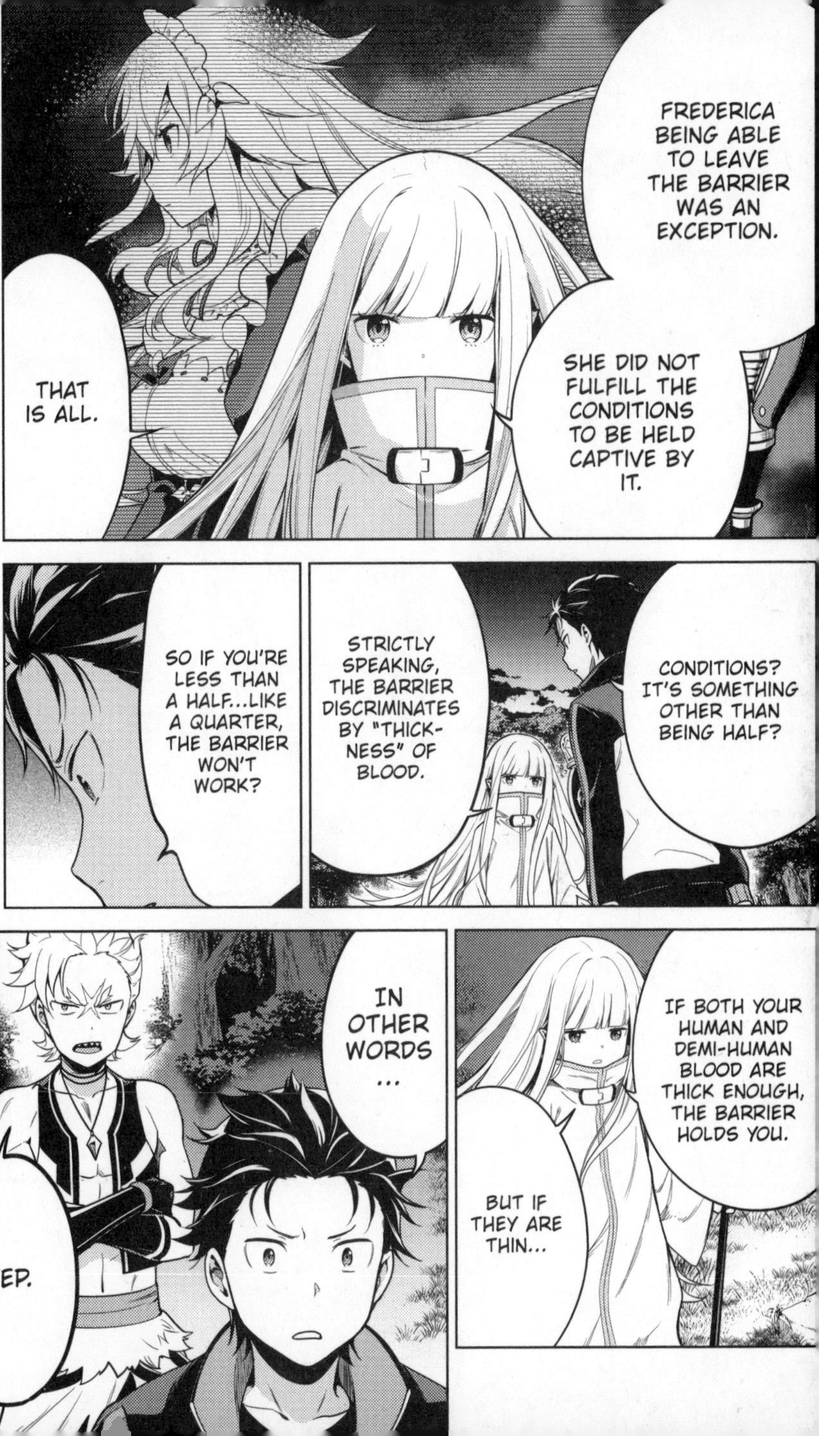
FREDERICA BEING ABLE TO LEAVE THE BARRIER WAS AN EXCEPTION.
SHE DID NOT FULFILL THE CONDITIONS TO BE HELD CAPTIVE BY IT.
THAT IS ALL.
CONDITIONS? IT'S SOMETHING OTHER THAN BEING HALF?
STRICTLY SPEAKING, THE BARRIER DISCRIMINATES BY "THICK-NESS" OF BLOOD.
SO IF YOU'RE LESS THAN A HALF...LIKE A QUARTER, THE BARRIER WON'T WORK?
IF BOTH YOUR HUMAN AND DEMI-HUMAN BLOOD ARE THICK ENOUGH, THE BARRIER HOLDS YOU.
BUT IF THEY ARE THIN...
IN OTHER WORDS...
YEP.

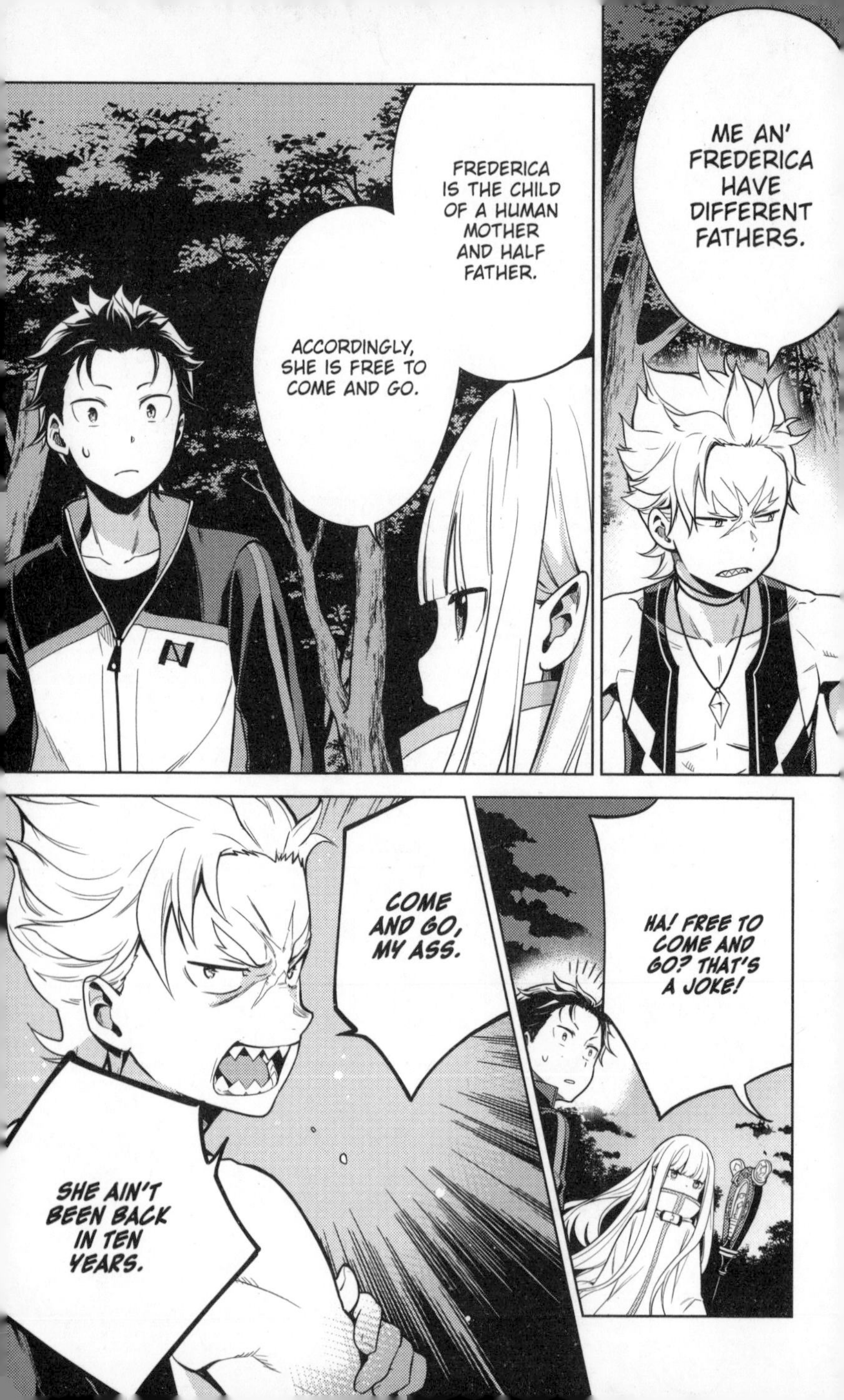
ME AN' FREDERICA HAVE DIFFERENT FATHERS.
FREDERICA IS THE CHILD OF A HUMAN MOTHER AND HALF FATHER.
ACCORDINGLY, SHE IS FREE TO COME AND GO.
HA! FREE TO COME AND GO? THAT'S A JOKE!
COME AND GO, MY ASS.
SHE AIN'T BEEN BACK IN TEN YEARS.

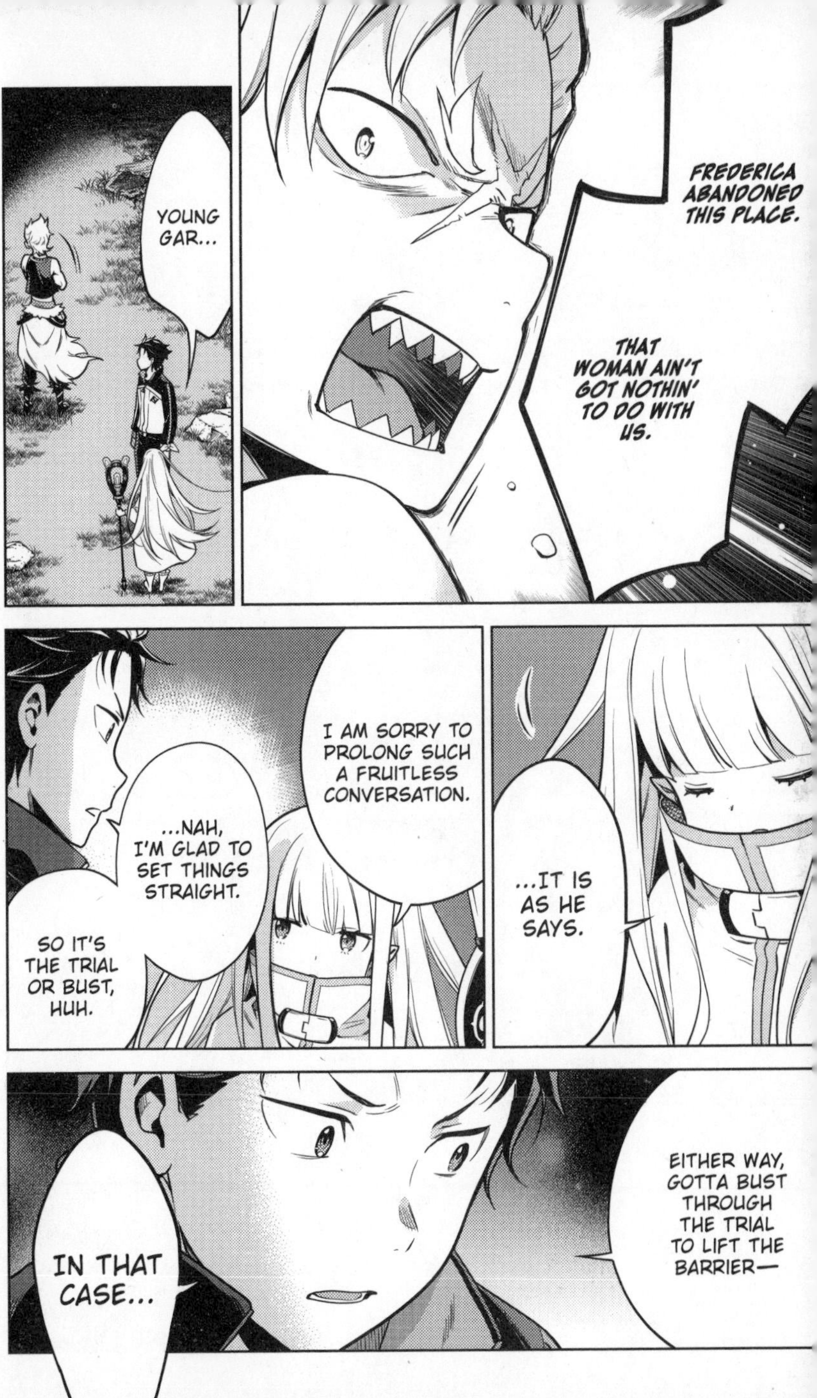
FREDERICA ABANDONED THIS PLACE.
THAT WOMAN AIN'T GOT NOTHIN' TO DO WITH US.
YOUNG GAR...
...IT IS AS HE SAYS.
I AM SORRY TO PROLONG SUCH A FRUITLESS CONVERSATION.
...NAH, I'M GLAD TO SET THINGS STRAIGHT.
SO IT'S THE TRIAL OR BUST, HUH.
EITHER WAY, GOTTA BUST THROUGH THE TRIAL TO LIFT THE BARRIER—
IN THAT CASE...

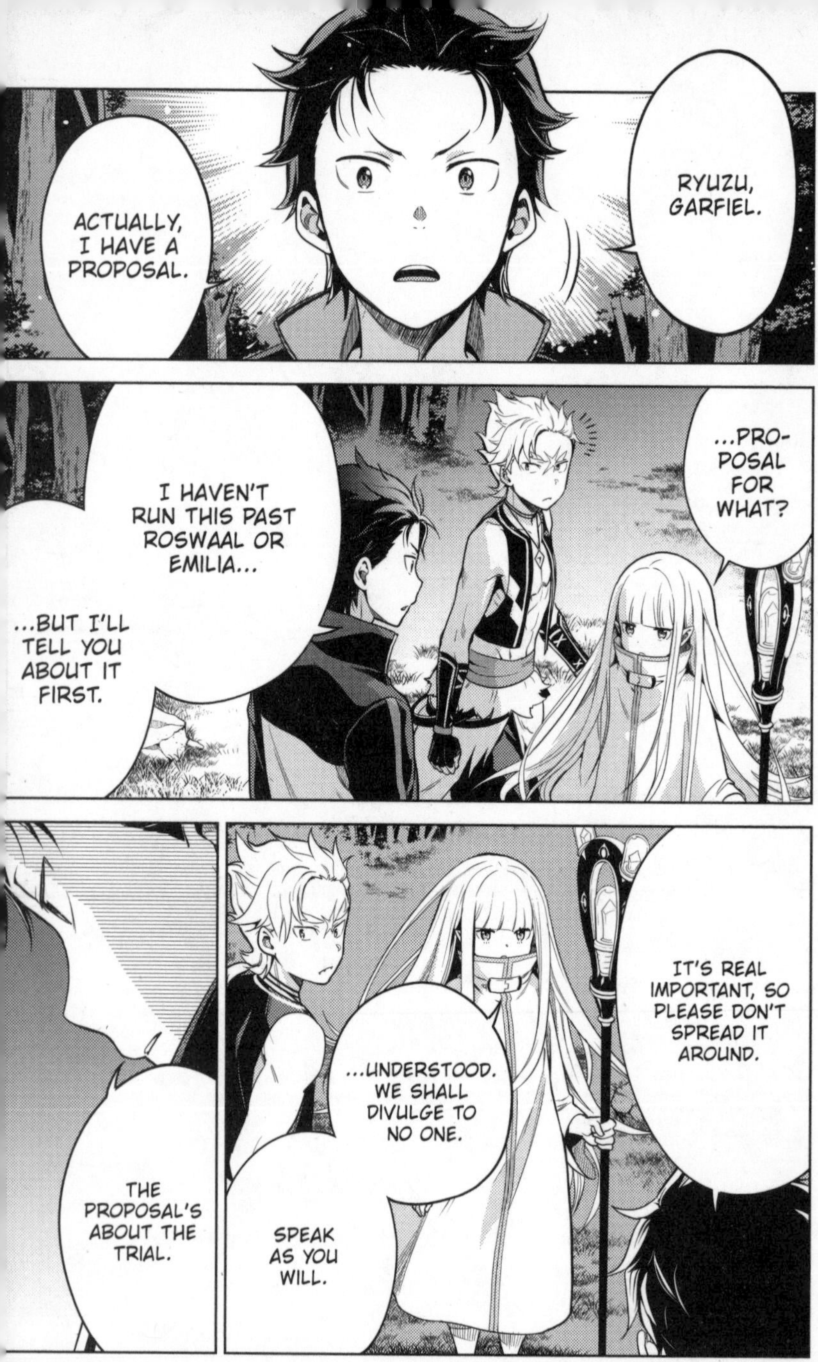
RYUZU, GARFIEL.
ACTUALLY, I HAVE A PROPOSAL.
...PRO-POSAL FOR WHAT?
I HAVEN'T RUN THIS PAST ROSWAAL OR EMILIA...
...BUT I'LL TELL YOU ABOUT IT FIRST.
IT'S REAL IMPORTANT, SO PLEASE DON'T SPREAD IT AROUND.
...UNDERSTOOD. WE SHALL DIVULGE TO NO ONE.
SPEAK AS YOU WILL.
THE PROPOSAL'S ABOUT THE TRIAL.

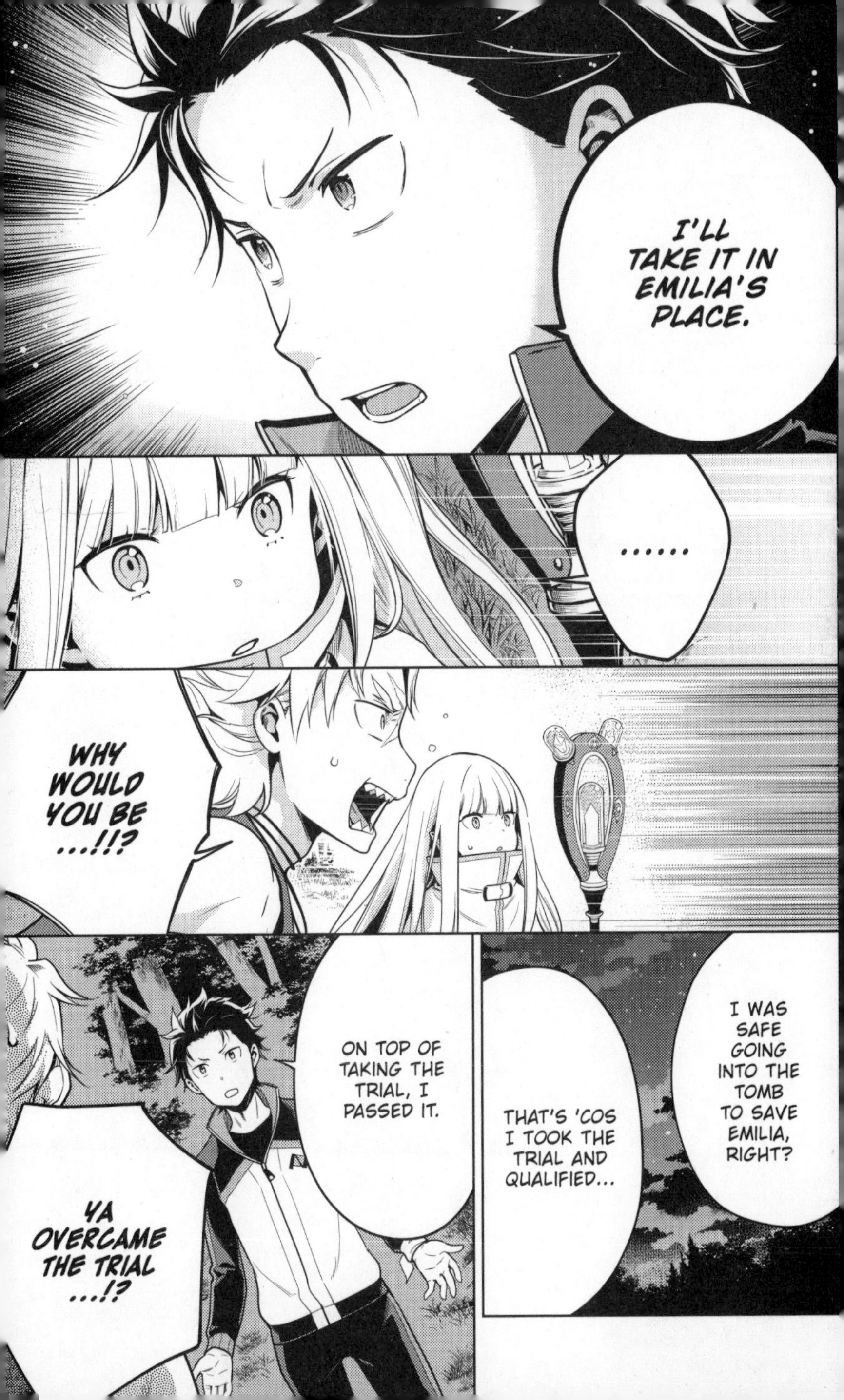
I'LL TAKE IT IN EMILIA'S PLACE.
......
WHY WOULD YOU BE ...!!?
I WAS SAFE GOING INTO THE TOMB TO SAVE EMILIA, RIGHT?
THAT'S 'COS I TOOK THE TRIAL AND QUALIFIED...
ON TOP OF TAKING THE TRIAL, I PASSED IT.
YA OVERCAME THE TRIAL ...!?

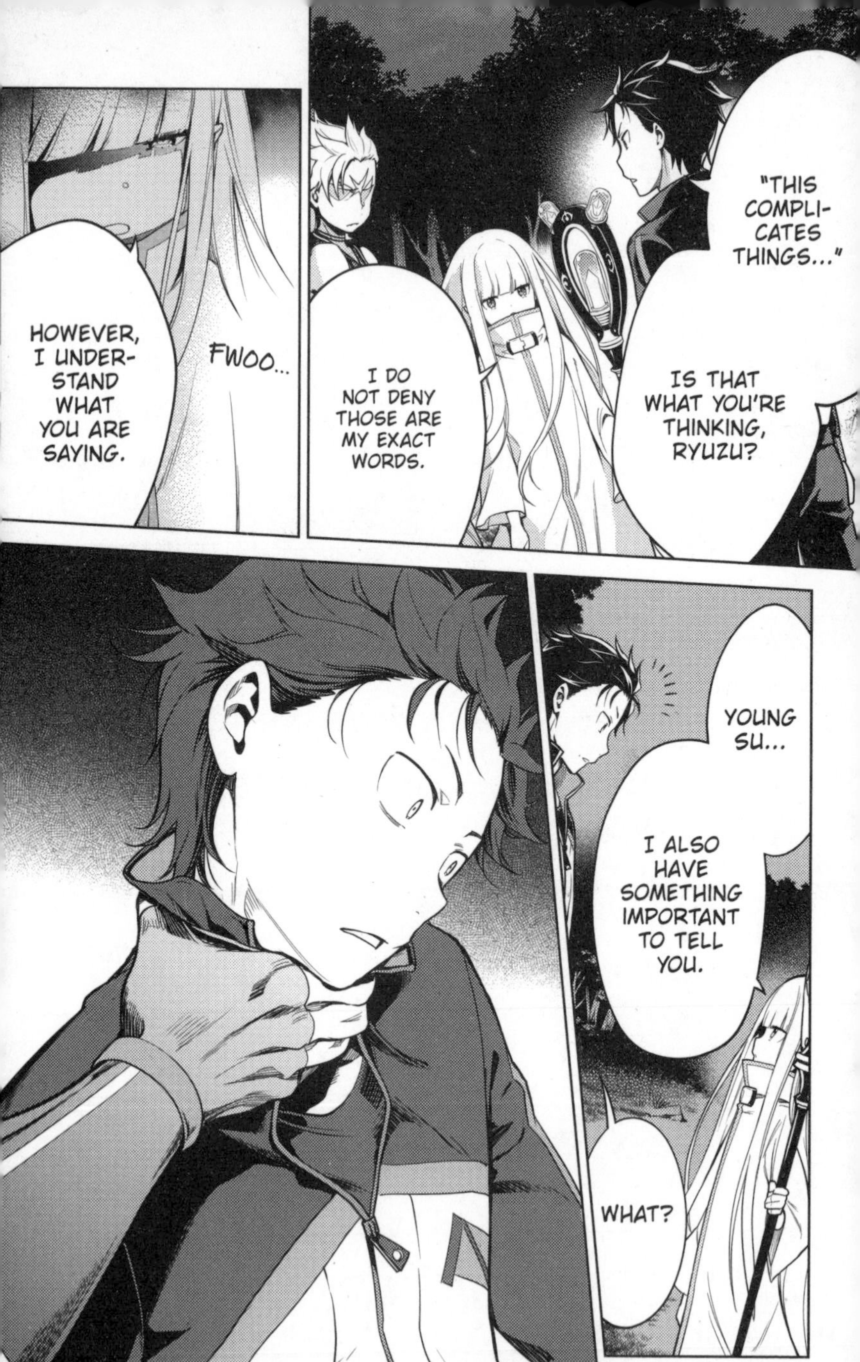
"THIS COMPLICATES THINGS..."
IS THAT WHAT YOU'RE THINKING, RYUZU?
I DO NOT DENY THOSE ARE MY EXACT WORDS.
FWOO...
HOWEVER, I UNDERSTAND WHAT YOU ARE SAYING.
YOUNG SU...
I ALSO HAVE SOMETHING IMPORTANT TO TELL YOU.
WHAT?

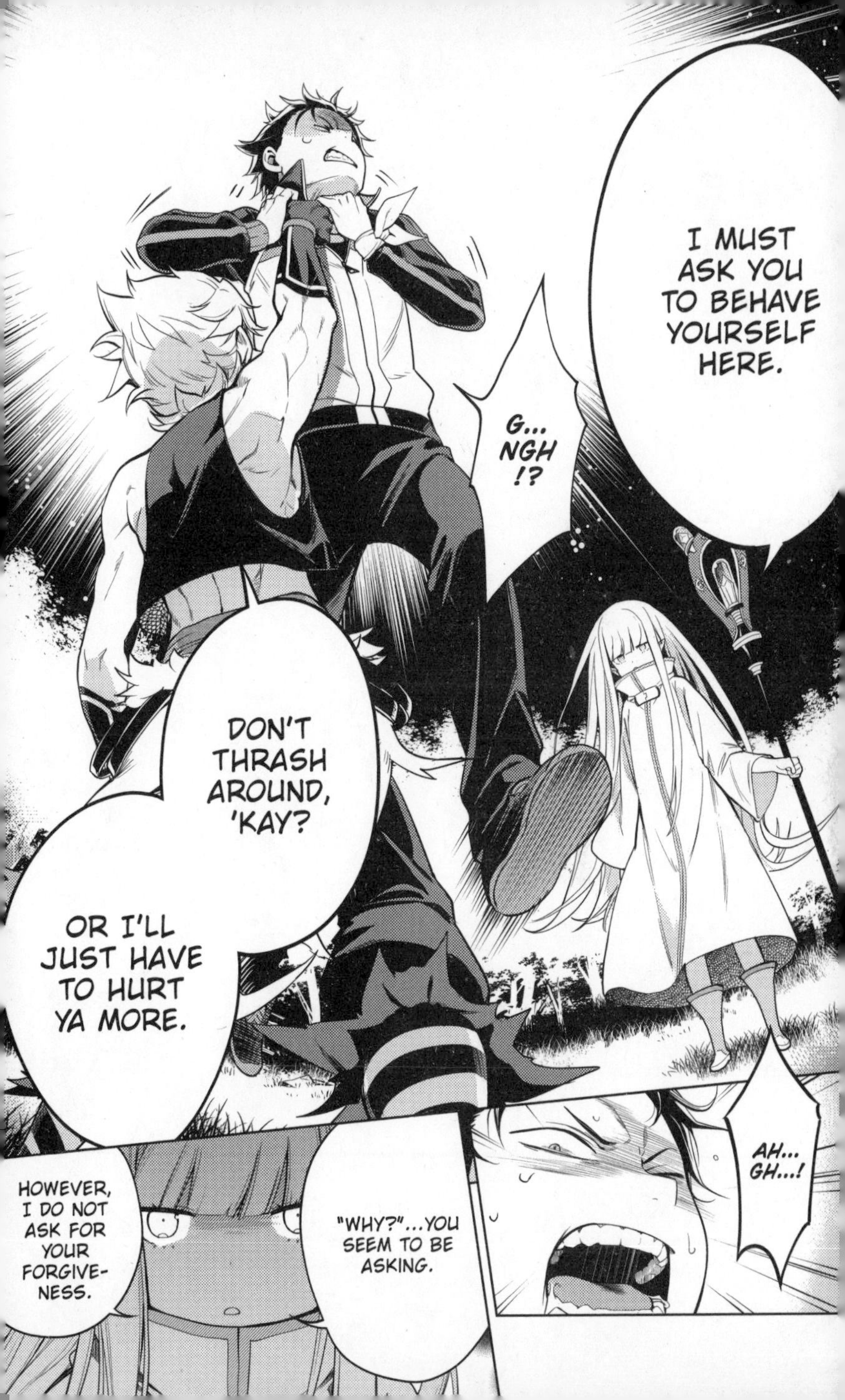
I MUST ASK YOU TO BEHAVE YOURSELF HERE.
G... NGH !?
DON'T THRASH AROUND, 'KAY?
OR I'LL JUST HAVE TO HURT YA MORE.
AH... GH...!
"WHY?"...YOU SEEM TO BE ASKING.
HOWEVER, I DO NOT ASK FOR YOUR FORGIVE-NESS.

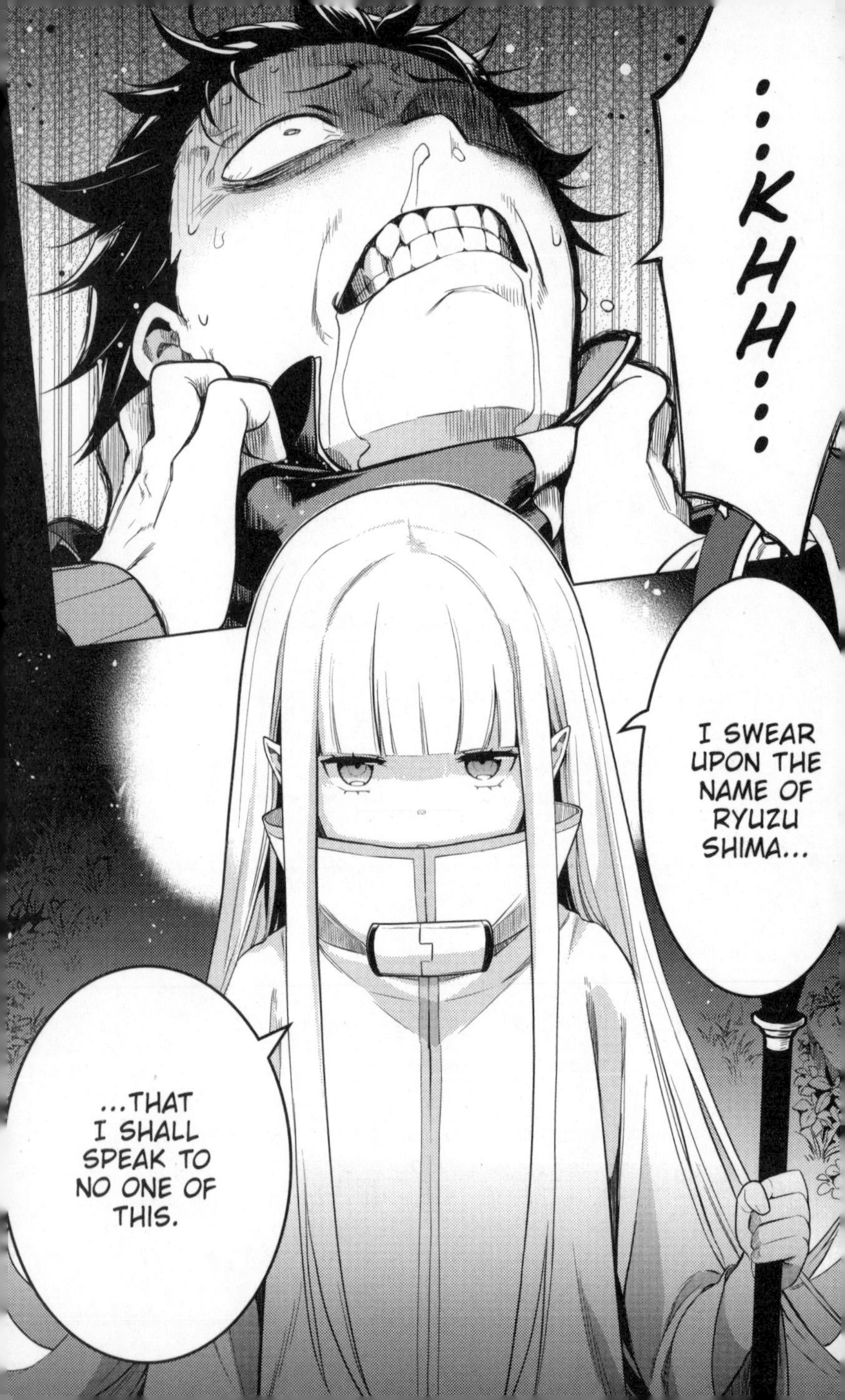
...KHH...
I SWEAR UPON THE NAME OF RYUZU SHIMA...
...THAT I SHALL SPEAK TO NO ONE OF THIS.

Episode 18
Friend

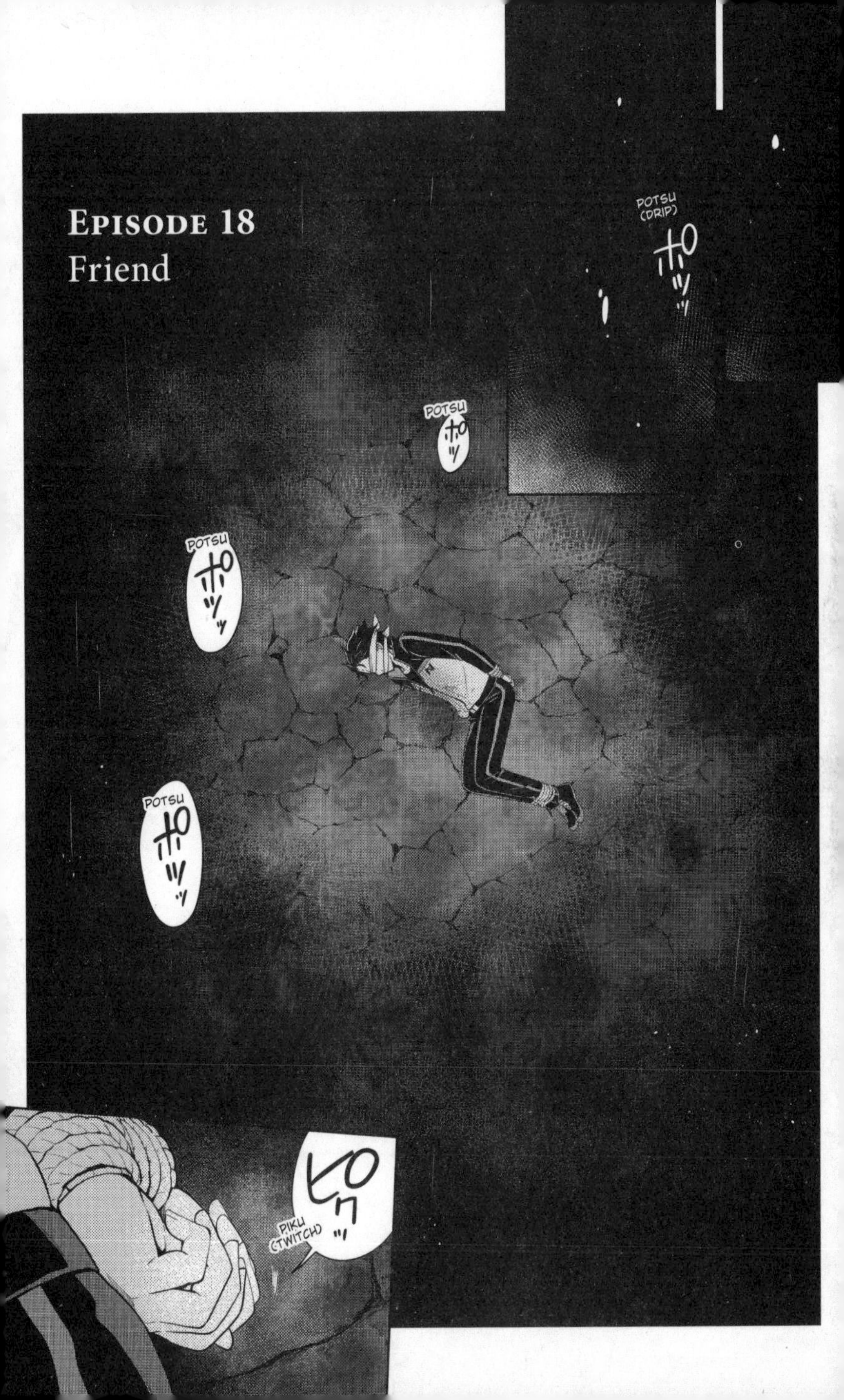
POTSU (DRIP)
ポツッ
POTSU
ポツッ
POTSU
ポツッ
POTSU
ポツッ
ピクッ
PIKU (TWITCH)

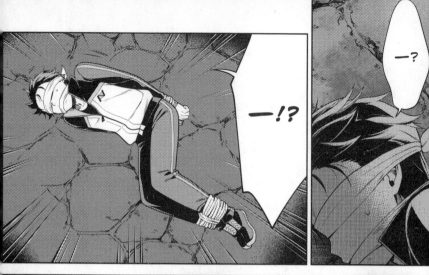

—!?

—?

KSHH!

KSHH!

FROM THE LOOKS OF IT...

...!

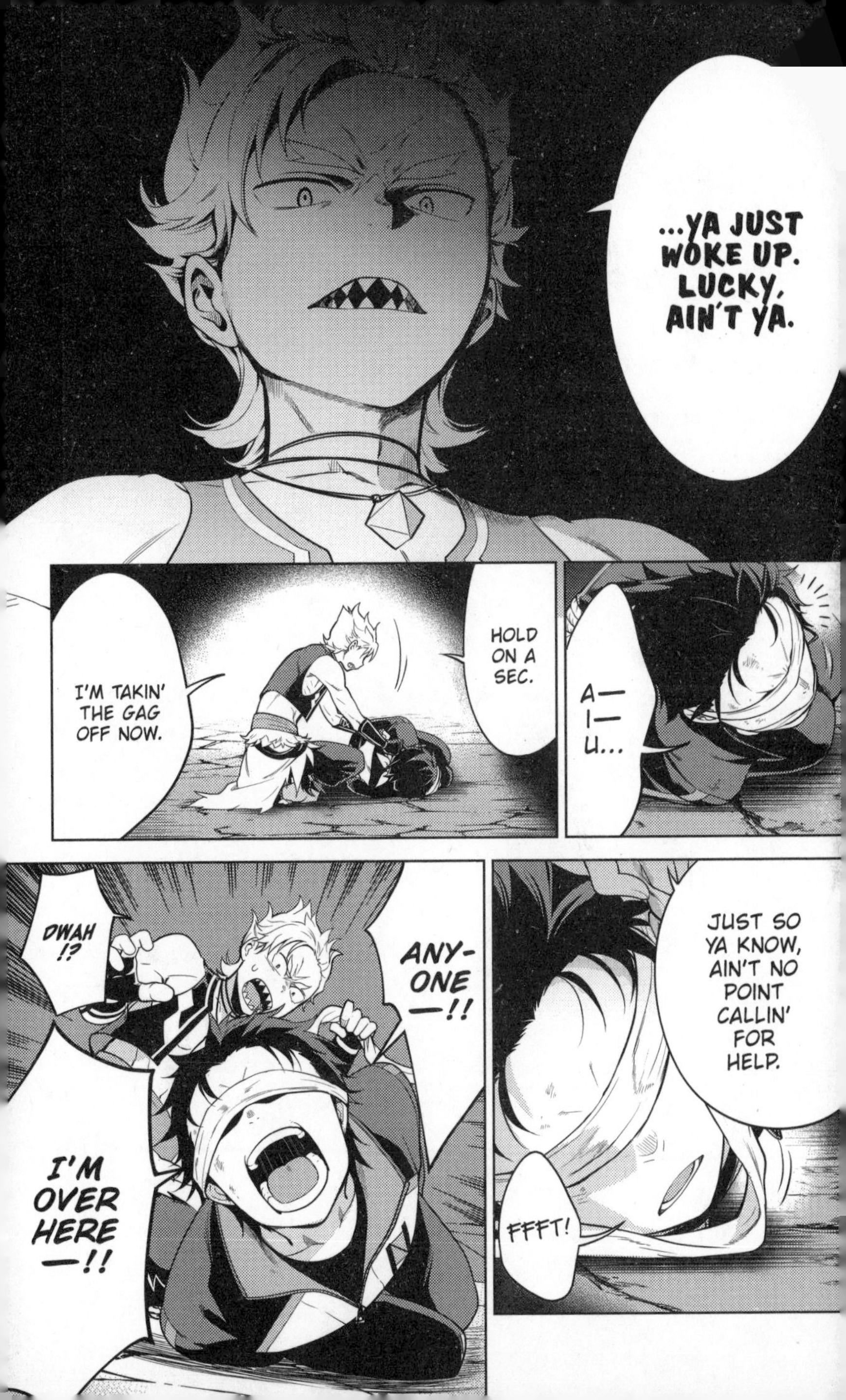
...YA JUST WOKE UP. LUCKY, AIN'T YA.
A— I— U...
HOLD ON A SEC.
I'M TAKIN' THE GAG OFF NOW.
JUST SO YA KNOW, AIN'T NO POINT CALLIN' FOR HELP.
FFFT!
ANY-ONE—!!
DWAH!?
I'M OVER HERE—!!

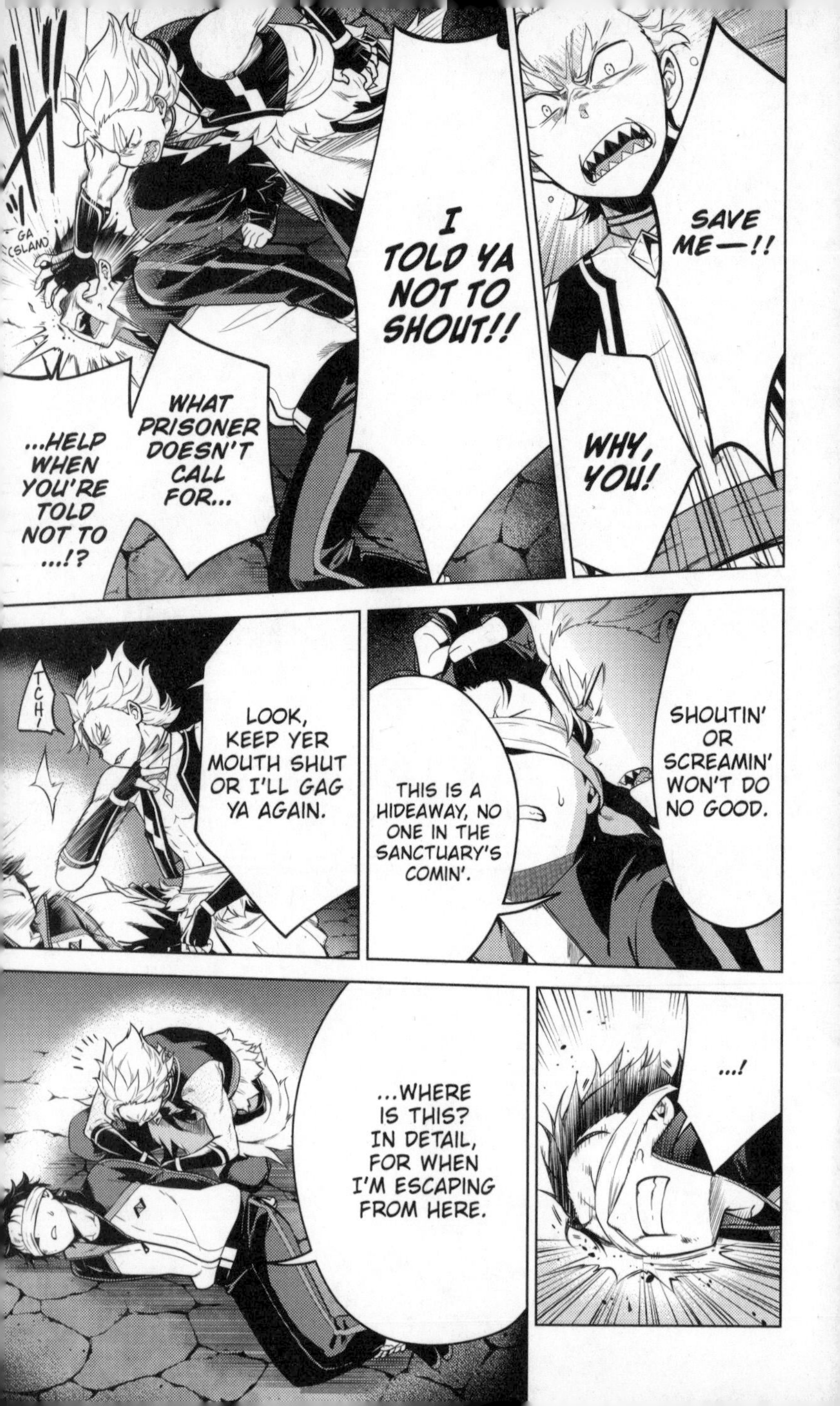
SAVE ME—!!
WHY, YOU!
I TOLD YA NOT TO SHOUT!!
GA (SLAM)
WHAT PRISONER DOESN'T CALL FOR...
...HELP WHEN YOU'RE TOLD NOT TO ...!?
SHOUTIN' OR SCREAMIN' WON'T DO NO GOOD.
THIS IS A HIDEAWAY, NO ONE IN THE SANCTUARY'S COMIN'.
TCH!
LOOK, KEEP YER MOUTH SHUT OR I'LL GAG YA AGAIN.
...!
...WHERE IS THIS? IN DETAIL, FOR WHEN I'M ESCAPING FROM HERE.

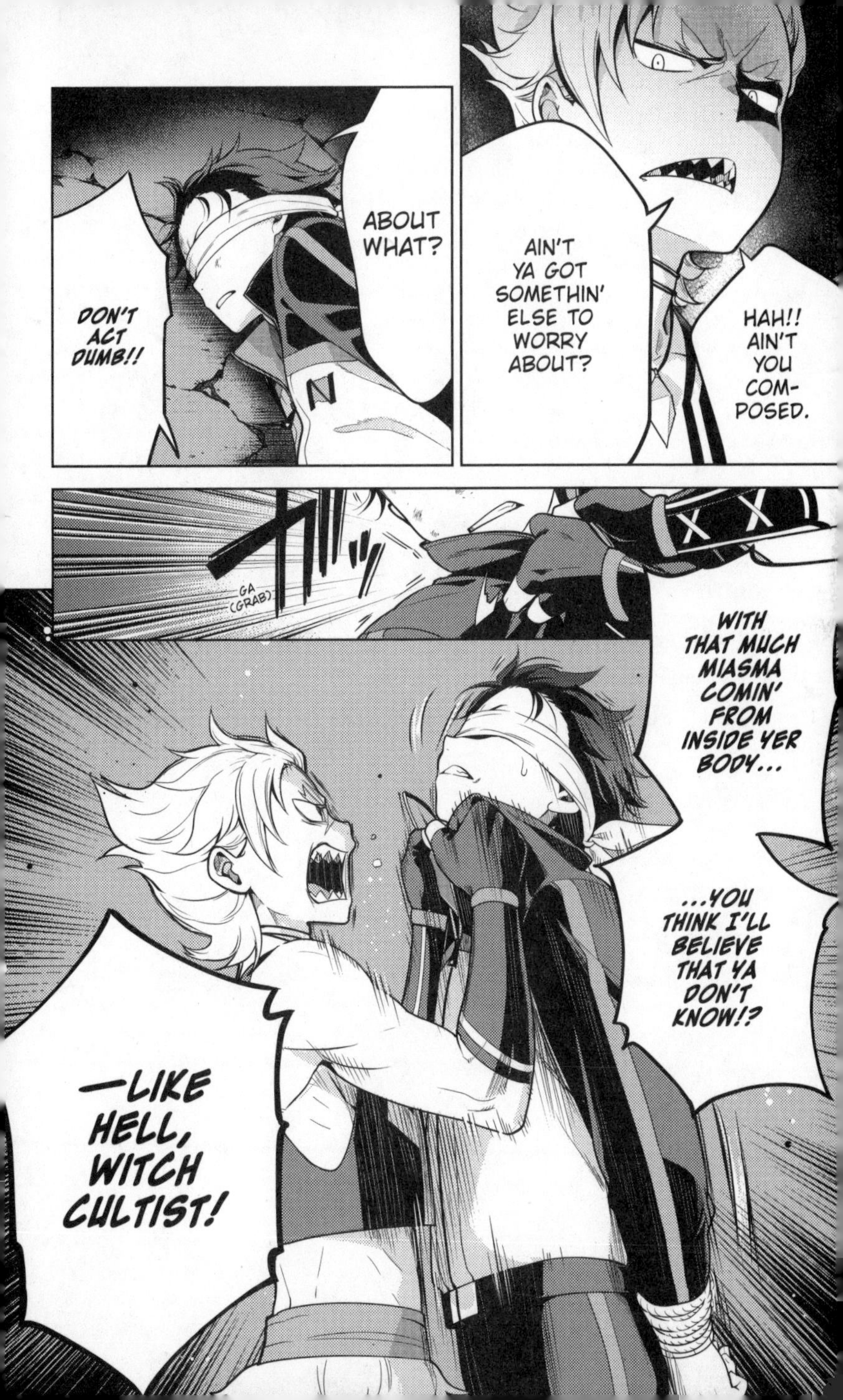
HAH!! AIN'T YOU COM-POSED.
AIN'T YA GOT SOMETHIN' ELSE TO WORRY ABOUT?
ABOUT WHAT?
DON'T ACT DUMB!!
GA (GRAB)
WITH THAT MUCH MIASMA COMIN' FROM INSIDE YER BODY...
...YOU THINK I'LL BELIEVE THAT YA DON'T KNOW!?
—LIKE HELL, WITCH CULTIST!

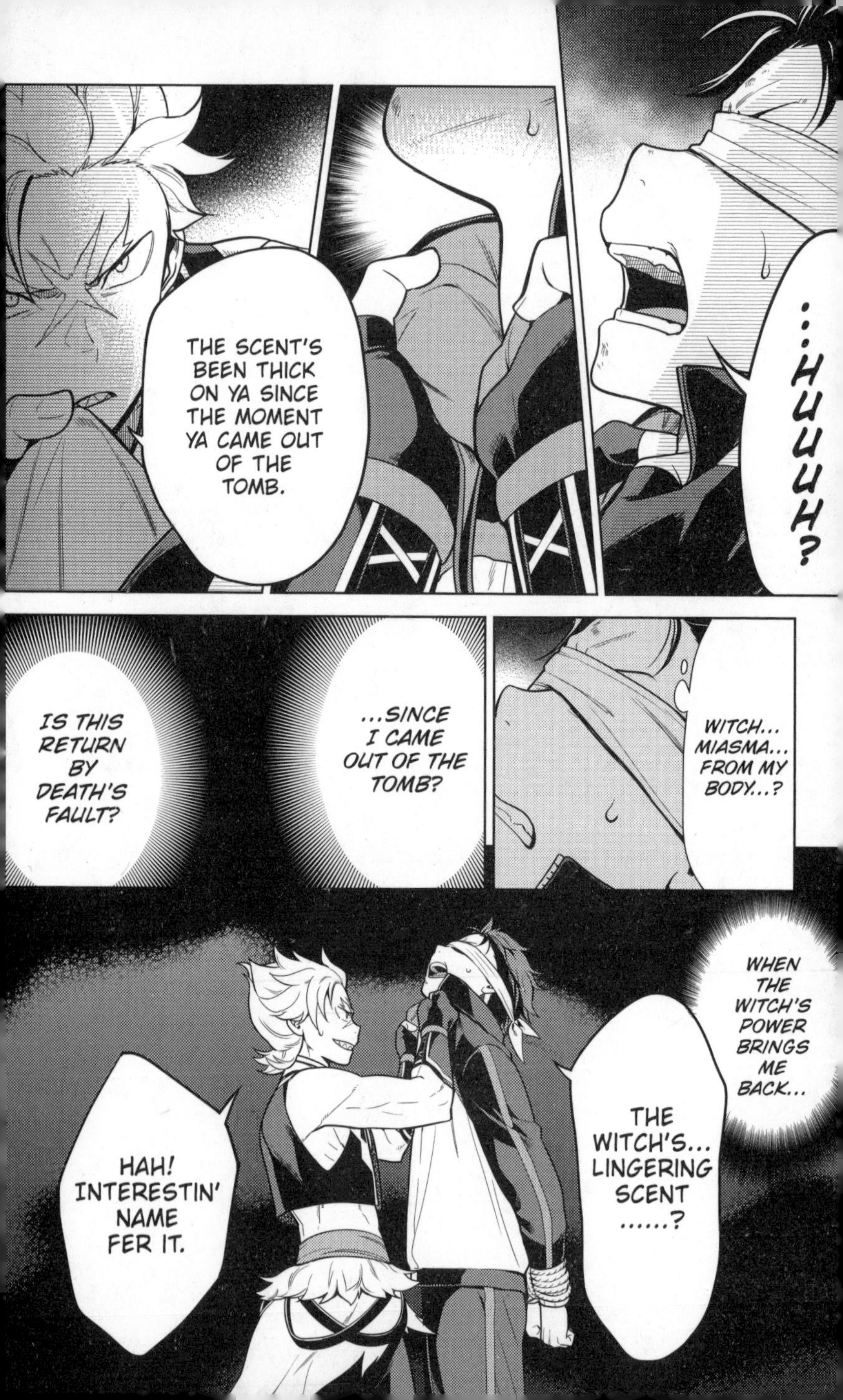
...HUUUH?
THE SCENT'S BEEN THICK ON YA SINCE THE MOMENT YA CAME OUT OF THE TOMB.
WITCH... MIASMA... FROM MY BODY...?
...SINCE I CAME OUT OF THE TOMB?
IS THIS RETURN BY DEATH'S FAULT?
WHEN THE WITCH'S POWER BRINGS ME BACK...
THE WITCH'S... LINGERING SCENT ......?
HAH! INTERESTIN' NAME FER IT.

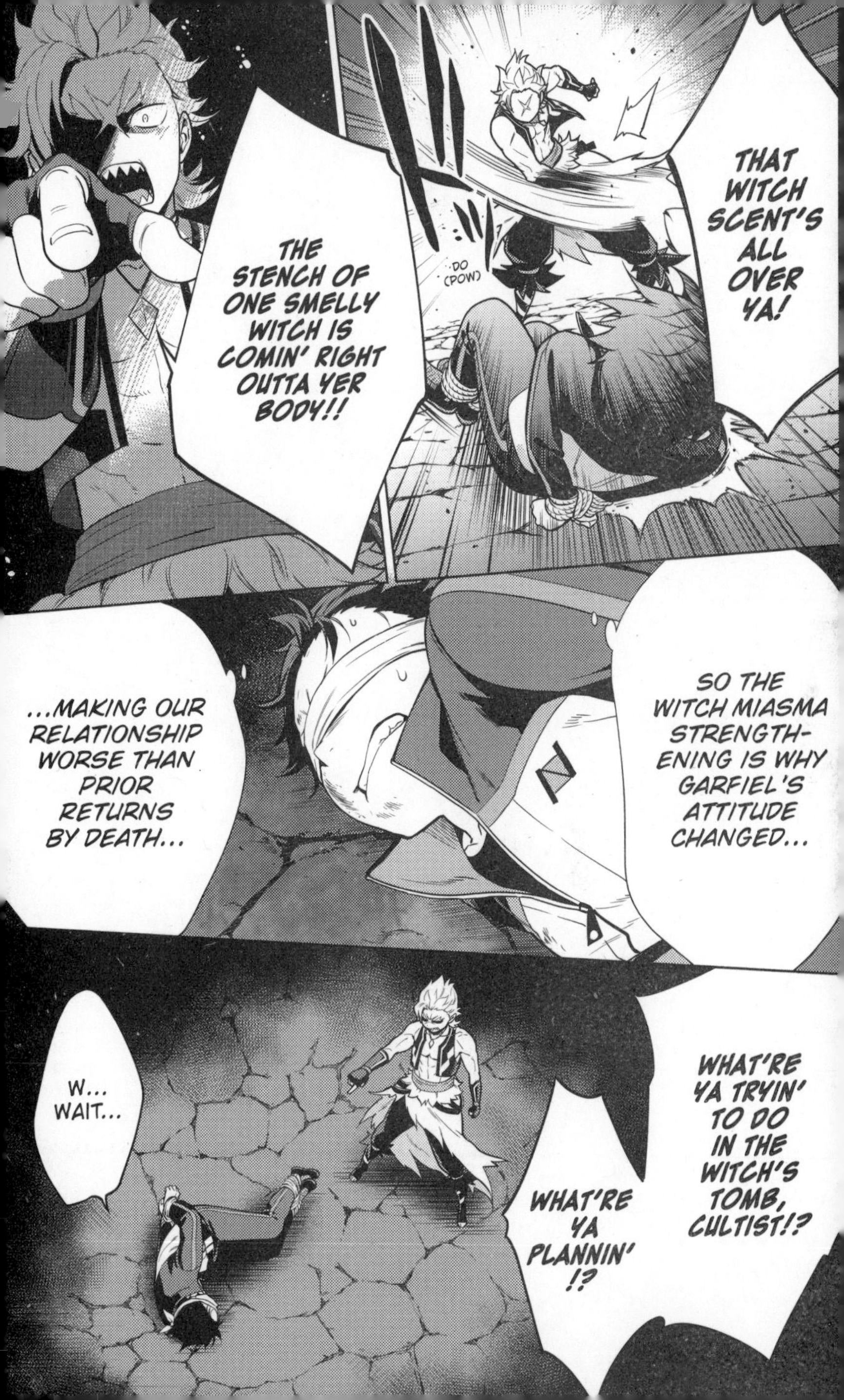
THAT WITCH SCENT'S ALL OVER YA!
DO (POW)
THE STENCH OF ONE SMELLY WITCH IS COMIN' RIGHT OUTTA YER BODY!!
SO THE WITCH MIASMA STRENGTH-ENING IS WHY GARFIEL'S ATTITUDE CHANGED...
...MAKING OUR RELATIONSHIP WORSE THAN PRIOR RETURNS BY DEATH...
WHAT'RE YA TRYIN' TO DO IN THE WITCH'S TOMB, CULTIST!?
WHAT'RE YA PLANNIN' !?
W... WAIT...

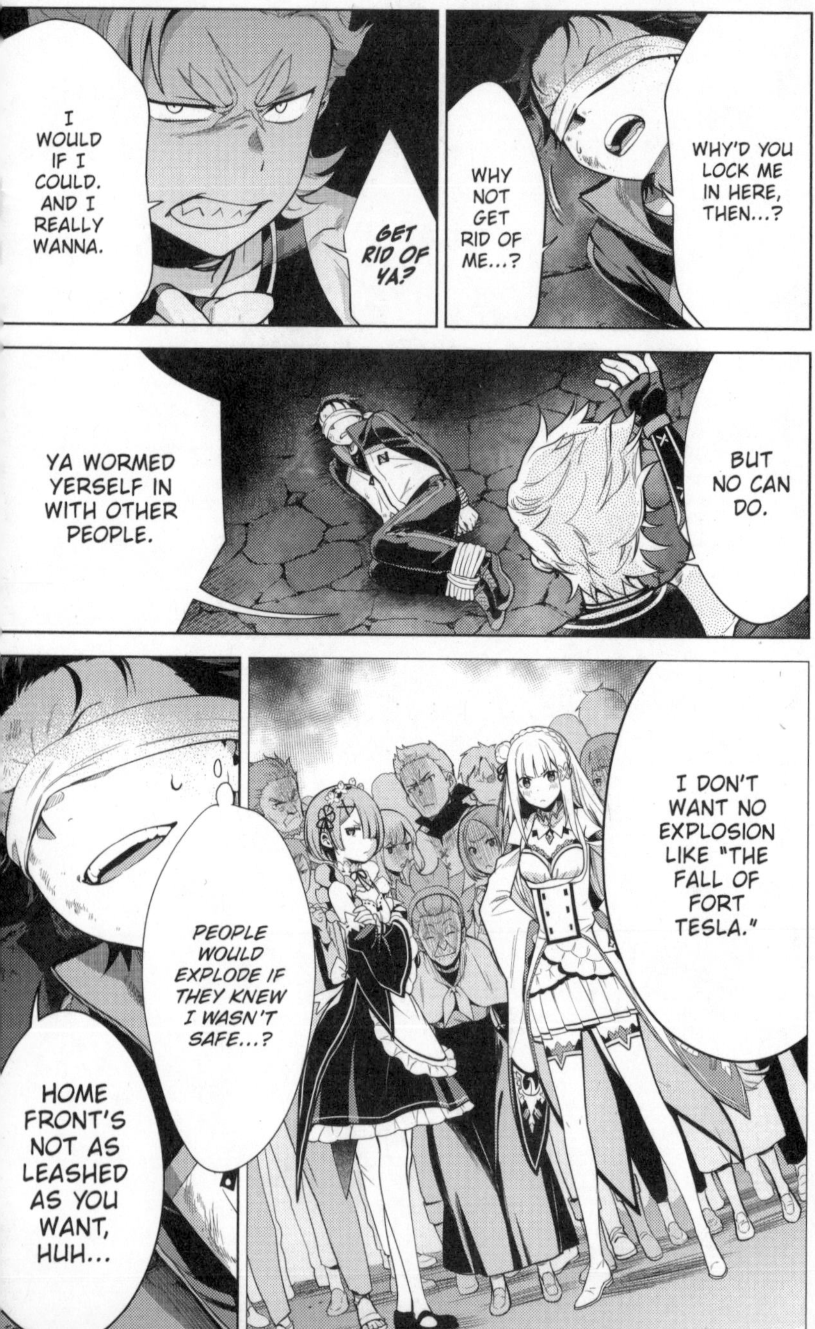
WHY'D YOU LOCK ME IN HERE, THEN...?
WHY NOT GET RID OF ME...?
GET RID OF YA?
I WOULD IF I COULD. AND I REALLY WANNA.
BUT NO CAN DO.
YA WORMED YERSELF IN WITH OTHER PEOPLE.
I DON'T WANT NO EXPLOSION LIKE "THE FALL OF FORT TESLA."
PEOPLE WOULD EXPLODE IF THEY KNEW I WASN'T SAFE...?
HOME FRONT'S NOT AS LEASHED AS YOU WANT, HUH...

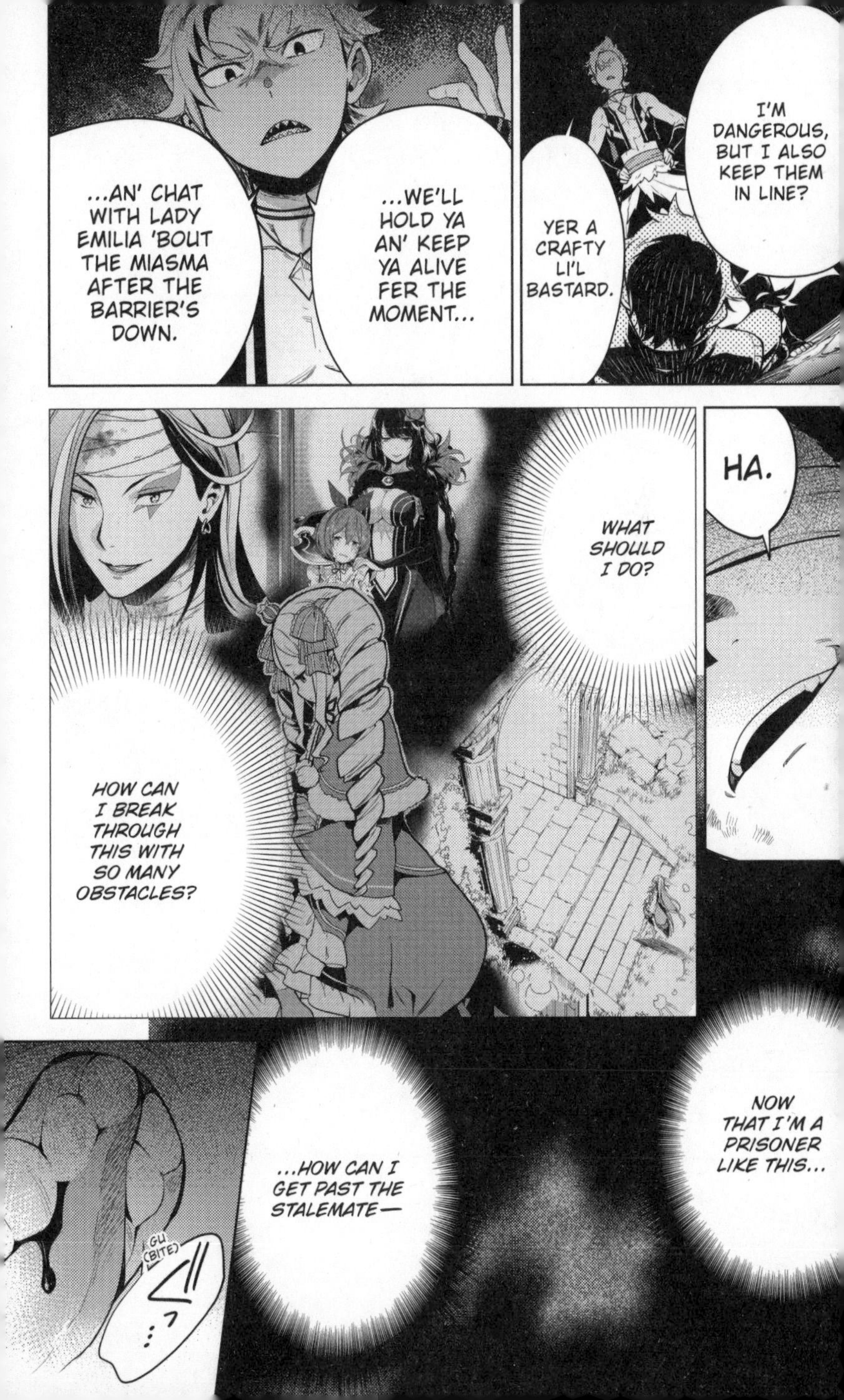
I'M DANGEROUS, BUT I ALSO KEEP THEM IN LINE?
YER A CRAFTY LI'L BASTARD.
...WE'LL HOLD YA AN' KEEP YA ALIVE FER THE MOMENT...
...AN' CHAT WITH LADY EMILIA 'BOUT THE MIASMA AFTER THE BARRIER'S DOWN.
HA.
WHAT SHOULD I DO?
HOW CAN I BREAK THROUGH THIS WITH SO MANY OBSTACLES?
NOW THAT I'M A PRISONER LIKE THIS...
...HOW CAN I GET PAST THE STALEMATE—
GU (BITE)
...?

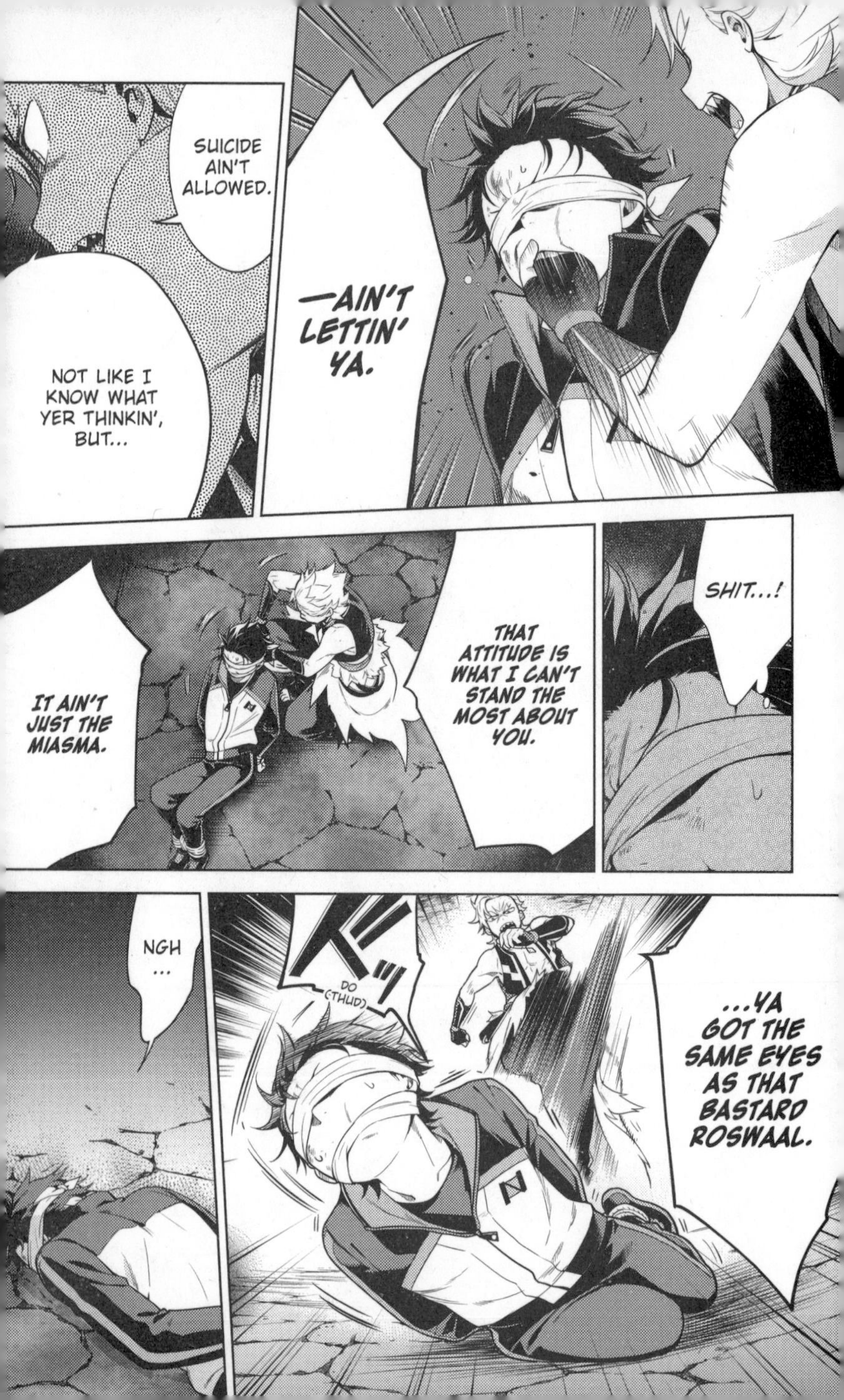
—AIN'T LETTIN' YA.
SUICIDE AIN'T ALLOWED.
NOT LIKE I KNOW WHAT YER THINKIN', BUT...
SHIT...!
THAT ATTITUDE IS WHAT I CAN'T STAND THE MOST ABOUT YOU.
IT AIN'T JUST THE MIASMA.
...YA GOT THE SAME EYES AS THAT BASTARD ROSWAAL.
DO (THUD)
NGH ...

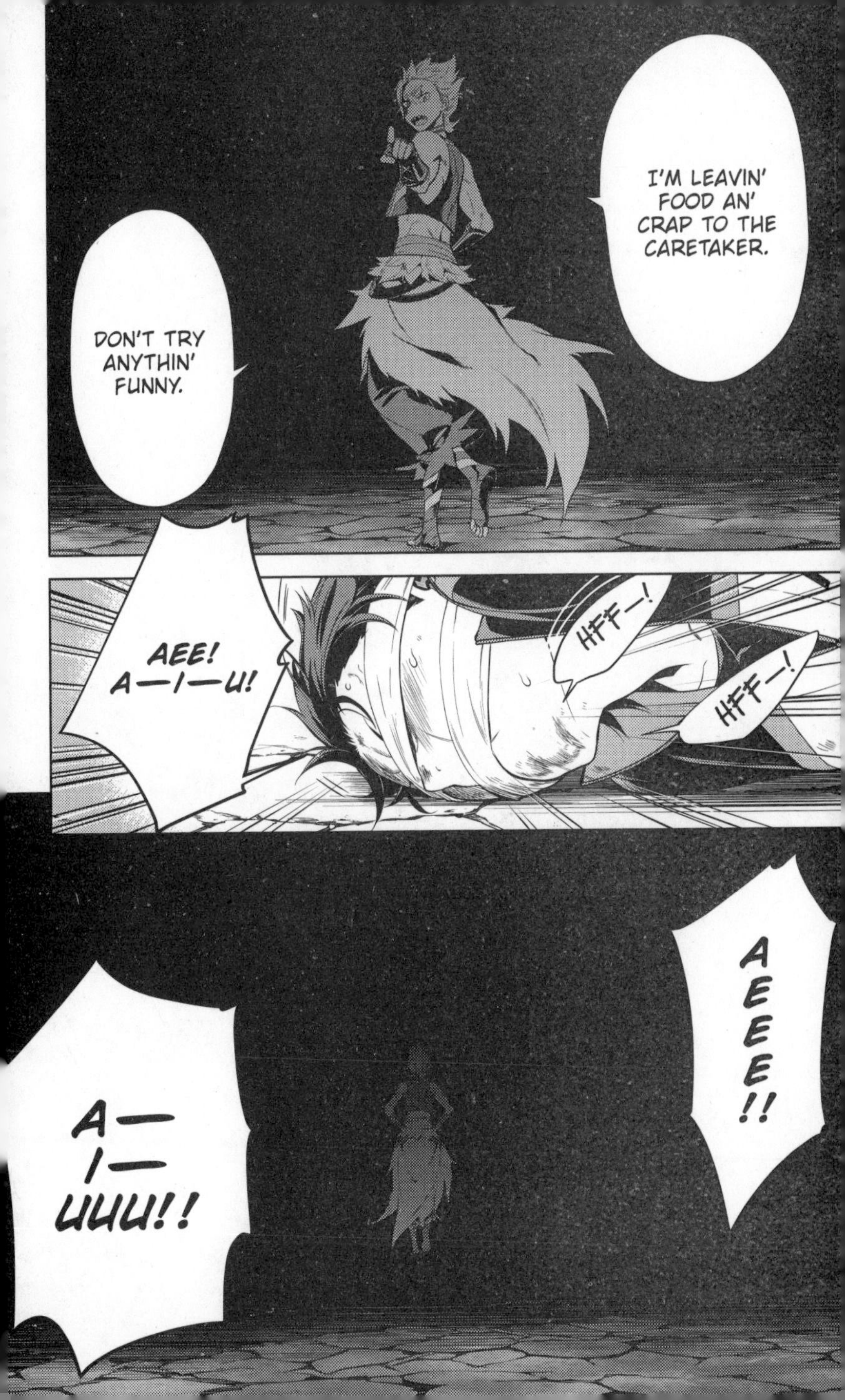
I'M LEAVIN' FOOD AN' CRAP TO THE CARETAKER.
DON'T TRY ANYTHIN' FUNNY.
HFF—!
HFF—!
AEE! A—I—U!
AEEE!!
A— I— UUU!!

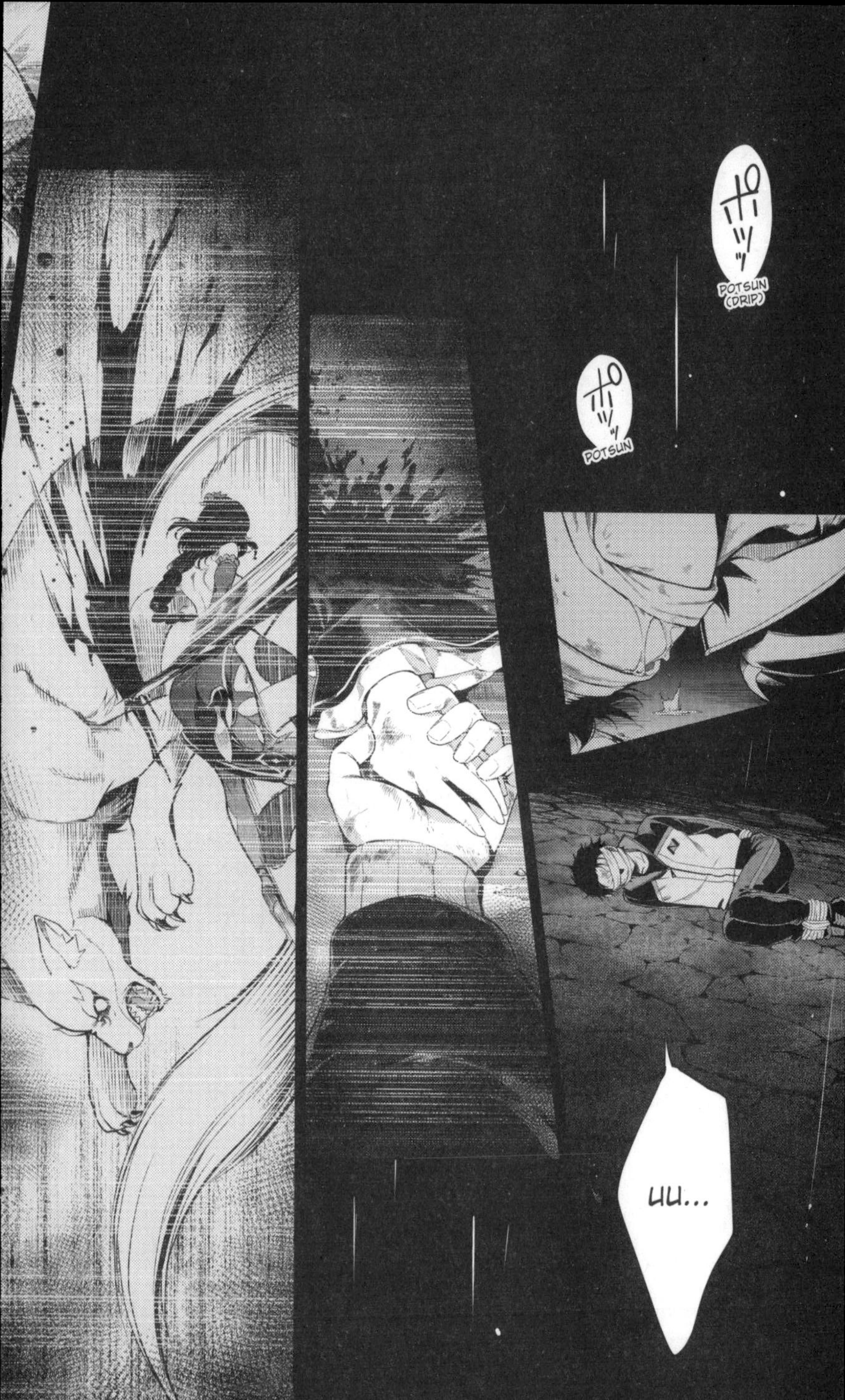
POTSUN
(DRIP)
POTSUN
UU...

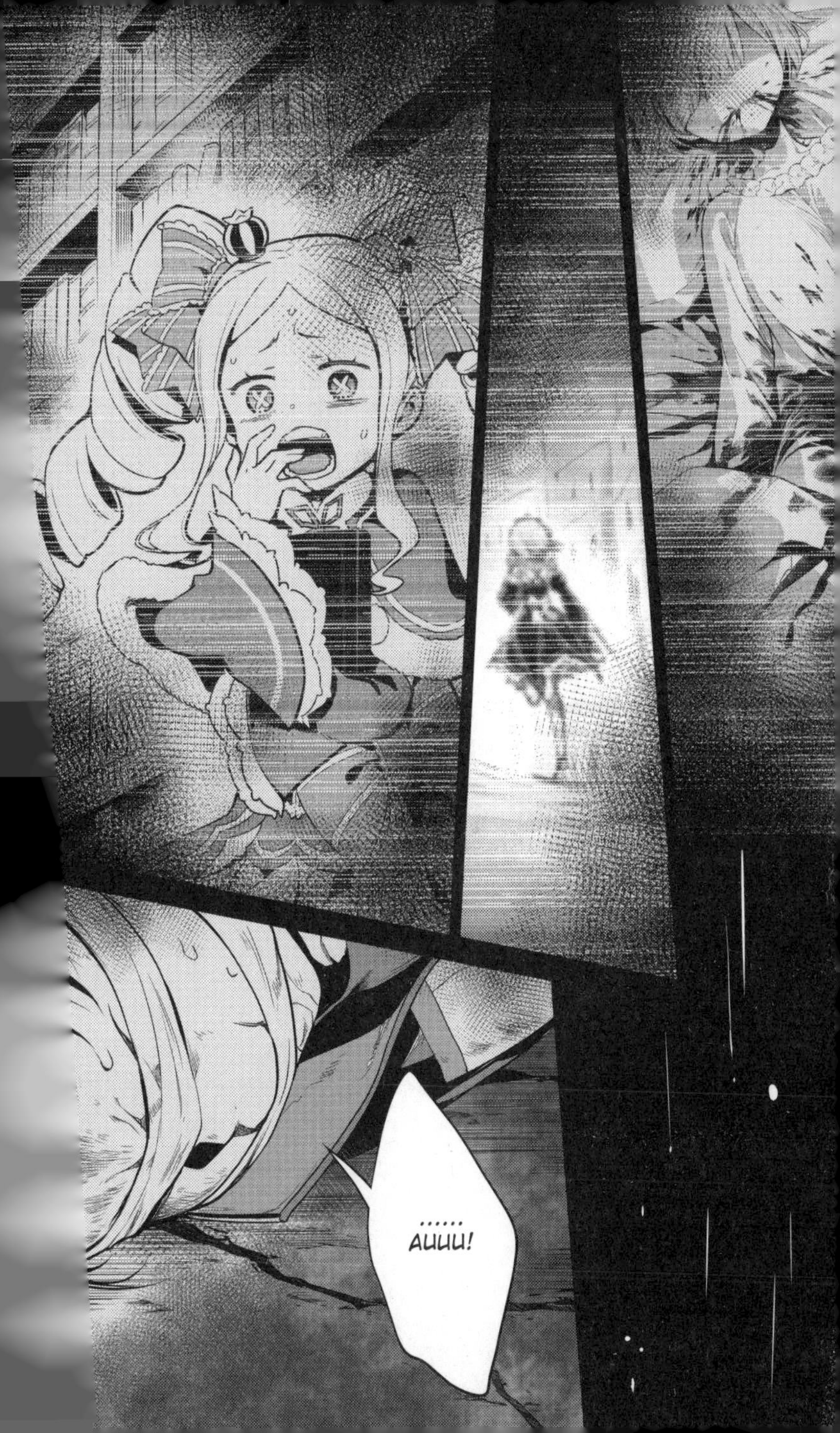

......
AUUU!

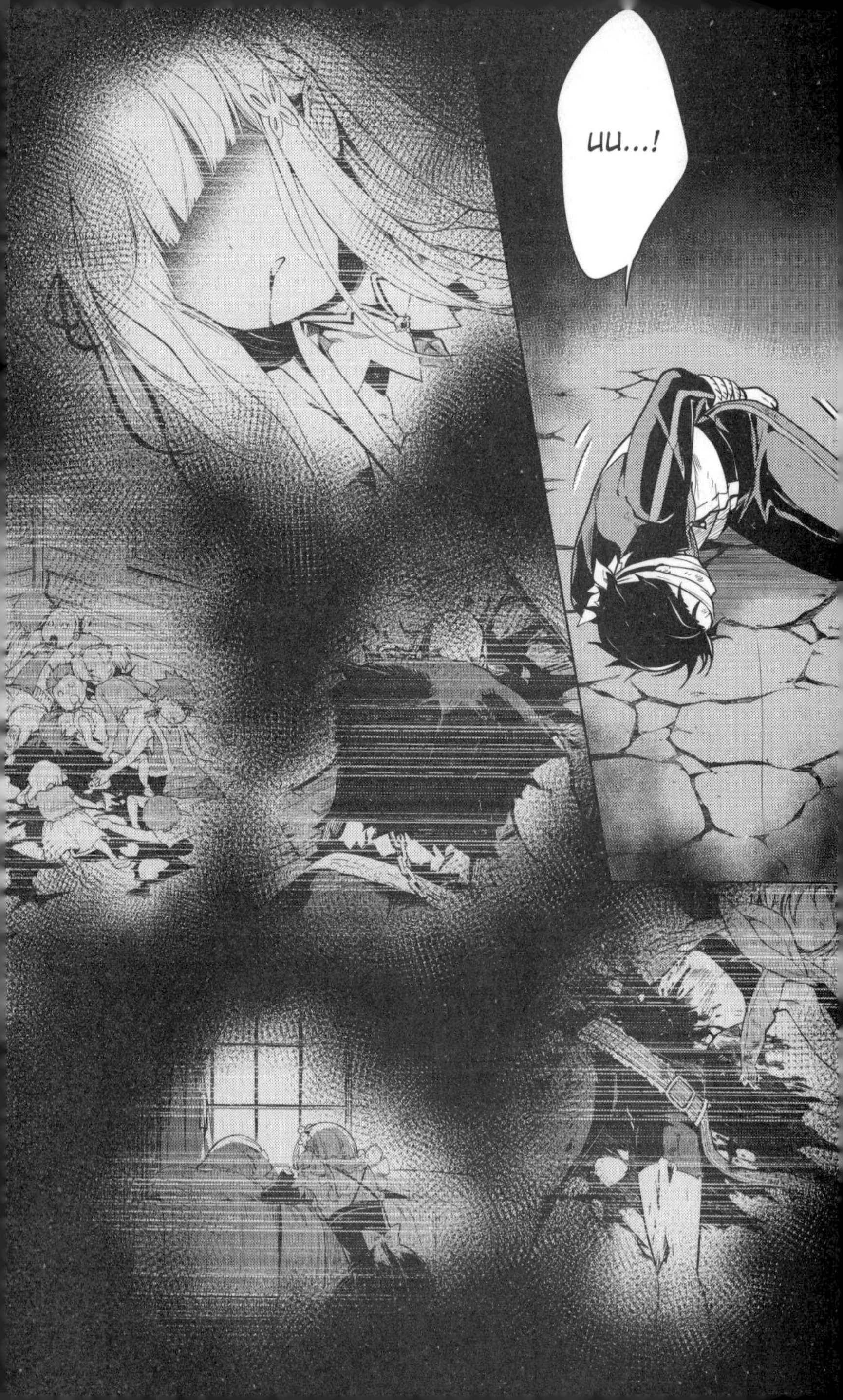
UU...!

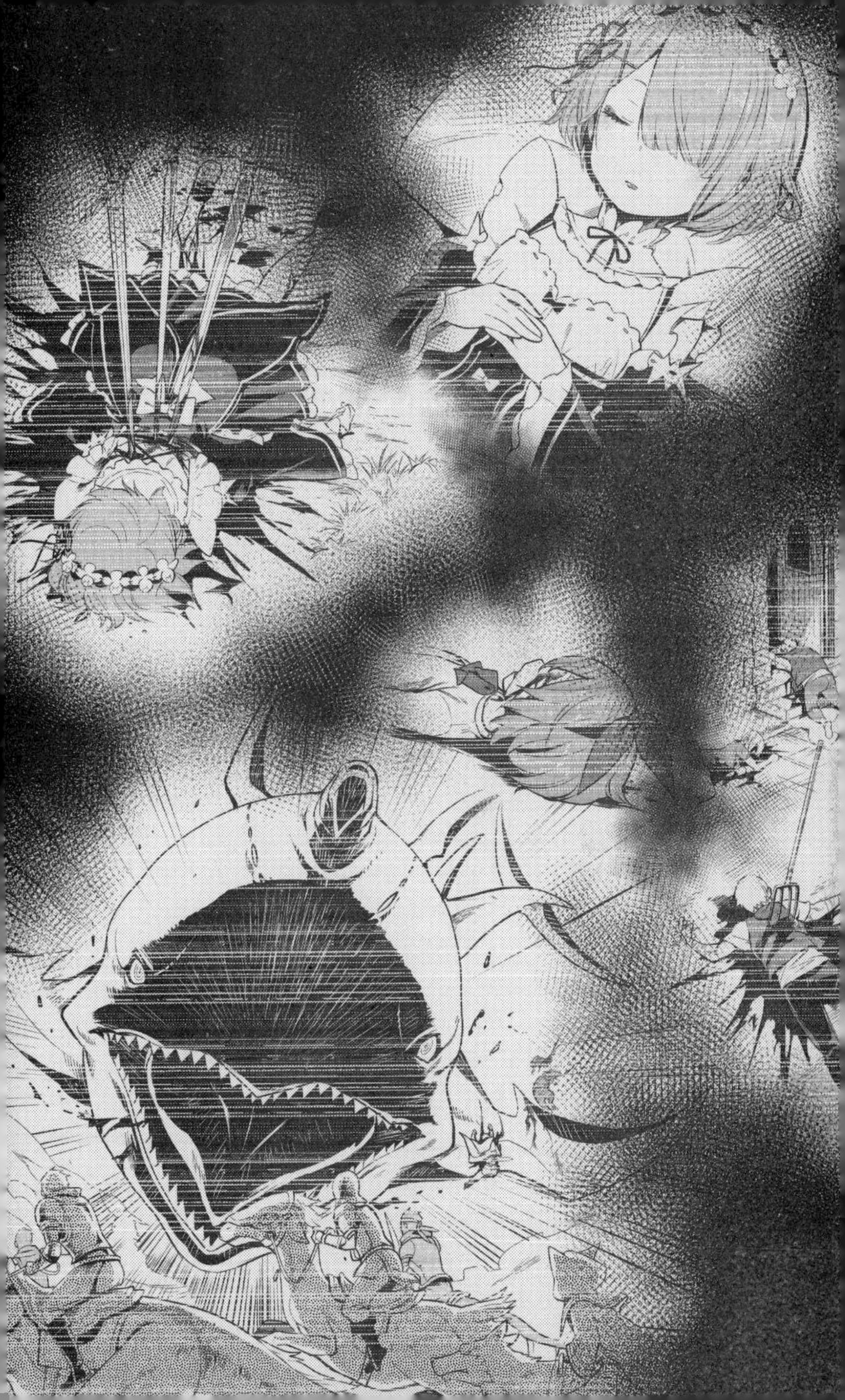

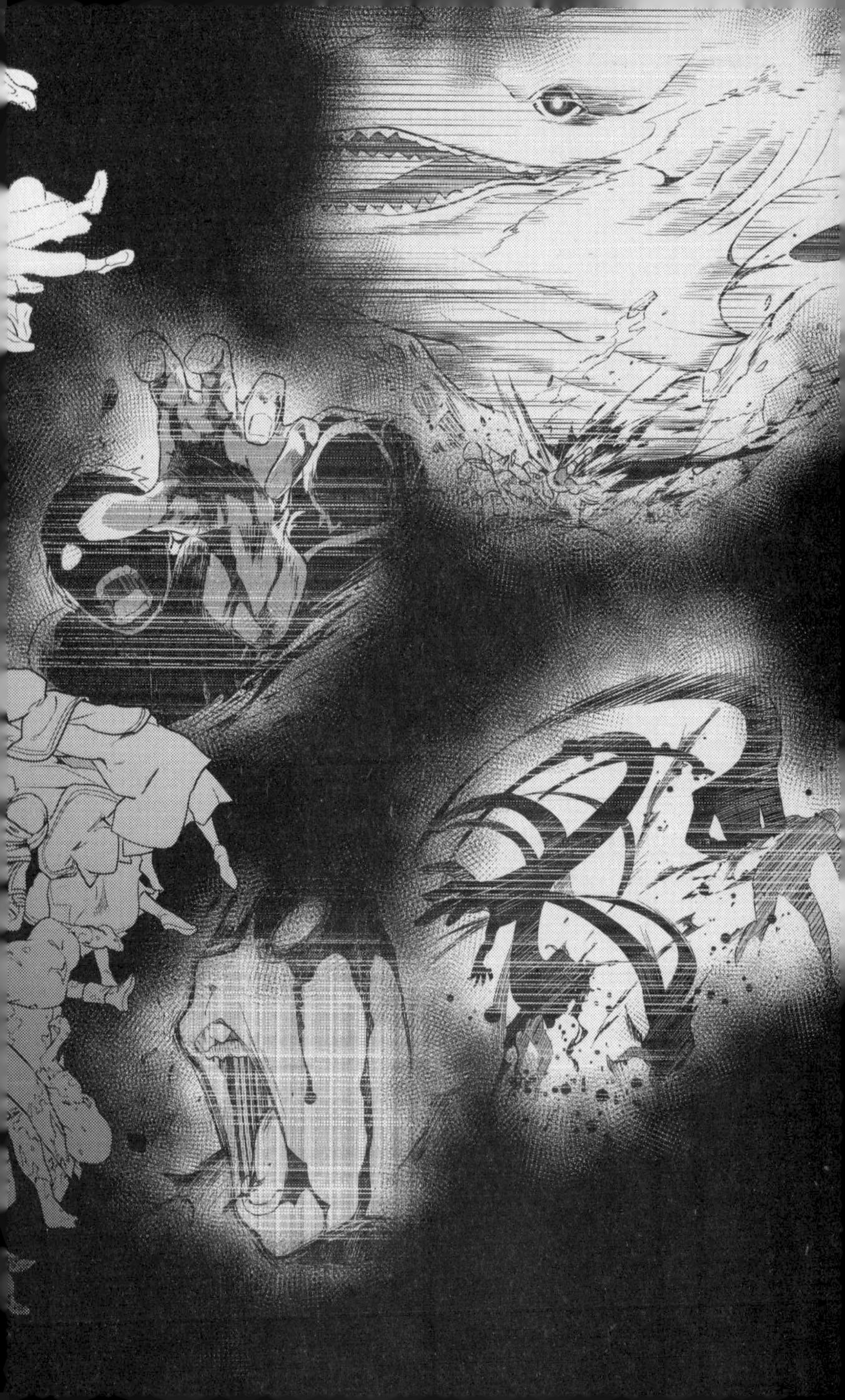

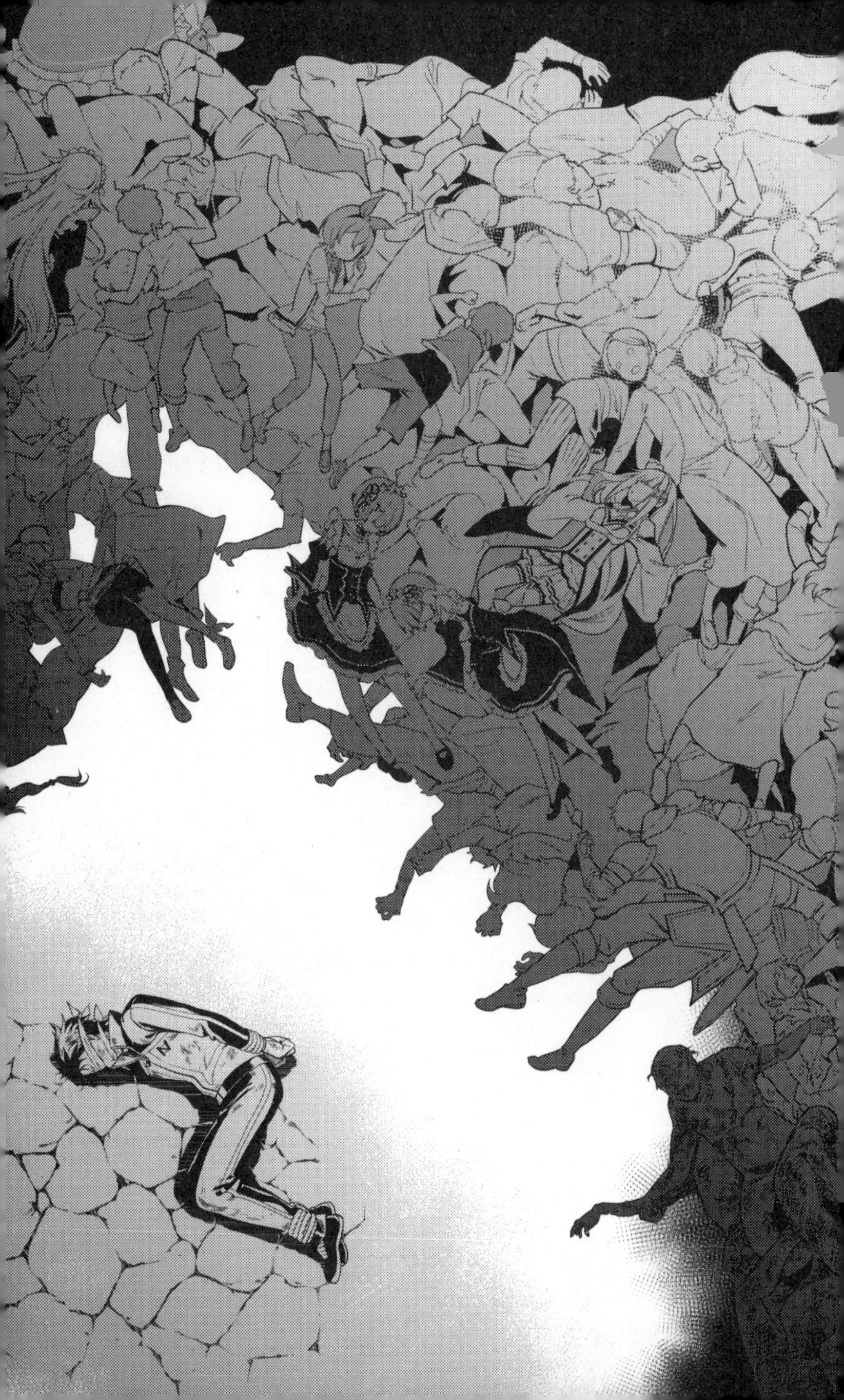

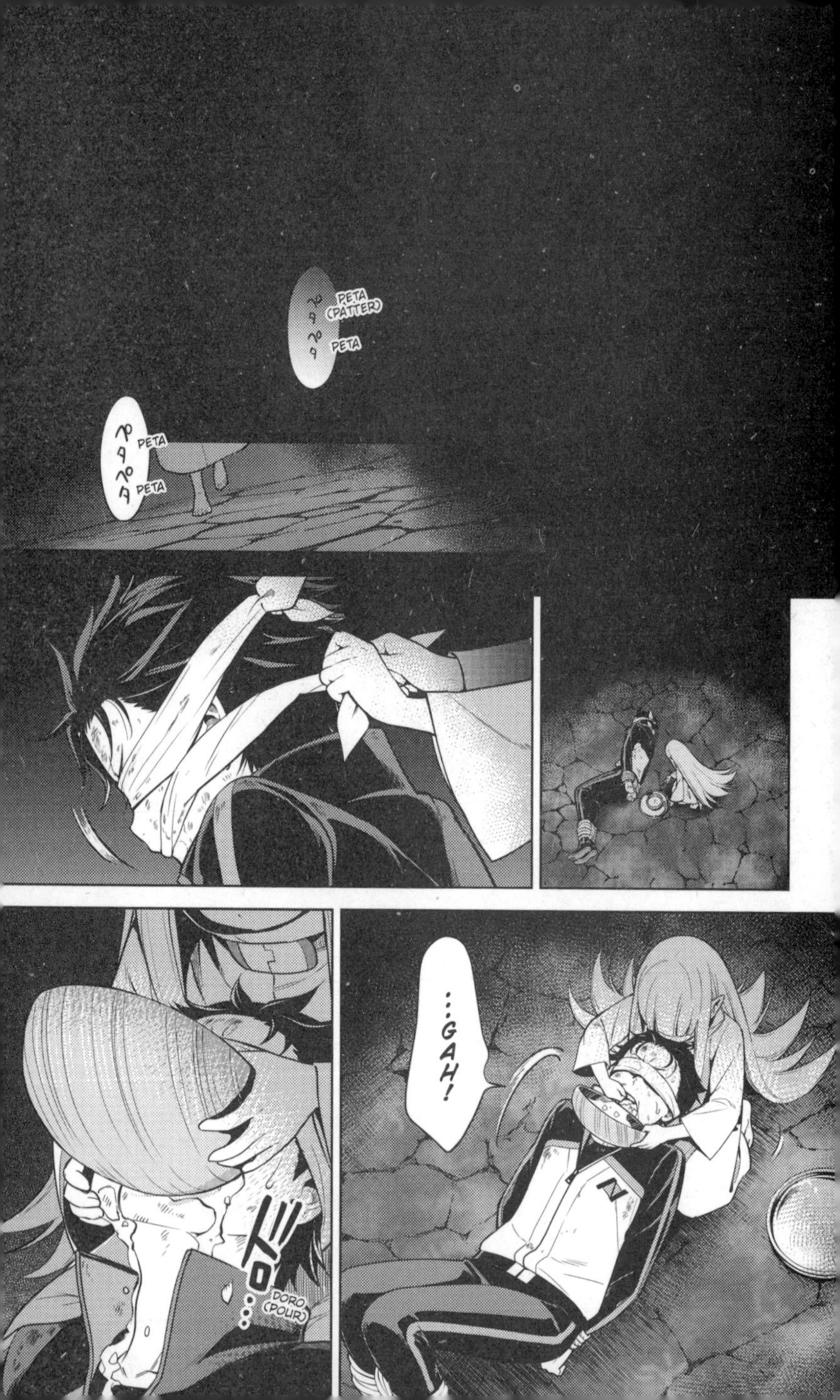
PETA (PATTER) PETA
PETA PETA
...GAH!
DORO (POUR)

KOFF!

KOFF!

GOSO
(RUSTLE)

—JUST...

PETA

PETA

PETA

PETA

...WHEN
AND
HOW CAN
I DIE...?

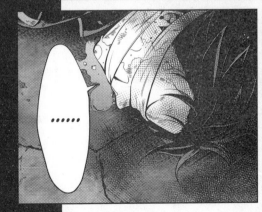

......

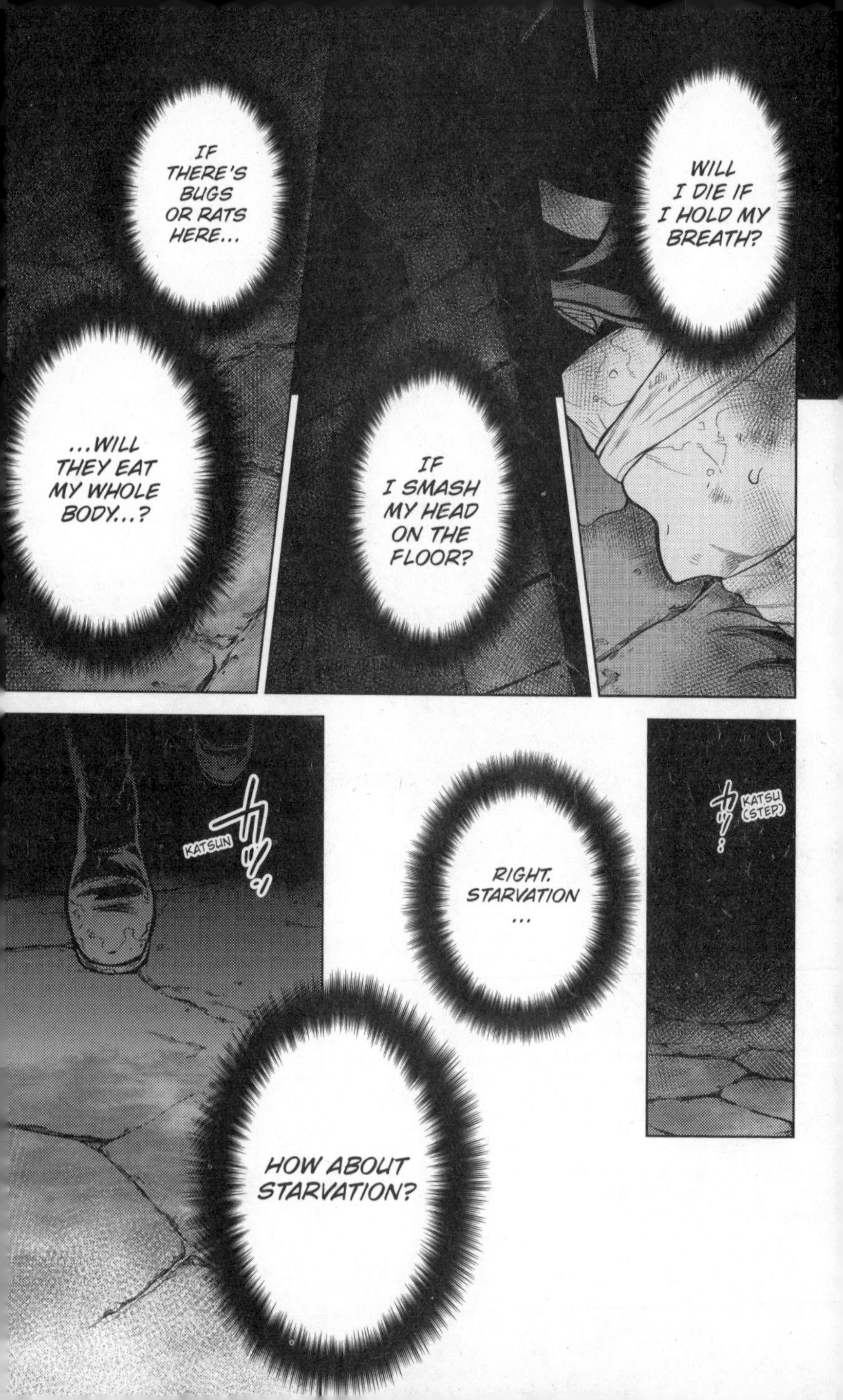
WILL I DIE IF I HOLD MY BREATH?
IF I SMASH MY HEAD ON THE FLOOR?
IF THERE'S BUGS OR RATS HERE...
...WILL THEY EAT MY WHOLE BODY...?
KATSU (STEP)
RIGHT. STARVATION ...
KATSUN
HOW ABOUT STARVATION?

CAN I DIE IF I REFUSE FOOD?

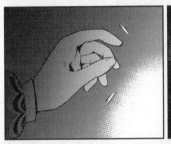

ZA (JERK)

HI! HI!

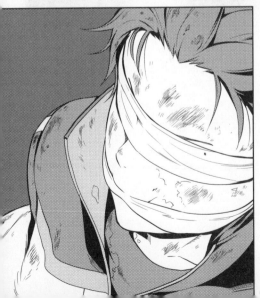

...I IMAGINED YOU WOULD BE IN A TERRIBLE STATE, BUT THIS IS EVEN GRAVER THAN I PRESUMED.

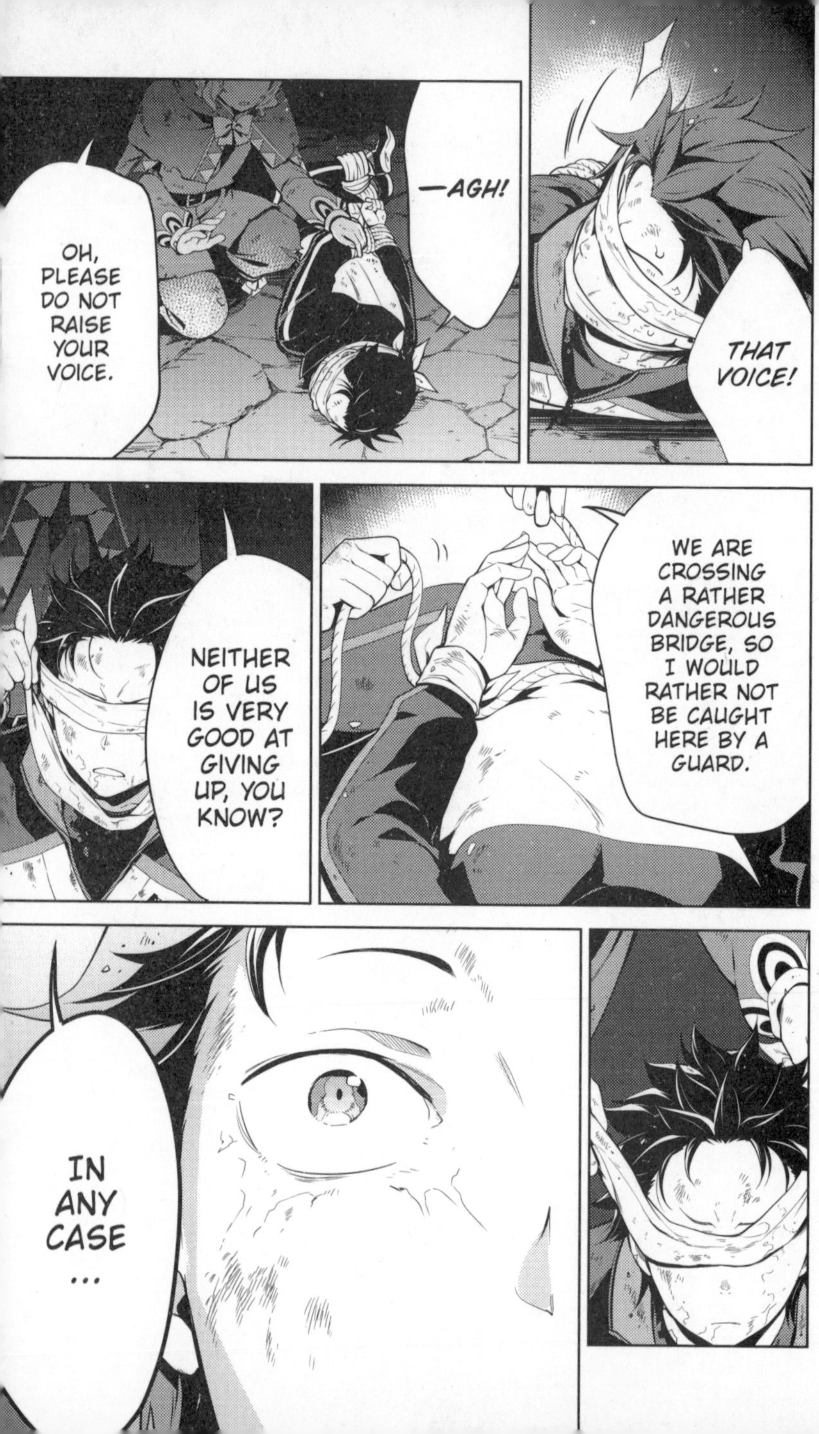
THAT VOICE!
—AGH!
OH, PLEASE DO NOT RAISE YOUR VOICE.
WE ARE CROSSING A RATHER DANGEROUS BRIDGE, SO I WOULD RATHER NOT BE CAUGHT HERE BY A GUARD.
NEITHER OF US IS VERY GOOD AT GIVING UP, YOU KNOW?
IN ANY CASE ...

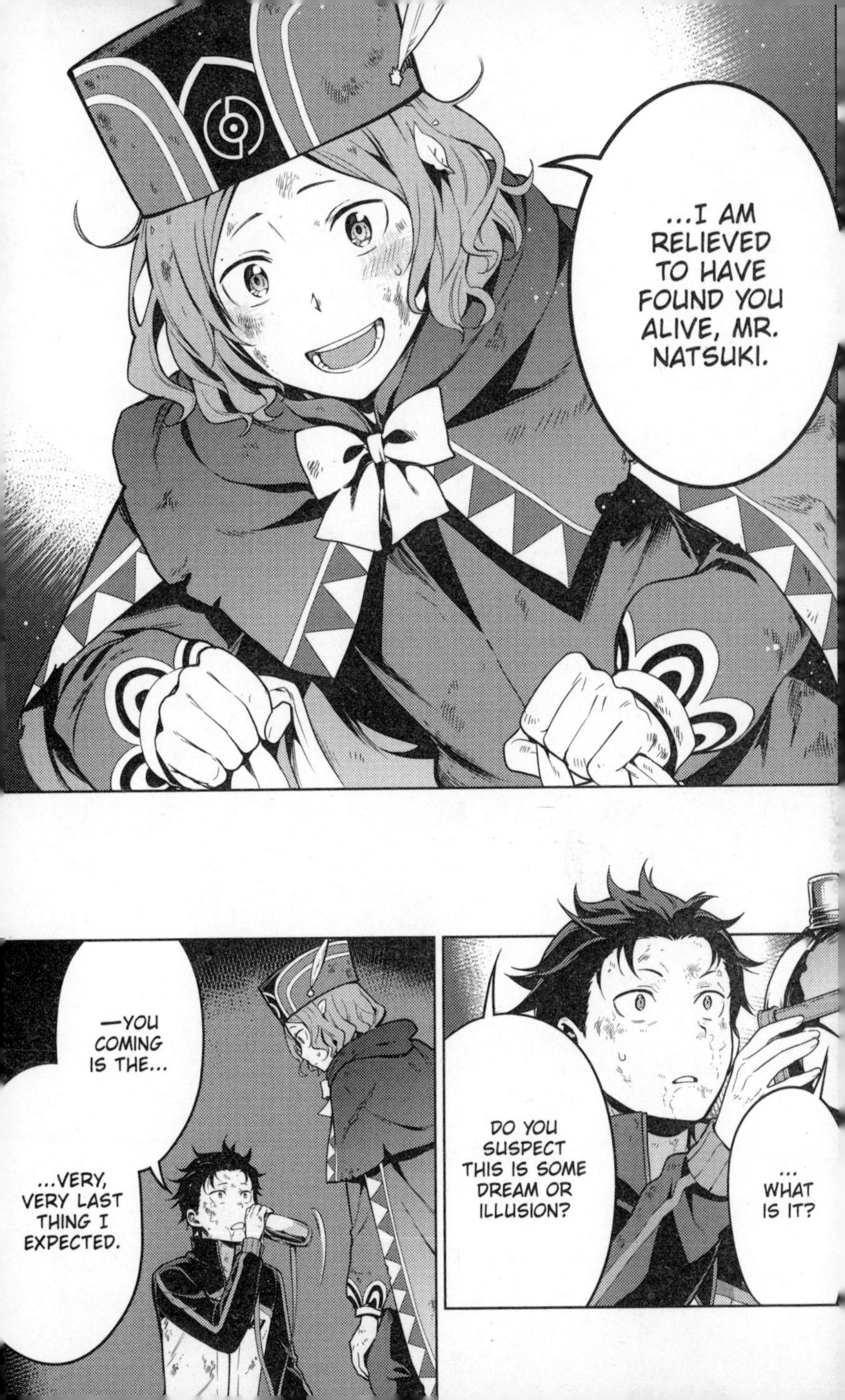
...I AM RELIEVED TO HAVE FOUND YOU ALIVE, MR. NATSUKI.
... WHAT IS IT?
DO YOU SUSPECT THIS IS SOME DREAM OR ILLUSION?
—YOU COMING IS THE...
...VERY, VERY LAST THING I EXPECTED.

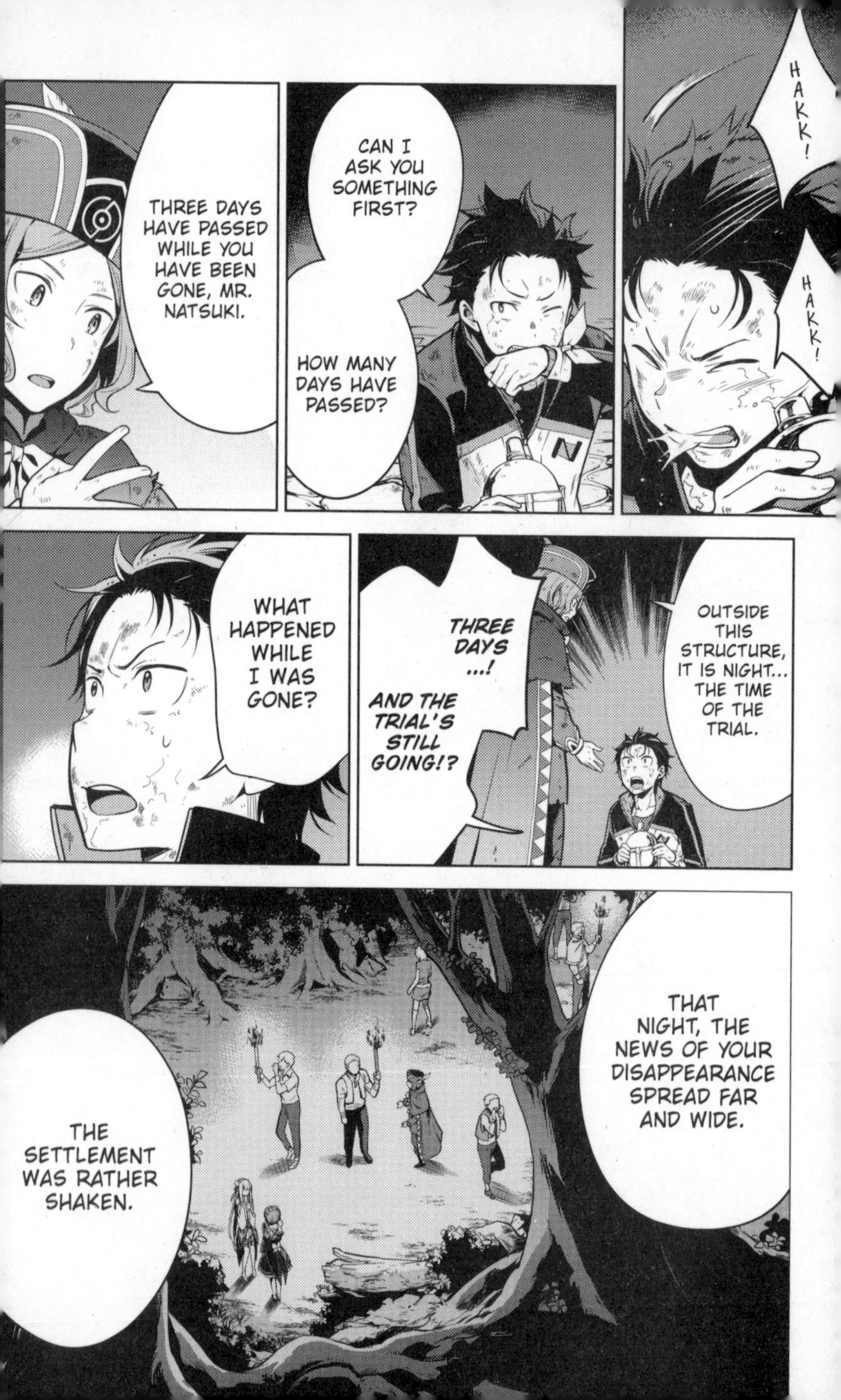
HAKK!
HAKK!
CAN I ASK YOU SOMETHING FIRST?
HOW MANY DAYS HAVE PASSED?
THREE DAYS HAVE PASSED WHILE YOU HAVE BEEN GONE, MR. NATSUKI.
OUTSIDE THIS STRUCTURE, IT IS NIGHT... THE TIME OF THE TRIAL.
THREE DAYS ...!
AND THE TRIAL'S STILL GOING!?
WHAT HAPPENED WHILE I WAS GONE?
THAT NIGHT, THE NEWS OF YOUR DISAPPEARANCE SPREAD FAR AND WIDE.
THE SETTLEMENT WAS RATHER SHAKEN.

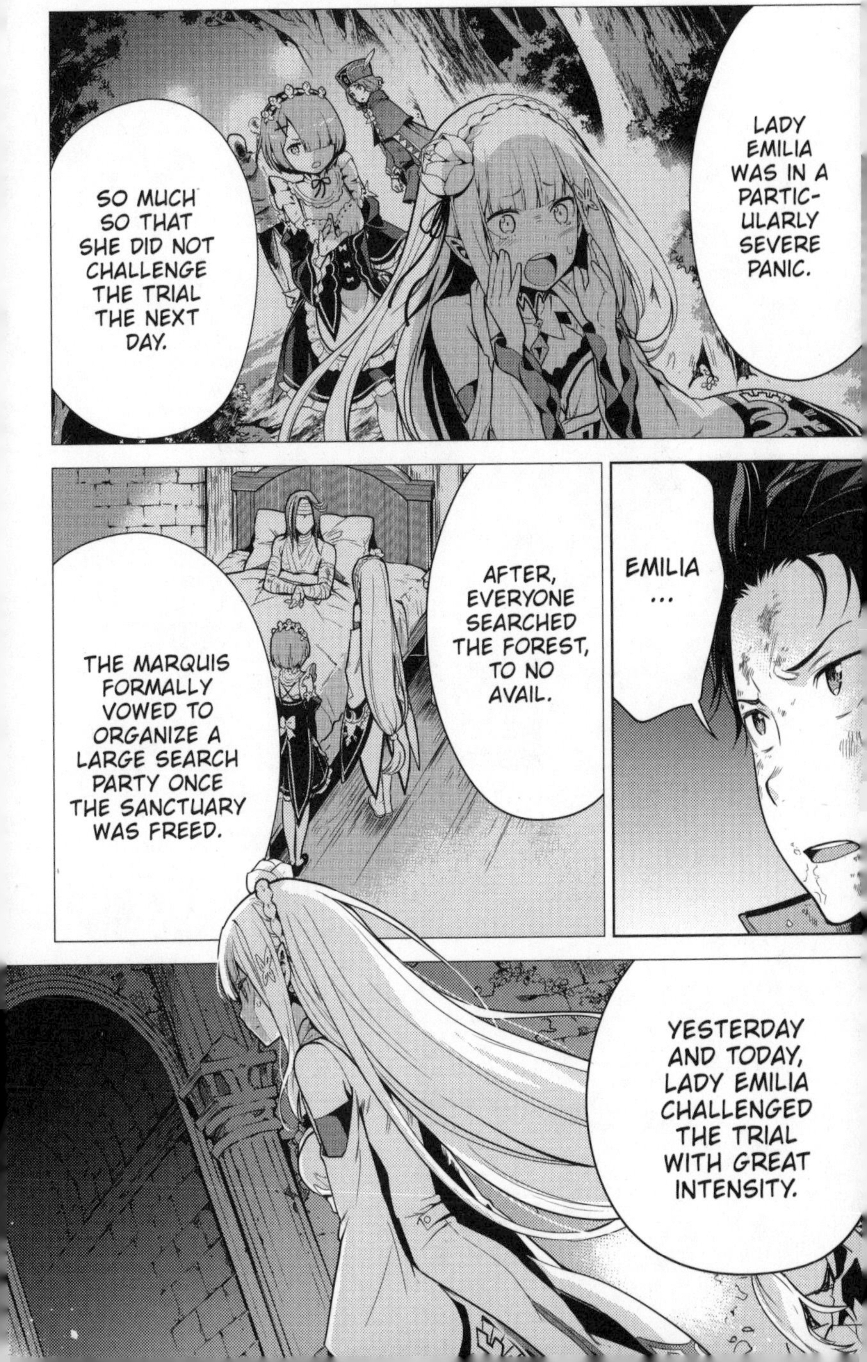
LADY EMILIA WAS IN A PARTICULARLY SEVERE PANIC.
SO MUCH SO THAT SHE DID NOT CHALLENGE THE TRIAL THE NEXT DAY.
EMILIA...
AFTER, EVERYONE SEARCHED THE FOREST, TO NO AVAIL.
THE MARQUIS FORMALLY VOWED TO ORGANIZE A LARGE SEARCH PARTY ONCE THE SANCTUARY WAS FREED.
YESTERDAY AND TODAY, LADY EMILIA CHALLENGED THE TRIAL WITH GREAT INTENSITY.

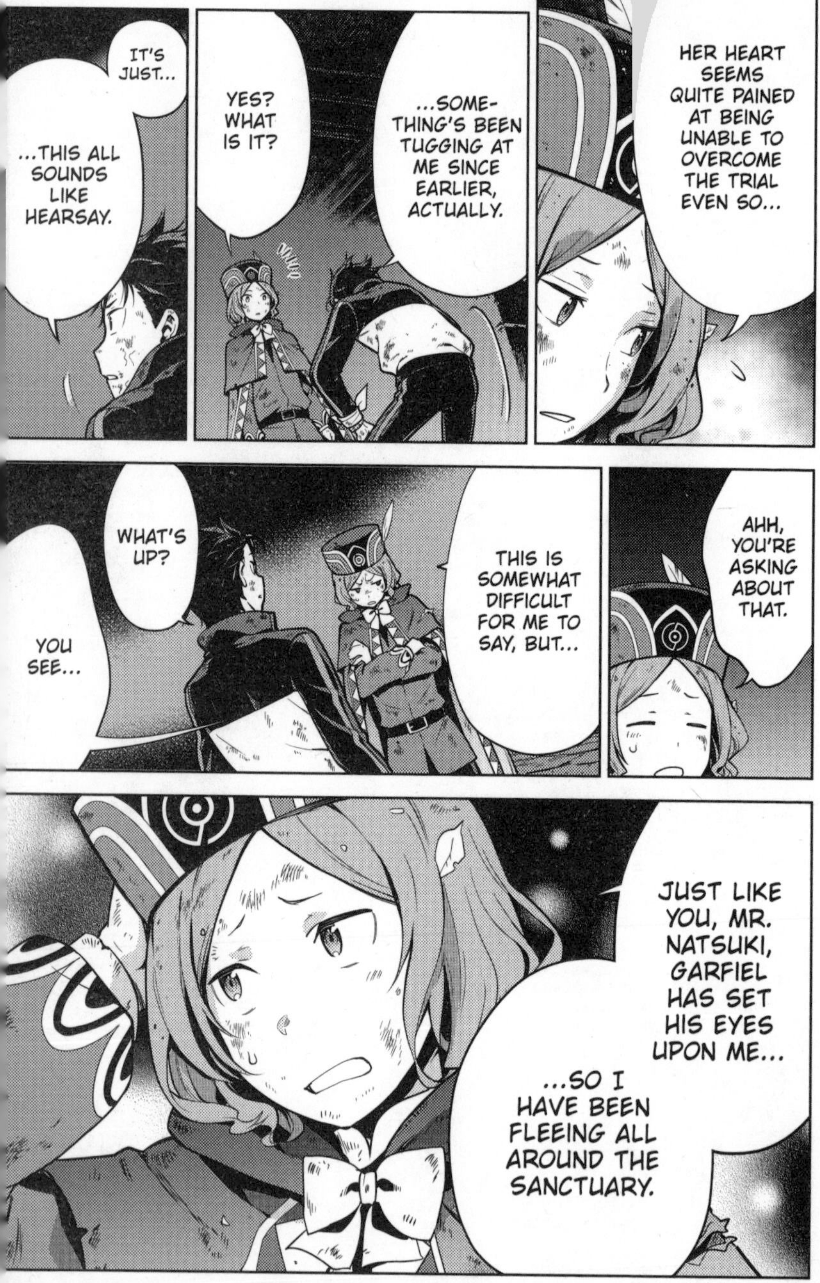
HER HEART SEEMS QUITE PAINED AT BEING UNABLE TO OVERCOME THE TRIAL EVEN SO...
...SOME-THING'S BEEN TUGGING AT ME SINCE EARLIER, ACTUALLY.
YES? WHAT IS IT?
IT'S JUST...
...THIS ALL SOUNDS LIKE HEARSAY.
AHH, YOU'RE ASKING ABOUT THAT.
THIS IS SOMEWHAT DIFFICULT FOR ME TO SAY, BUT...
WHAT'S UP?
YOU SEE...
JUST LIKE YOU, MR. NATSUKI, GARFIEL HAS SET HIS EYES UPON ME...
...SO I HAVE BEEN FLEEING ALL AROUND THE SANCTUARY.

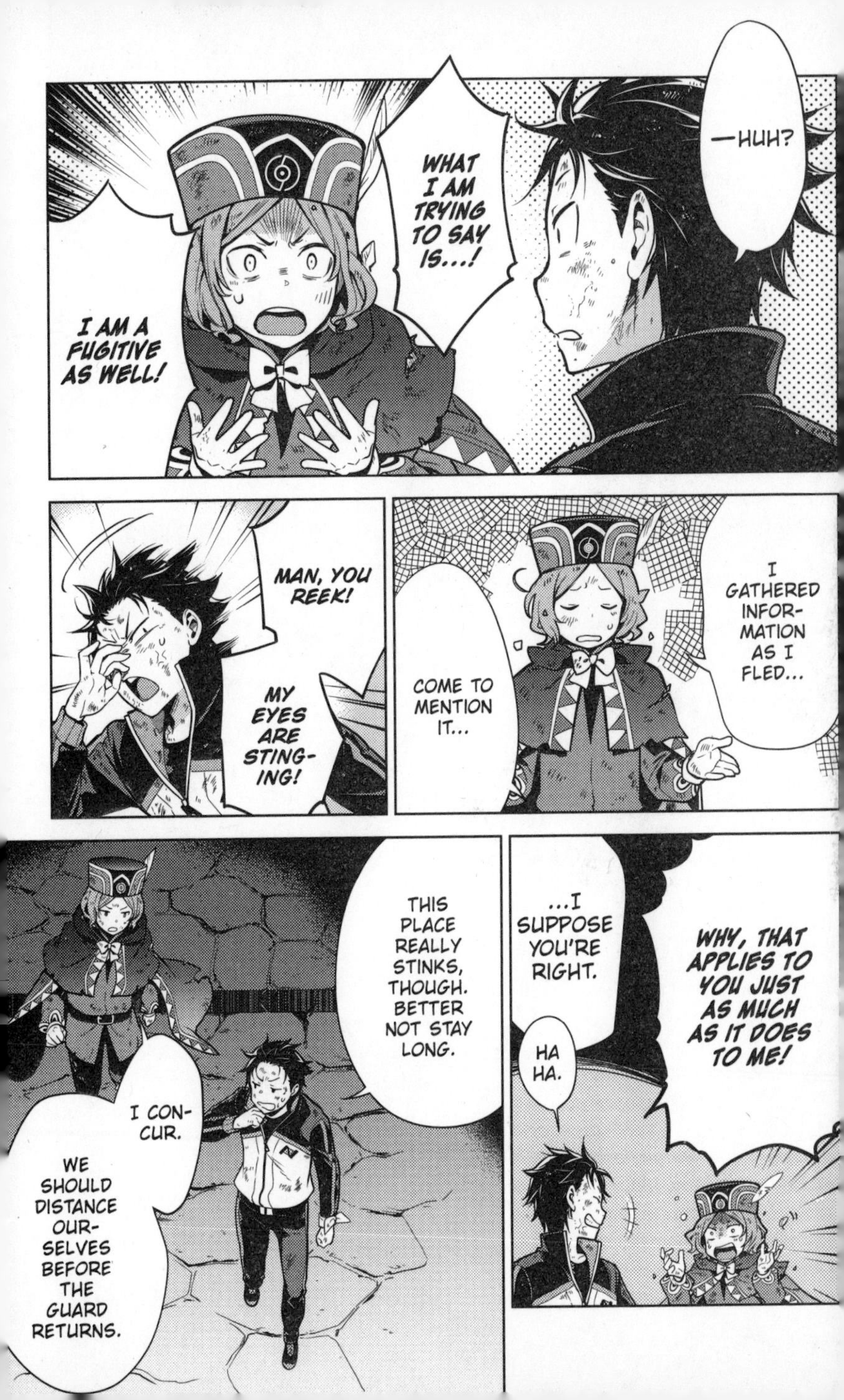
—HUH?
WHAT I AM TRYING TO SAY IS...!
I AM A FUGITIVE AS WELL!
I GATHERED INFOR-MATION AS I FLED...
COME TO MENTION IT...
MAN, YOU REEK!
MY EYES ARE STING-ING!
WHY, THAT APPLIES TO YOU JUST AS MUCH AS IT DOES TO ME!
...I SUPPOSE YOU'RE RIGHT.
HA HA.
THIS PLACE REALLY STINKS, THOUGH. BETTER NOT STAY LONG.
I CON-CUR.
WE SHOULD DISTANCE OUR-SELVES BEFORE THE GUARD RETURNS.

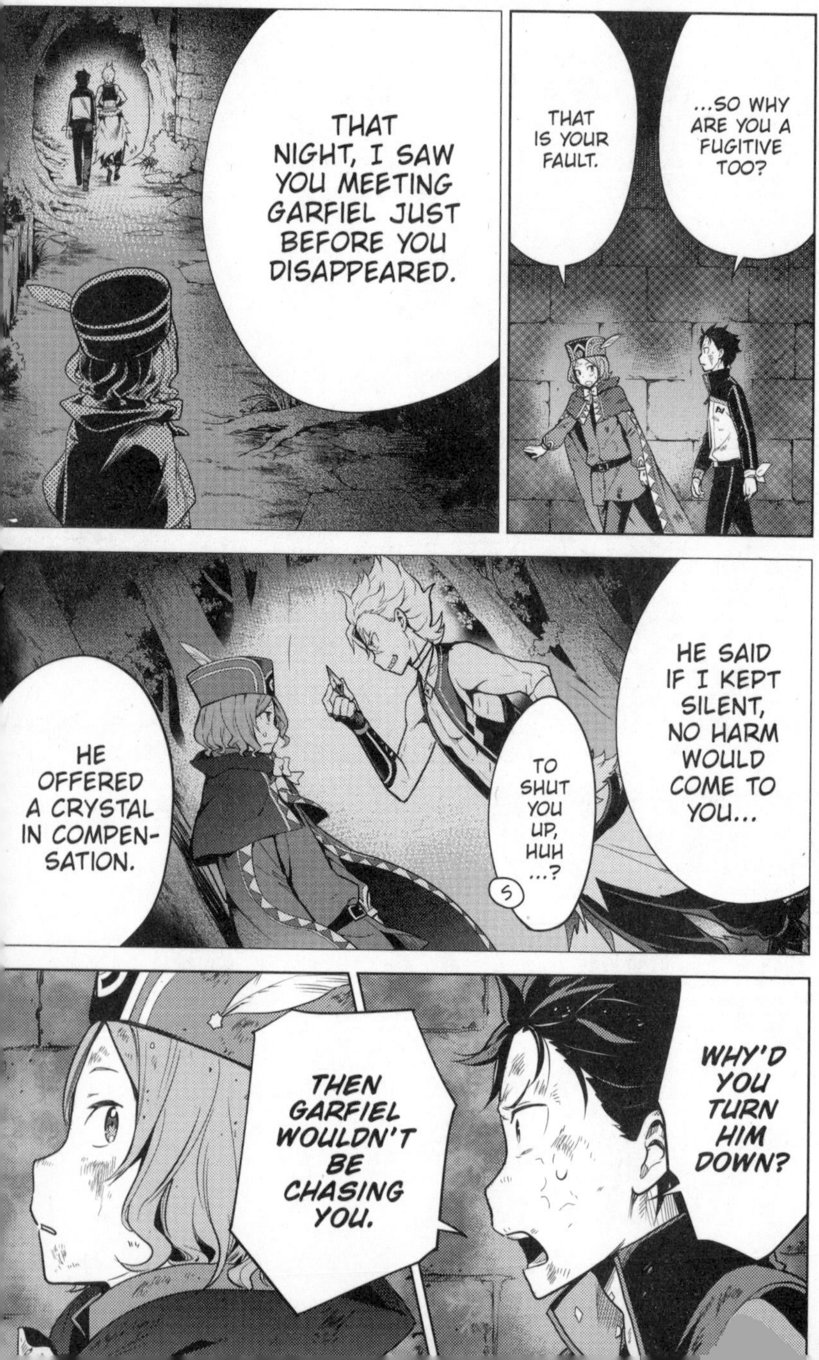
...SO WHY ARE YOU A FUGITIVE TOO?
THAT IS YOUR FAULT.
THAT NIGHT, I SAW YOU MEETING GARFIEL JUST BEFORE YOU DISAPPEARED.
HE SAID IF I KEPT SILENT, NO HARM WOULD COME TO YOU...
TO SHUT YOU UP, HUH ...?
S
HE OFFERED A CRYSTAL IN COMPEN-SATION.
WHY'D YOU TURN HIM DOWN?
THEN GARFIEL WOULDN'T BE CHASING YOU.

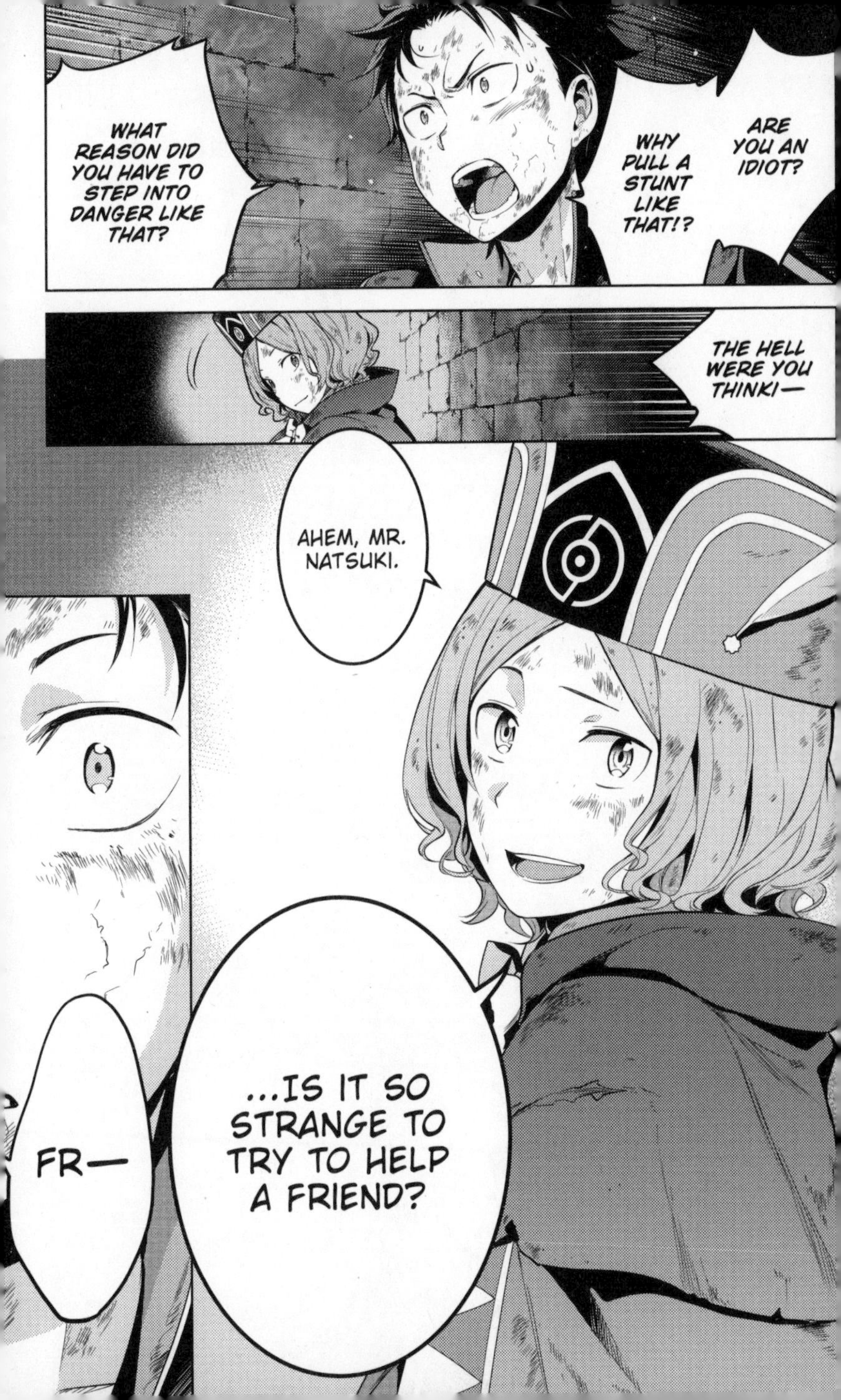
ARE YOU AN IDIOT?
WHY PULL A STUNT LIKE THAT!?
WHAT REASON DID YOU HAVE TO STEP INTO DANGER LIKE THAT?
THE HELL WERE YOU THINKI—
AHEM, MR. NATSUKI.
...IS IT SO STRANGE TO TRY TO HELP A FRIEND?
FR—

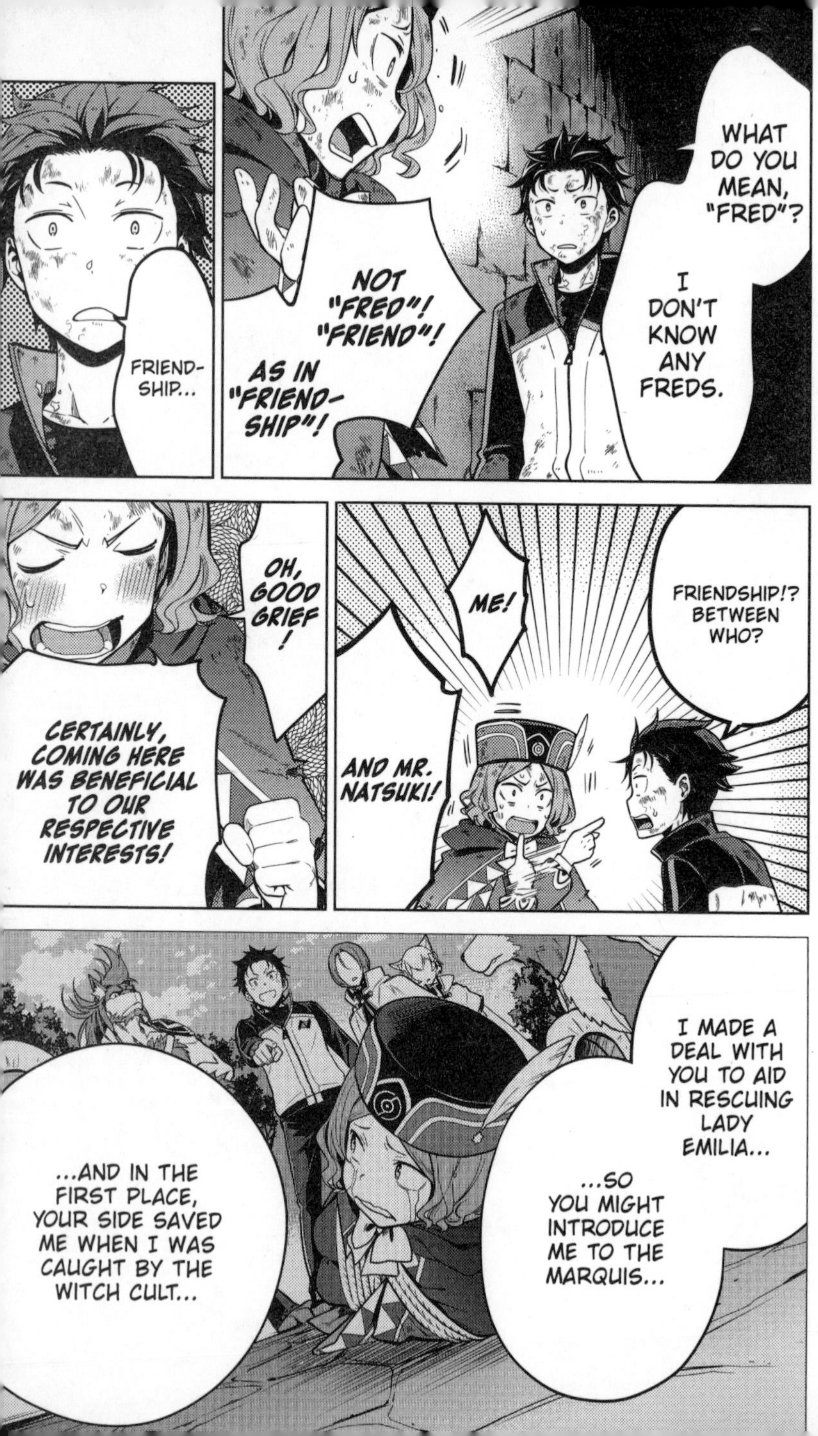
WHAT DO YOU MEAN, "FRED"?
I DON'T KNOW ANY FREDS.
NOT "FRED"! "FRIEND"!
AS IN "FRIENDSHIP"!
FRIENDSHIP...
FRIENDSHIP!? BETWEEN WHO?
ME!
AND MR. NATSUKI!
OH, GOOD GRIEF!
CERTAINLY, COMING HERE WAS BENEFICIAL TO OUR RESPECTIVE INTERESTS!
I MADE A DEAL WITH YOU TO AID IN RESCUING LADY EMILIA...
...SO YOU MIGHT INTRODUCE ME TO THE MARQUIS...
...AND IN THE FIRST PLACE, YOUR SIDE SAVED ME WHEN I WAS CAUGHT BY THE WITCH CULT...

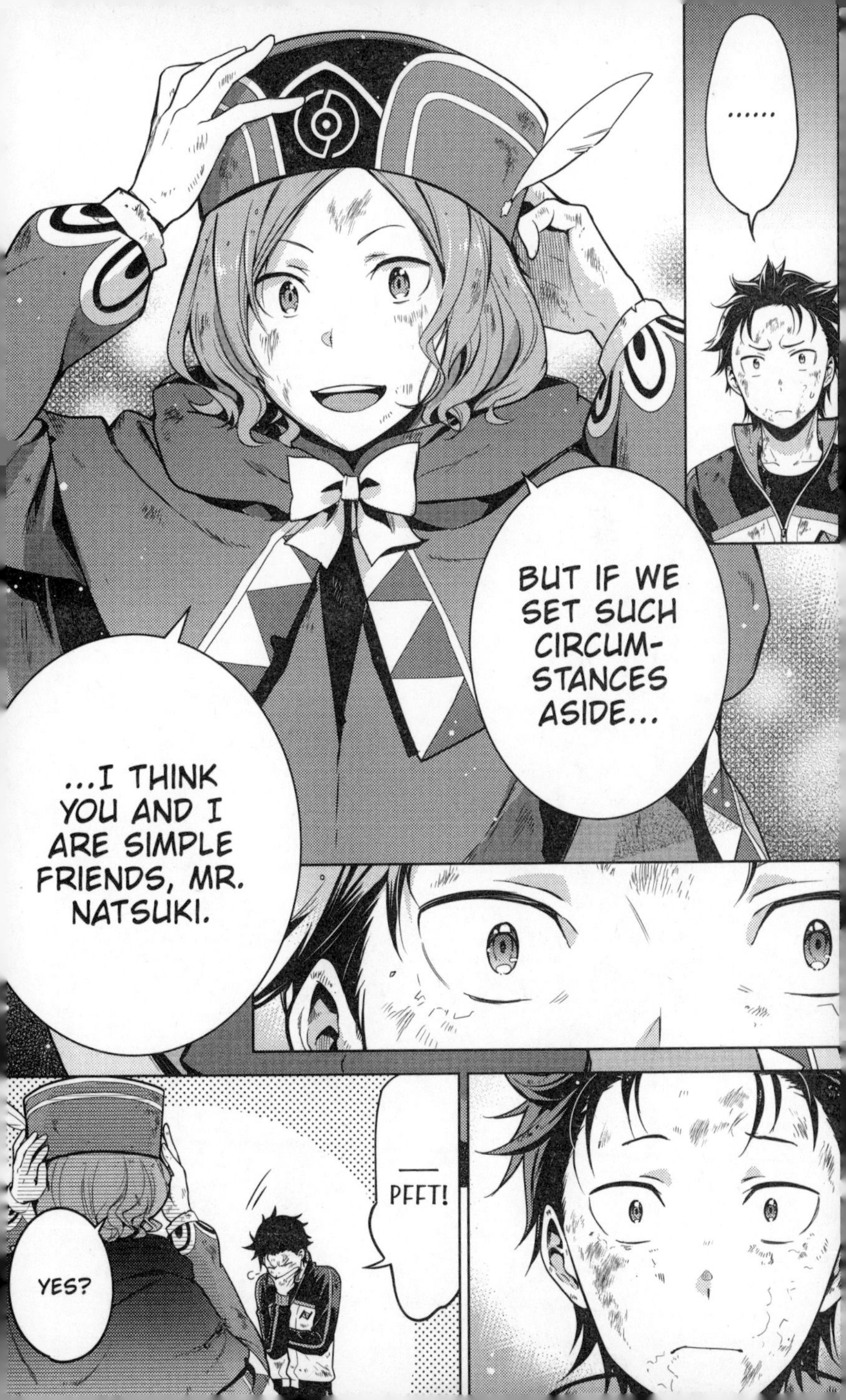
......
BUT IF WE SET SUCH CIRCUM-STANCES ASIDE...
...I THINK YOU AND I ARE SIMPLE FRIENDS, MR. NATSUKI.
—PFFT!
YES?

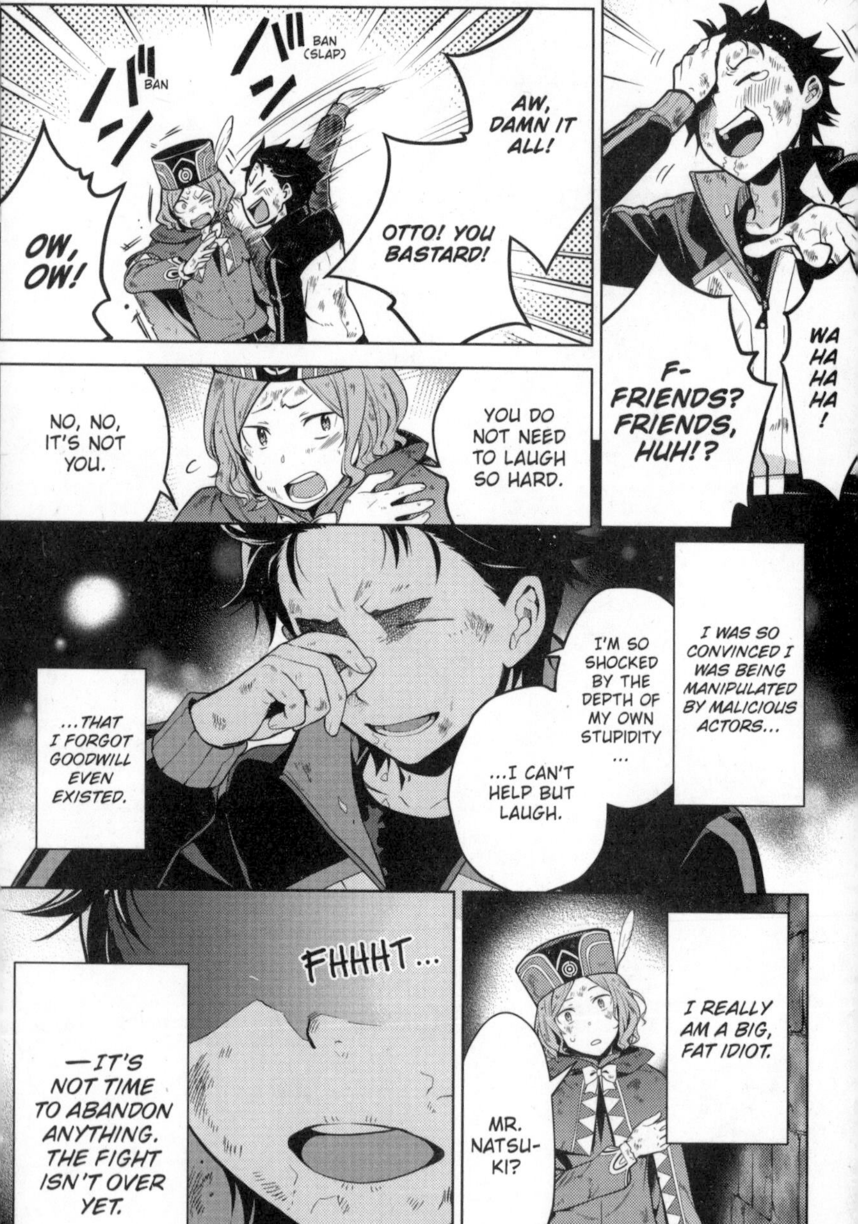
WA HA HA HA!
F-FRIENDS? FRIENDS, HUH!?
AW, DAMN IT ALL!
OTTO! YOU BASTARD!
BAN (SLAP)
BAN
OW, OW!
YOU DO NOT NEED TO LAUGH SO HARD.
NO, NO, IT'S NOT YOU.
I WAS SO CONVINCED I WAS BEING MANIPULATED BY MALICIOUS ACTORS...
I'M SO SHOCKED BY THE DEPTH OF MY OWN STUPIDITY...
...I CAN'T HELP BUT LAUGH.
...THAT I FORGOT GOODWILL EVEN EXISTED.
I REALLY AM A BIG, FAT IDIOT.
MR. NATSUKI?
FHHHT...
—IT'S NOT TIME TO ABANDON ANYTHING. THE FIGHT ISN'T OVER YET.